Astrology and the Academy

Cinnabar Books
PO Box 1071
Bristol BS991HE,
UK.

Cinnabar@caol.demon.co.uk

First published 2004

ISBN 1-898485-07-0

Edited by Nicholas Campion, Patrick Curry, Michael York.
Copy editing: Alice Ekrek.
Production: Alice Ekrek and Nicholas Campion

British Library Cataloguing in Publication Data
A catalogue card for this book is available from the British Library

Printed by Cromwell Press
Trowbridge, Wiltshire BA14 0XB

ASTROLOGY

AND THE

ACADEMY

Papers from the inaugural conference of the Sophia Centre, Bath Spa University College held on 13-14 June 2003.

Edited by Nicholas Campion, Patrick Curry and Michael York

CINNABAR BOOKS, BRISTOL

Contents

Acknowledgements

The organizers of the conference would like to acknowledge the Urania Trust (http://www.uraniatrust.org/) for its generous sponsorship of this publication, the Sophia Trust (http://www.sophia-project.org.uk/) for its funding of the Sophia Centre, and the academic staff and Commercial Facilities Department at Bath Spa University College for their support of the conference on Astrology and the Academy. Thanks in particular to Alice Ekrek for copy-editing.

Erratum: The paper by Joanna Komorowska entitled 'The Lure of Egypt or How to Sound Like a Reliable Source' contains Greek characters which were printed incorrectly in this edition of *Astrology and the Academy*. If you have not received an appended copy please contact the Administrator at: Sophia-centre@bathspa.ac.uk phone: +44 (0)1225 876147 fax: +44 (0)1225 876230 for the correct version. We apologise for any inconvenience caused.

The Editors

The Sophia Centre

Bath Spa University College
Newton Park, Newton St. Loe, Bath BA2 9BN, UK.
www.bathspa.ac.uk/sophia

The Sophia Centre is a ground-breaking initiative within the School of Historical and Cultural Studies at Bath Spa University College, founded in 2002 and funded by the Sophia Trust.*

The Centre has two academic goals:

a. 'to undertake the academic and critical examination of astrology and its practice', and;

b. 'to pursue research, scholarship and teaching in the relationship between astrological, astronomical and cosmological beliefs and theories, and society, politics, religion and the arts, past and present'.

The full time staff are Professor Michael York (Head of Centre and Principal Lecturer), Dr Patrick Curry and Dr Nicholas Campion (Senior Lecturers).

For further information please contact the Administrator at the address above, or by email: sophia-centre@bathspa.ac.uk Tel: 00 44 (0)1225 876147 Fax: 00 44 (0)1225 876230

For study possibilities at the Sophia Centre please see the section at the end of this book.

* http://www.sophia-project.org.uk

Contributors

Dr Nicholas Campion is Senior Lecturer in the Centre for the Study of Cultural Astronomy and Astrology, Bath Spa University College. He is the author of *The Great Year: Astrology, Millenarianism and History in the Western Tradition* (London: Penguin, 1994). Forthcoming books include *Cosmos: a Cultural History of Astrology* (London Books 2005) and *What do Astrologers Believe?* (Granta 2005). He is the editor of *Culture and Cosmos*.

Ruth Cintra became interested in astrology and spiritual matters in the 1980s when, along with her sister Renata, she went all over São Paulo to attend workshops and conferences. Thus was born the idea of TRIOM – Centro de Estudos Marina e Martin Harvey – a meeting place offering a variety of courses, a bookstore and publishing house. Ruth is responsible for the publishing branch of TRIOM, and her work includes translating from English, proof-reading, production and distribution of books.

Geoffrey Cornelius is a consultant astrologer with a background in philosophy and divination. He is a former President of the Astrological Lodge of London, and a co-founder of the Company of Astrologers. He has been active in UK astrological education since the 1970s, and was one of the initiators of the Sophia Project, advancing astrology at university level. He teaches Cosmology and Divination in the Mysticism and Religious Experience MA programme at the University of Kent, where he is engaged in post-graduate studies in divination.

Dr Patrick Curry is a Senior Lecturer in the MA programme at the Sophia Centre, Bath Spa University College. He holds a Ph.D. in the History and Philosophy of Science and is the author of several books on astrology, most recently *Astrology, Science and Culture* (with Roy Willis, Berg Books, 2004).

Dr Liz Greene has been a professional astrologer for nearly forty years. She is director of the London-based Centre for Psychological Astrology which she founded in 1983. In 1996 she created the CPA Press, which publishes transcribed seminars. She holds a doctorate in psychology and is a qualified Jungian analyst. She also holds a diploma in counselling from the Centre for Transpersonal Psychology in London and the diploma from the Faculty of Astrological Studies, of which she is a lifetime Patron. She is the author of many books on astrological, psychological and mythological themes, as well as several computer-generated astrological interpretation programmes. Liz is also a visiting lecturer in the Department of Cultural Astronomy and Astrology at Bath Spa University College.

Dr Jacques Halbronn is the Head of the Bibliotheca Astrologica, Paris, France – an important library which contains astrological literature and information about astrological circles. The library is nourished by research material from J. Halbronn, and by his activities since 1974 as organiser of astrological conferences. His main publications are *Le monde juif et l'astrologie* (1985) and *Le texte prophétique en France Formation et fortune* (1999).

Mike Harding, A.D.E.P., U.K.C.P.reg., is an extistential psycho-therapist. He is a lecturer and supervisor at the School of Psychotherapy & Counselling, Regent's College with a particular interest in continental philosophy and the work of Wittgenstein. He is also a consultant astrologer, and has written extensively on both its technical and philosophical aspects.

Pat Harris received her diploma in astrological studies from the Faculty of Astrological Studies in 1982. She was awarded a Master's degree in Health Psychology in 1997 at Southampton University where she is now researching a doctorate in the applications of astrology to health psychology. She is the Administrative Assistant to the Research Group for the Critical Study of Astrology based at the University and is editor of *Correlation*, the Astrological Association journal of research in astrology.

Prof. Ronald Hutton is Professor of History at Bristol University, and the author of eleven books, of which the most relevant to the present subject is *Witches, Druids and King Arthur: Essays in Paganism, Myth and Magic* (Hambledon and London, 2003).

Prudence Jones is an independent author and researcher who has published widely on the history of astrology and on European indigenous religion. Her university research was in ancient and mediaeval logic and she taught at Cambridge and at the University of Alberta. She is a past President of the Pagan Federation and Chair of the Association of Professional Astrologers. Recent publications include "Contemporary

Paganism: a Guide for the Perplexed" in the *Journal of New Age Studies* (Vol.1, 2004), and "Nineteenth Century Origins of the New Age Triple Moon Goddess" (forthcoming).

Dr Joanna Komorowska, graduate of the Institute of Classical Studies at the Jagiellonian University of Kraków, is author of several publications on ancient Greek astrology and drama. She teaches courses on ancient culture and history of ancient philosophy at the Paedagogical Academy of Kraków, Poland.

Jean Hinson Lall, MA in archetypal studies from Lesley University, is an astrological consultant and psychotherapist in Baltimore, Maryland, USA, and Director of the Institute for the Study of Imagination. She is currently engaged in postgraduate research in cosmology and divination at the University of Kent, Canterbury.

Dr Maarit Laurento has been a professional astrologer in Finland since 1997. In the past she has worked as a researcher in two Finnish universities. She runs an astrology office (business and private clients) in Helsinki and is the chair for Professional Astrologers in Finland.

Prof. Jesús Navarro began both his engineering and astrological studies in 1967. Previously Doctor of Engineering (1976) and Assistant Professor (1972-1978) at the Polytechnic University of Madrid, he is presently Full Professor in Electronics at the University of Zaragoza, where his research and teaching in astrology has also granted some academic support since the year 2000.

Prof. Anna Marie Roos is an assistant professor of history at the University of Minnesota Duluth. She has published articles in the history of early modern astronomy, medicine, and chemistry, as well as a monograph entitled *Luminaries in the Natural World: Perceptions of the Sun and the Moon in England, 1400-1720* (New York and Bern, 2001).

Dr Angela Voss is an astrologer and musician, currently convening courses in Cosmology and Divination for the MA in Mysticism and Religious Experience at the University of Kent, Canterbury, under the sponsorship of the Sophia Trust.

Derek Walters is the author of several books on the history and practice of Chinese astrology, as well as several books on fengshui and related matters. His first book, however, was an *Introduction to Chemistry*. As a member of the Scientific Organising Committee, he has presented papers to the International Conference for the Study of Ancient Chinese Astronomy and Traditional Culture, Academia Sinica, Nanjing, 1999, and Jiyuan, 2001, and a paper on Astronomical references in the Yi Jing to the World I Ching Conference in Taiwan in 2002. He holds regular seminars in Frankfurt and Munich, and has frequently lectured in Moscow, St Petersburg, and Odessa.

Foreword

Patrick Curry, Bath Spa University College

For once, the cliché is apt: this publication is historic. The papers collected here were given at the first conference hosted by the Sophia Centre, at Bath Spa University College, where it is once again possible – after more than three hundred years – to study astrology in an academic institution. In the Anglophone world, at least, astrology was chased out of the academy in the late seventeenth-century. The astrologer John Butler, writing to Elias Ashmole from Oxford in 1680, lamented,

> But do you hear the news from Alma Mater? All Astrology must be banished, and that also as it shall not so much as find room in the imaginations of men! Then what shall become of me? And of us all Astrologers?[1]

The MA taught at the Sophia Centre is in the subject of 'Cultural Astronomy and Astrology'. Cultural astronomy is more inclusive, including any cultural meaning, past or present, of the cosmos, but not surprisingly, a considerable part of the course is taken up with astrology: in its various forms, the oldest and most widespread instance of cultural astronomy in the world today.

Concerning astrology, we favour a broad definition: "the practice of relating the heavenly bodies to lives and events on Earth, and the tradition that has thus been generated".[2] (Note that this construal can include, but does not depend on, a causal relationship between the stars and humanity; the former can equally well be 'signs'.)

Our remit at the Sophia Centre is clear: "to undertake the academic and critical examination of astrology and its practice" and "to pursue research, scholarship and teaching in the relationship between astrological, astronomical and cosmological beliefs and theories, and society, politics, religion and the arts, past and present".[3]

We are therefore not in the business of teaching people how to practice astrology (for which there are already various schools). Nor are we directly concerned with the scientific truth or otherwise of astrology. Our province is the human *meanings* of astrology. This can include the former kind of question, of course, but in keeping with contemporary science studies, positive and negative scientific results are treated symmetrically; the production of both are equally fair game. But we are by no means limited to such questions, since astrology has a range of human meanings that its strictly scientific analysis do not begin to exhaust. (Indeed, since "The practice of science is itself a *practice*"[4] – that is, inescapably by and for human beings – there is, *strictu sensu*, no such thing as purely scientific.)

Our principal charge at the Sophia Centre is a double one: to be as academically rigorous as possible while fully respecting the integrity of the phenomenon. This challenge contrasts sharply with a common double failing of recent centuries. On the one hand, astrology as such has frequently been studied outside the academy with less than adequate respect for critical canons. (To pick just one example: the endlessly recycled story of Isaac Newton rebuking Edmond Halley for his ignorance of astrology, for which there is no evidence whatever.) Of course, this situation is nothing if not predictable: astrology has been excluded from just the institutions where such canons matter.

On the other hand, however, within the academy astrology has too often been examined as purely a failed version of something else: an ersatz religion, or pseudo-science, or vulgar rather than educated belief. (Significantly – on account of the continuities and common ground it reveals – all three favour the epithet 'superstition'.) But what Ann Geneva wrote about astrology in the seventeenth-century holds true, in essence, at any point in its history, including the present: it

> was not a science. It was not a religion. It was not magic. Nor was it astronomy, mathematics, puritanism, neo-Platonism, psychology, meteorology, alchemy or witchcraft. It used some of these as tools; it held tenets in common with others; and some people were adept at several of these skills. But in the final analysis it was only itself: a unique divinatory and prognostic art embodying centuries of accreted methodology and tradition.[5]

In short, a prerequisite for studying astrology properly and adequately is to respect it as a fully human pursuit and experience, with as much 'right' to be considered such as any other.

When it comes to the nuts-and-bolts of such study, however, astrology is almost always paired with at least one other human body of practice and theory ('discourse', let us say). This too is right, and does not contradict the imperative just described, because like all human activities, astrology does not exist in a void but in an ongoing set of complex and contradictory relationships with other discourses. In the case of astrology, these include myth, magic, religion, natural philosophy and science, politics...

What, in fact, are the minimal requirements for astrology to be possible? Surely they include not only *an astrologer*, but *a world*: Earth, Sun, planets and arguably stars. But this is still insufficient, for there also has to be a body of collective lore, knowledge and/or wisdom: which, looked at diachronically, is *a tradition*, but synchronically, *a ritual*. (Hence, perhaps, the primacy of three intellectual traditions here: history, anthropology, and – because the entire discussion is predicated on it – philosophy.). The challenge, then, is to study astrology without *either* essentialising it *or* reducing entirely to its contexts and relations.

Of course, it might still be asked: why bother to study astrology? But such a question would reveal more about the questioner's likely assumptions and prejudices than the subject itself. We have already argued that astrology is first and foremost a human activity. Is there anything people do that should *off-limits* to critical intellectual inquiry? The onus is surely on those who think so to argue that case, rather than for us to have to defend including astrology.

Furthermore, astrology is a particularly rich vein. It is sufficiently ancient, ubiquitous and hardy enough (having survived many attempts to extirpate it) to suggest that it embodies a relatively fundamental human need, and/or meets a basic human need. Being so old and complex, it can throw fascinating light on the other discourses it has been partly formed by and partly itself formed (if only through its rejection). Yet at the same time, there is nothing else quite like it!

The exclusion of astrology from the general cultural conversation of our society has resulted not only in its impoverishment but also the loss of what it has to offer. It is high time for astrology to come in out of the cold.

Endnotes

1. John Butler, *[Astrologia], or, The most Sacred and Divine Science of Astrology...* (London, 1680), n.p.
2. Patrick Curry, "Astrology", in Kelly Boyd (ed.), *Encyclopedia of History and Historical Writing* (London: Fitzroy Dearborn, 1999), p. 55.
3. From the Heads of Agreement between the Sophia Trust and BSUC.
4. Mary Midgley, *Science and Poetry* (London: Routledge, 2001), p. 94.
5. Ann Geneva, *Astrology and the Seventeenth-Century Mind: William Lilly and the Language of the Stars* (Manchester: Manchester University Press, 1985), p.9.

Introduction: Cultural Astronomy

Nicholas Campion, Bath Spa University College

What astronomy is not an astronomy in a culture?

Michael Hoskin[1]

Cultural astronomy: the use of astronomical knowledge, beliefs or theories to inspire, inform or influence social forms and ideologies, or any aspect of human behaviour. Cultural astronomy also includes the modern disciplines of ethnoastronomy and archaeoastronomy.

Nicholas Campion[2]

Astronomy is more than the science of the stars. It is intimately connected to our ideas of ourselves, our purpose and place in the universe. Currently it is fuelling myths, beliefs and ideologies as much as at any time in its history. We may point to the neo-paganism which draws spiritual sustenance from such sites as Stonehenge. There is the belief in UFOs, borne out of modern science and science fiction, perhaps with ancient roots in angelic and demonic visitations, which in the last decade has exploded in ever more detailed doctrines of alien visitation and abduction. On a more sober level we have the manipulation of the space race to provide propaganda for the cold war. In the post-1989 world the USA continues to use its space programme to reinforce images of the American dream; space has become the new frontier, and 1997's Mars Rover mission was designed to touch down on 4 July, the anniversary of the declaration of independence. George W. Bush's announcement in January 2004 of plans to create lunar colonies and send a manned mission to Mars was an unmistakeable response to the emerging space programmes of countries such as India and, more especially, China. Then there is the social impact of the new cosmology, explored in terms of quantum physics by Danah Zohar and Ian Marshall.[3] If the political impact of Copernicus'[4] and Newton's[5] discoveries is now well recognised, then we have hardly begun to question what effect Einstein may have had on twentieth century politics. At least Denis Cosgrove has explored the impact of the shock of the first photographs of the earth from space.[6] That's before we consider the archaic survival of ancient ritual calendars which still form the basis of the religious year in all the world's major religions. Even in Christianity, which so prominently rejects its historical links to the sky, with the exception of the Bethlehem star, Christ's birth is still celebrated on 25th December, the Roman winter solstice and feast of Sol Invictus, the unconquered sun god; his resurrection, meanwhile, is commemorated on the first Sun-day following the first full moon after the spring equinox. Such rules may be meaningless to modern church-goers, but are a living legacy of the moral cosmology of the Hebrew prophets of three thousand years ago.

Then there is the question of astrology's popularity which, in the modern west, is as strong as it has been for centuries. Its survival strikes many people as something of a historical problem: how in a modern rational, scientific world could such an irrational, unscientific belief flourish? Given that such words as 'rational' and 'scientific' are highly problematic and open to differing interpretations, astrology's contemporary revival does require study and explanation. Does it represent the late flowering of an outmoded and ultimately doomed superstition or is it, as Bauer and Durant argue, 'part and parcel of late modernity'?[7] Whatever the answer to this question, the study of astrology in its cultural context in the Sophia Centre is explicitly linked to the wider, emerging discipline of cultural astronomy.

Cultural Astronomy

Cultural Astronomy is a recent discipline, defined only in the 1990s. It emerged out of the slightly less recent discipline of archaeoastronomy, the study of the astronomical alignment, orientation or symbolism embodied in (usually ancient) buildings and monuments. Its antecedents may be traced back to the handful of enthusiasts who were fascinated by Stonehenge's possible astronomical function, notably John Aubrey in 1666 and William Stukely in 1724.[8] It was not, though, until the 1860s that Charles Piazzi Smyth began to look further afield and take an interest in the astronomy of the Great Pyramid,[9] and the 1890s-1900s that Sir Norman Lockyer systematically surveyed not just British megalithic sites but Greek and Egyptian temples. Lockyer's work is largely responsible for the idea that it was customary for ancient people to align their sacred monuments with precise solar, lunar and stellar positions.[10] Lockyer, of course was an astronomer, and the archaeologists' generally scathing response to his work began an academic turf war, which continues to this day, over who has the right to speak for ancient cultures. While Lockyer's views on Egyptian and Greek temples have attracted little attention amongst Egyptologists and classical historians, the continuing arguments concerning megalithic astronomy have essentially focused on competing *a priori* views of ancient culture; archaeologists, whose knowledge of astronomy is often negligible, tend to assume that Neolithic people were by definition unable to perform the intellectual feats which Lockyer ascribed to them while astronomers, for their part, have been accused of ignoring archaeological evidence. However, the whole question of ancient astronomy remained an obscure one until the mid-1960s, when two influential books were published. The first was Gerald Hawkins' 1965 *Stonehenge Decoded*,[11] which claimed that Stonehenge was a giant computer which might be used to predict eclipses. In 1966 the astronomer Fred Hoyle was asked by the archaeological journal *Antiquity* to check (and hopefully refute) Hawkins eclipse predictor model. Although Hoyle found flaws in Hawkins' model, he instead produced a simpler, more effective, one. Hoyle compared the builders of Stonehenge to NASA scientists, challenging the conventional archaeological idea of Neolithic people as savages.[12] While Hawkins' work attracted wide attention, Alexander Thom's *The Stone Circles of Britain*, published in 1967, caused less of a public stir. It was, though, more difficult for archaeologists to cope with on account of the sheer extent of the precise surveys he used to substantiate his claim that megalithic sites were both laid out according to exact geometrical principles and precise solar, lunar and stellar alignments.

The cultural backdrop to Hawkins' and Thom's books was provided by two distinct cultural currents. First, and most obvious, was the 'space race', which began with the launch of Sputnik in 1957 and then moved via Yuri Gagarin's first manned space flight in 1961 to the Apollo moon landing in 1969. It was therefore natural, if anachronistic, for Hoyle to directly compare the megalith builders to NASA scientists and for astronomers, about to achieve their greatest triumph, to acquire a new set of distinguished ancient ancestors. The second was the social and political revolution of the 1960s: the widespread use of psychedelic drugs from 1965 onwards, the 1967 'Summer of Love' and the political radicalism of 1968, the 'May Days' in Paris and the anti-Vietnam war protests. The notion that megalithic culture was highly sophisticated encouraged its adoption as a pre-Christian, pre-scientific, pre-industrial alternative to the supposedly 'alienated' civilisation of the modern west which the disaffected radicals were busily rejecting.[13] From this perspective Stonehenge has become the Westminster Abbey, perhaps the St. Peter's, of New Age, neo-pagan, Wiccan, and alternative and ecological spiritualities, a monument which supposedly recognises humanity's need for harmony with the seasons, sun, moon and stars rather than its dependence on a distant God. The marriage between Thom, Hawkins and the emerging alternative spiritualities was effected by John Michel who, in the late 1960s, was writing, and summarising their new theories, in the pages of *International Times*, the London-based 'underground newspaper'. Michel's *The View over Atlantis*, [14] first published in 1969, is as much the seminal text of modern 'earth mysteries' and sacred geography, as Hawkins' and Thom's work is of archaeoastronomy.

Between them, then, Thom and Hawkins were responsible for the idea that Neolithic Britons were much like modern scientists, with an exact astronomy and precise surveying techniques, rather than stone-age savages. This had three effects:

1. It fed straight into the New Age movement, providing an ancient lineage for ideas of the interdependence of heaven and earth.
2. It presented a major challenge to orthodox archaeologists, overturning (a) views of the Neolithic period as essentially barbarous and (b) the belief that civilisation spread outwards from the Middle East, the 'cradle' of civilisation.
3. It encouraged the study of possible astronomical alignments in other cultures, particularly native American and central American.

Intrigued by astronomical investigations of megalithic sites, working separately to Thom and Hawkins, and attracting far less attention, Alexander Marshak had published his first work arguing for the existence of lunar calendars dating back to 30,000 BCE in 1964.[15] He identified these stone-age calendars in notches on antlers, tusks and bones. Marshak's work attracted little criticism and was largely ignored by archaeologists, but provides the only pervasive material evidence of a culture of astronomy in the late palaeolithic period. It was four years later, in 1968, that the term 'archaeoastronomy' was reputedly coined by Euan MacKie.

Prompted by the archaeological controversy over Hawkins' and Thom's theories, the Royal Society and the British Academy held a joint symposium in 1972 entitled 'The Place of Astronomy in the Ancient World'.[16] From these and other discussions it soon became clear to the first archaeoastronomers that astronomical evidence alone, was not enough to make a case. For example, questions of intent were raised: if an astronomical alignment is identified at a particular monument, how can it be argued that the alignment was intentional rather than coincidental?

Statistics might provide one answer: if a certain number of similar sites indicate similar alignments then it may be reasonably concluded that they were intended by the builders. Yet, a site such as Stonehenge is unique and its purpose might have been different to that of other, smaller circles and may therefore not be susceptible to statistical evidence. Perhaps, then, it was argued, ethnographic and anthropological evidence might provide additional confirmatory evidence for the existence of ancient astronomy. It was in this context, in 1973, that Elizabeth Chesley Baity compiled her extensive survey of all the material published to date on astronomy in ancient cultures (excepting civilisations such as Egypt and Mesopotamia for which the literature was widely known), and the term 'ethnoastronomy' entered common usage.[17] It was then recognised that multi-disciplinary approaches were required. As John Carlson wrote in 1978,

> Archaeoastronomy is a centrifugal science, yet the focus is on a central problem in the development of civilisation and technological man. It yields results at the interfaces between many traditional disciplines and makes contributions in unexpected and personally rewarding ways. These new results enrich not only the individual disciplines but also contribute to the general understanding of the origins of science and the roots of human culture.[18]

By 1977 there was sufficient interest for John Carlson to found the periodical *Archaeoastronomy Bulletin* (later renamed simply *Archaeo-astronomy*) as the house journal of the Center of Archaeoastronomy[19] and, in the following year, the *Journal for the History of Astronomy* launched an annual supplement, also called *Archaeoastronomy.*[20] In September 1983, the Center of Archaeoastronomy organised, jointly with the National Air and Space Museum, the first international conference on ethnoastronomy at the Smithsonian Institute in Washington DC.[21] A strong emphasis on studies based on the Americas indicated both an expanding area of interest in academia, unencumbered by the baggage that was brought to studies of Megalithic culture by western archae-ologists. The overwhelming focus on the non-western and pre-modern defined the area in anthropological rather than sociological terms, that is, about 'them' rather than 'us'.

Separately, the first Conference on Archaeoastronomy was organised in Oxford in 1981. This conference was to be the ancestor of an ongoing series of 'Oxford' conferences, named after the founding venue. The second conference was held in Mexico in 1986, the third in St. Andrews in 1990.[22] At the time of writing the seventh in the series is scheduled to be held in Flagstaff, Arizona in June 2004. The term 'Cultural Astronomy' first appeared in the volume of papers derived from the third conference,[23] but failed to replace the preferred 'astronomy in culture'. The term ('cultural astronomy' was not generally used until, separately, it became part of the sub-title for *Culture and Cosmos* in 1997.[24]) In recent years two academic groups have been formed to bring students of these areas together – SEAC[25] (the European Society for the Study of Astronomy in Culture) and ISAAC[26] (the International Society for the Study of Archaeoastronomy and Astronomy in Culture). In 2000 *Archaeoastronomy* became ISAAC's official journal, with the new subtitle, *the Journal of Astronomy in Culture*. In the same year the discipline gained academic recognition with the appointment of Clive Ruggles as the world's first Professor of Archaeoastronomy at Leicester University.

During its progress through the 1970s to 1990s the new academic discipline of archaeoastronomy tended to withdraw from the extreme position taken by Hawkins and Thom in relation to Megalithic culture and argue for the existence only of more limited alignments incorporating such obvious points as the solar solstices and lunar standstills, or orientations which were frequently approximate – for example, to the east in general – rather than to a particular point on the horizon.[27] These more limited claims should, in theory, have been more acceptable to archaeologists, although the profession as a whole remains indifferent to, or ignorant of, the evidence for Neolithic astronomy. Again, the politics of knowledge are evident. Neolithic culture, to use Barbara Bender's phrase, has become part of a 'contested landscape'.[28] The notion of a sophisticated Megalithic civilisation, though not necessarily Hawkins' and Thom's work in particular, has been appropriated by the advocates of the highly popular publishing genre which has come to be known as 'alternative archaeology', pioneered in the 1990s by such figures as Adrian Bauval and Graham Hancock.[29] Alternative archaeology pits itself against its academic cousin by insisting that the latter routinely suppresses evidence for a universal ancient civilisation. The counter-argument is that alternative archaeologists play fast and loose with the evidence, sacrificing rigour in pursuit of mythology. Although alternative archaeology as a discipline has roots in late eighteenth and nineteenth-century concepts of an ancient universal civilisation, particularly those propagated by H.P Blavatsky and the Theosophical Society,[30] it may be said to represent a third distinct consequence of Hawkins' and Thom's work, along with academic archaeoastronomy on the one hand, and the romantic ancient astronomy of alternative spirituality on the other.

The History of Astrology

The significance of astrology to the history of ideas, religion and science is no longer in question, the case having been made by Otto Neugebauer in 1951.[31] Before Neugebauer wrote, of course, Lynn Thorndike's epic *History of Magic and Experimental Science* had made the argument convincingly and in great detail.[32] A select group of other scholars have examined astrology's role in specific periods and cultures, notably in the ancient Middle East, the classical world and in medieval and Renaissance Europe. There were, though, two significant developments in 1984. A conference on the history of astrology was organised at London University's Warburg Institute[33] and the Astrological Lodge of London held the first of its annual seminars on the history of astrology seminars.[34] The idea of a journal on the history of astrology was first mooted after the Warburg conference but not actually implemented until 1997, with the launch of *Culture and Cosmos.* It was in recognition of the fact that astrology exists only within a cultural context, and that many if its areas of interest, such as its relationship with religion, are shared with the history of astronomy, that the new journal was given the subtitle, *a journal of the history of astrology and cultural astronomy*, as an explicit recognition of the fact that astrology exists in a cultural framework.

Astrology may be defined as the use of celestial phenomena to interpret and predict events on earth or, as Patrick Curry writes in this volume, 'the practice of relating the heavenly bodies to lives and events on earth, and the tradition that has thus been generated'.[35]

However, in order to flourish, astrology requires a philosophical context based on a general belief that movements and changes in the heavens are significant for humanity. Astrology may be studied for itself and the art and technique of horoscope interpretation may be learnt, but it may also be examined as a phenomenon. This is what is done when its history is investigated: its social and political aspects, or its relation with religion, art and literature. The study of history, including that of astrology, is profoundly important for an understanding of the culture within which it flourishes. For example, questions may be asked about astrology, in relation to both the past and the present, which can inform us about its contemporary nature. If it is asked why people believe in astrology, an astrologer might answer 'because it's true', a sceptic because people are prone to self-delusion. But, if it is then asked why most students of astrology, perhaps eighty-percent, are women, different questions may follow. Are women better at perceiving the truth than men? Or are they, as astrology's sceptical critics would have it, more gullible?[36] Whatever the answer, it is clear that astrology exists within a cultural context, in this case gender, and to ignore that is to preclude any consideration of its nature and function.

This, it must be said, is an argument which finds influential support from amongst prominent astrologers. In the 1970 foreword to his 1936 work, *The Astrology of Personality*, Dane Rudhyar, the founder of humanistic and psychological astrology, announced that he was creating a new astrology specifically to cope with the consequences of the social and psychological upheavals of the 1960s in the face of which, he believed, previous forms of astrology were proving inadequate.[37] Alexander Ruperti, Rudhyar's interpreter and fellow member of Alice Bailey's Arcane School, stated in a lecture in the Czech Republic in the early 1990s that the notion that 'an astrology with a capital A which exists somewhere, has always existed, and which we should all submit ourselves or be faithful to…is merely the result of our imagination'.[38] There is, therefore, according to Ruperti, no such thing as an astrology which has any independent, objective existence; there are only astrologers interpreting their relationship with the universe through the manipulation of astrological symbols. Each astrologer has his or her own astrological system, dependent on time, place and cultural context.[39] No astrological interpretation is undertaken irrespective of the astrologer's own location within a tradition of learning.

Astrology might therefore be reasonably classified as a species of 'cultural astronomy'. This is not a definition of what astrology may be in itself. It does not concern its essential nature, whether as an art, craft, science, pseudo-science or form of divination. It is an attempt to categorise it within an emerging system of disciplines and sub-disciplines. It says nothing about whether astrology is true or false, science or divination, objectively 'out there' or subjectively 'in here'. Yet such a classification may help bi-pass some of the problems which arise from competing views of what actually constitutes astrology. For example, the Moon's influence on the tides was an astrological phenomenon according to Claudius Ptolemy in the second century,[40] but is hardly considered so today. By contrast, planetary influences were excused from attacks on astrology in the middle ages,[41] being considered part of the natural framework of the cosmos, but today are seen as thoroughly astrological. If it is accepted that the boundaries of what might be considered to come under the heading of 'astrology' are negotiable and vary between different times, cultures, adherents and critics, then the distinctions between astrology, astral-religion, sacred calendars and all other applications of the sky to culture begin to blur. All become different aspects of cultural astronomy.

To quote Clive Ruggles,

> What do people see when they look at the night sky? The answer is as much a cultural as an astronomical one. Thus, the study of cultural astronomies is concerned with the diversities of ways in which cultures, both ancient and modern, perceive celestial objects and integrate them into their view of the world. This fact, by definition, illustrates that a society's view of and beliefs about the celestial sphere are inextricably linked to the realm of politics, economics, religion, and ideology. In this sense, cultural astronomy is but part of the wider endeavor of investigating and interpreting human culture.[42]

The Work and Origins of the Sophia Centre

The Sophia Centre was conceived in a conversation between myself and Dr Marion Bowman, then head of the Study of Religions department at Bath Spa University College, on 7th December 1999. (The name Sophia, from the Greek for wisdom, is taken from the Sophia Project, which funded the Centre's creation, and was originally chosen by Charles Harvey.) After some discussion the title chosen for both the Centre as an academic entity and for the MA which it teaches was 'Cultural Astronomy and Astrology', from the subtitle of *Culture and Cosmos*. (The Sophia Centre is the physical building within which the academic centre is housed). The Centre's foundation is the first academic recognition of this new discipline.

The Centre opened its doors for teaching at 6 pm on Monday 7th October 2002. Its work is essentially interdisciplinary, within the parameters set by its location in the School of Historical and Cultural Studies. It is historical, sociological and anthropological, and crosses the boundaries between the departments of History, Cultural Studies and Media Studies. However, its identification with the Study of Religions department is present in its phenomenological emphasis. The essence of phenomenology is that 'differing belief systems are examined as perceived in their own terms, rather than by adopting a reductionist stance'.[43] As defined by Edmund Husserl in 1913, the phenomenological approach requires that all inquiries into any area of human endeavour touching on consciousness pay due respect to the 'I', the individual's subjective experience, rather than attempt to explain it away or reduce it to quantitative measurement.[44] Husserl's phenomenological approach was adapted to the new discipline of the study of religions by Ninian Smart. It was Smart who largely defined the discipline's approach as one of 'methodological neutralism' or 'agnosticism',[45] as opposed to the religious commitment which was once assumed to be a prerequisite of the study of theology.[46] In other words, the phenomenon under investigation should, as far as possible, be understood on its own terms. This is an ambitious project, for the phenomenologist has first to 'bracket' off his or her own bias, in line with the requirements of true, classical scepticism, and for this to happen such bias has first to be identified and acknowledged. The goal is to understand the many varieties of human experience rather than explain them away or search for the causes which render them meaning-less as forms of psychological or social deviation. The meaning which human beings attach to stories, symbols and, within the context of the Sophia Centre, the sky, have to be respected in order to be understood.

There are parallel currents which support this project. For example, archaeoastronomy has accepted the need to examine not just supposed astronomical alignments in isolation, but the phenomenology of landscape. For example, rather than analysing Stonehenge from a survey, we should actually walk about the landscape as our Neolithic ancestors would have done.[47] What would such a person have actually experienced on walking up the avenue to the great stone circle?

Clive Ruggles is a pioneer of this phenomenological approach. Revising Thom's thesis of precise astronomical alignments, he argued for an alternative approach, considering that

> What has been bequeathed to us is a set of more esoteric – and perhaps ultimately far more interesting - associations between the ceremonial architecture of life and death and the sun and moon, associations that manifest aspects of otherwise largely unfathomable systems of prehistoric thought.[48]

He added that,

> Ironically in view of the 'science v. symbolism' debates in archaeoastronomy in the early 1980s, answers are not to be found by searching for proto-Western science but in the very symbolism that was once seen as its antithesis. If we see non-Western systems of thought as substituting (superstitious) myth, ritual and ceremony for (rational) explanation, we fail to recognize that the conceptual structures underlying them themselves constitute mechanisms for explanation that are perfectly logical and coherent in their own terms. Correspondences such as that between the Barasana Caterpillar Jaguar constellation and earthly caterpillars, have explanatory power within a non-Western world-view, and symbolic expressions of such correspondences – such as that between quartz and moon-light – possess the power to express perceived reality in such a framework.[49]

The system of correspondences which Ruggles identifies as central to the megalithic world view is also the fundamental astrological world view – that all things are linked by what would once have been seen as essential, inner connections, but which would now more often be considered symbolic. This conclusion may have significance for other areas of the history of astronomy, assuming that we can take modern astrology and make certain generalisations about ancient astrology, and about megalithic culture. Clive Ruggles argues that we can. He asked,

> why should the archaeologist, and in particular the student of Neolithic and Bronze Age Wessex, be interested in the perception of astronomical phenomena? A general answer is that in many, if not virtually all, non-Western world-views celestial phenomena are not separated from terrestrial ones, but form part of an integrated whole with complex interconnections. The association may often be viewed as closer in nature to modern astrology than modern astronomy.[50]

Further questions are suggested: if modern astrology may inform us about the experience of the megalithic astronomer, what is the experience of the modern astrologer? Is there an astrological experience? Such a question is central to the Sophia Centre's phenomenological emphasis.

The discussions held at the Oxford conferences were extended into a new series of conferences, those on the Inspiration of Astronomical

Phenomena[51] (INSAP). There have, to date, been four conferences: 1994 in Castel Gandolfo, Italy, 1999 in Malta, 2000 in Palermo and 2003 in Oxford, with the fifth scheduled for the Adler Planetarium, Chicago, in 2005. The conferences are designed to include artists, art historians, astronomers, historians, physicists, indeed, people from any and every discipline, gathering to compare notes and share ideas. The non-western, pre-modern emphasis characteristic of ethnoastronomy and cultural astronomy in the 1980s was broadened and the topics covered at an INSAP conference might be ancient and distant, or immediate and contemporary. One presentation may be delivered by an artist incorporating cosmological themes in ceramics, the next by a physicist concerned with celestial images on ancient Greek coins. It was my privilege to attend the conferences in Malta in 1999 and Palermo in 2000,[52] to co-organise the 2003[53] conference with Valerie Shrimplin. In many ways the range of topics covered at the INSAP conferences, the respect for practitioners as well as critics and academics, and the blurring of the far too rigid distinctions between art and science have provided an inspiration for much of the syllabus at the Sophia Centre. That syllabus is interdisciplinary; it is anthropological, historical, literary, psychological, phenomenological, and both historical and contemporary.

In the broadest sense, then, the Sophia Centre's remit is to understand the many ways in which human beings use the sky as a historical backdrop to inspire the stories they tell about our place in the cosmos.

Endnotes

1. Michael Hoskin, review of *Astronomies and Cultures*, ed. Clive L. N. Ruggles and Nicholas J. Saunders (University of Colorado Press, Niwot, Col., 1993), in *Archaeoastronomy: supplement to the Journal for the History of Astronomy*, 1996 vol. 27, number 21, p 885-7.

2. Campion, Nicholas, 'Editorial', in *Culture and Cosmos*, Spring/Summer 1997, Vol. 1, no 1, p. 2.

3. Zohar, Danah and Ian Marshall, *The Quantum Society*, London: Bloomsbury Publishing, 1993.

4. Hutchison, Keith, 'Towards a Political Iconology of the Copernican Revolution' in Curry, Patrick (ed.) *Astrology, Science and Society*, Woodbridge, Suffolk: Boydell Press, 1987, pp 95-142.

5. Becker, Carl, *The Heavenly City of the Enlightenment Philosophers*, (Storrs Lectures), New Haven and London: Yale University Press 1932; Becker, Carl, *The Declaration of Independence: a study in the history of political ideas*, New York, 1922.

6. Cosgrove, Denis, *Apollo's Eye: A Cartographic Genealogy of the Earth in the Western Imagination*, Baltimore, Johns Hopkins University Press 2001.
7. Bauer, John and Durant, Martin, 'British Public Perceptions of Astrology: An Approach from the Sociology of Knowledge', *Culture and Cosmos*, 1997, Vol. 1 no 1, pp. 55-72, p. 72.
8. See Chippindale, Christopher, *Stonehenge Complete*, London: Thames and Hudson 1994.
9. Smyth, Charles Piazzi, *Our Inheritance in the Great Pyramid*, 1864, Smyth, Charles Piazzi, *Life and Work of the Great Pyramid*, 3 Vols., 1867.
10. Lockyer, Norman, *The Dawn of Astronomy*, London: Cassell and Company Ltd., 1894; Lockyer, Norman, *Stonehenge and British Stone Monuments Astronomically Considered*, London: MacMillan 1906.
11. Hawkins, Gerald, *Stonehenge Decoded*, New York: Dorset Press 1965.
12. See Hoyle, Fred, 'Speculations on Stonehenge', *Antiquity*, 1966, Vol. 40, pp. 262-76. See also Hoyle, Fred, *From Stonehenge to Modern Cosmology*, San Francisco, W.H. Freeman, 1972.
13. Campion, Nicholas, 'From Stonehenge to Seattle: Eco-Protest, Archaeoastronomy and New Age Cosmology', in Salvatore Serio (ed.), *Proceedings of the INSAP III Conference, Memoire della Societa Astronomica Italiana*, 2002, Special number 1, pp. 202-5.
14. Michel John, *The View over Atlantis*, London: The Garnstone Press, revised edition 1972, [1969].
15. Marshak, Alexander 'Lunar Notation on Upper Palaeolithic Remains, *Science*, 1964, Vol. 146, p. 743; see also Marshak, Alexander, *The Roots of Civilisation*, Mt. Kisco, New York and London: Moyer Bell Ltd., 1991.
16. 'The Place of Astronomy in the Ancient World', *Philosophical Transactions of the Royal Society*, London, A. Vol. 276, pp. 1-276.
17. Baity, Elizabeth Chesley, 'Archaeoastronomy and Ethnoastronomy So Far', *Current Anthropology*, Vol.14, no 4, October 1973, pp 389-431.
18. John Carlson in *Archaeoastronomy Bulletin*, November 1978, Vol. II, no 1, p. 1.
19. The Center for Archaeoastronomy, PO Box 'X', College Park, MD 20741-3022, USA. tel: (301) 864-6637, FAX (301) 699-5337. The Centre's newsletter also carries news of the International Society for Archaeoastronomy and Astronomy in Culture. <http://www.wam.umd.edu/~tlaloc/archastro/>. The journal *Archaeoastronomy* is available from University of Texas Press, Journals Division, Box 7819, TX 7813-7819, USA.
20. *Journal for the History of Astronomy,* Science History Publications Ltd., 16 Rutherford Road, Cambridge, CB2 2HH, England.
21. The First International Conference on Ethnoastronomy: Indigenous Astronomical and Cosmological Traditions of the World, September 5-9 1983, Smithsonian Institution, Washington, program and abstracts available from The

Center for Archaeoastronomy, PO Box 'X', College Park, MD 20741-3022, USA.

22. Papers derived from the second conference were published as Aveni, Anthony F., *World Archaeoastronomy*, Cambridge: Cambridge University Press 1989. Papers derived from the third conference were published in Ruggles, Clive and Nicholas Saunders, *Astronomies and Cultures*, Niwot, Colorado: University Press of Colorado 1993 and Ruggles, Clive (ed.), *Archaeoastronomy in the 1990s*, Loughborough: Group D Publications, 1993. Papers from the sixth conference, held on Tenerife in 1999 were published as Esteban, César and Juan Antonio Belmonte (eds.), *Astronomy and Cultural Diversity, proceedings of the 1999 Oxford VI Conference on Archaeoastronomy and Astronomy in Culture*, Tenerife: Oranismo Autonomo de Museos del Cablido de Tenerife 2000.

23. Ruggles, Clive and Nicholas Saunders, 'The Study of Cultural Astronomy', in Ruggles, Clive and Nicholas Saunders, *Astronomies and Cultures*, Niwot CO: University of Colorado Press 1993, pp. 1-31.

24. http://www.cultureandcosmos.com

25. http://www.mikrob.com/seac. For papers from recent conferences see Ruggles, Clive, with Frank Prendergast and Tom Ray, Astronomy, *Cosmology and Landscape*, Proceedings of the SEAC 98 Meeting, Dublin, Ireland, September 1998, Bognor Regis: Ocarina Books 2001; Blomberg, Mary, Peter E. Blomberg and GöranHenriksson, *Calendars, Symbols, and Orientations: Legacies of Astronomy in Culture*, Proceedings of the 9th annual meeting of the European Society for Astronomy in Culture (SEAC), The Old Observatory, Stockholm, 27-30 August 2001, Stockholm: Uppsala Astronomical Observatory Report no 59 2003.

26. http://www.wam.umd.edu/~tlaloc/archastro/

27. For an authoritative survey of the academic discipline of archaeoastronomy see Ruggles, Clive, *Astronomy in Prehistoric Britain and Ireland,* New Haven and London: Yale University Press 1999.

28. See Barbara Bender (ed.), *Landscape: Politics and Perspectives,* Oxford and New York: Berg Publishers, 1993; Barbara Bender, *Stonehenge: Making Space*, Oxford and New York: Berg Publishers 1998.

29. See for example, Bauval, Robert and Adrian Gilbert, *The Orion Mystery: Unlocking the Secrets of the Pyramids,* London: Heinemann, 1994; Robert Bauval, John Grigsby, and Graham Hancock, *The Mars Mystery*, London: Michael Joseph 1998.

30. Blavatsky, H.P., *The Secret Doctrine*, volumes 1 and 2, facsimile of the original edition of 1888, Los Angeles: The Theosophy Company 1982.

31. Neugebauer, Otto, 'The History of Wretched Subjects', *Isis,* vol. 42, June 1951, reprinted in Neugebauer, Otto, *Astronomy and History: Selected Essays,* New York, Berlin, Heidelberg, Tokyo, 1983, p. 3, and *Culture and Cosmos*, Autumn/Winter 1997, Vol. 1 no 2, pp. 3-4.

32. Thorndike, Lynn, *History of Magic and Experimental Science*, 8 Vols., New York: Columbia University Press, 1923 – 58; see also Thorndike, Lynn, *The Place of Magic in the Intellectual History of Europe*, New York: Ames Press 1967 [1905].
33. The papers were published as Curry, Patrick (ed.) *Astrology, Science and Society*, Woodbridge, Suffolk: Boydell Press, 1987.
34. A selection of papers was published as Kitson, Annabella (ed.) *History and Astrology: Clio and Urania Confer*, London: Unwin Paperbacks 1989.
35. Curry, Patrick 'Astrology' in Kelly Boyd, ed., *The Encyclopaedia of Historians and Historical Writing*, 1999, p 55.
36. Sherriff, Lucy, 'Women are NOT from Gullibull', *The Skeptic*, 2001, Vol. 14 no 3, p.7.
37. Rudhyar, Dane, *The Astrology of Personality*, Garden City, New York: Doubleday 1970 [1936], p. xv.
38. Ruperti, Alexander, *Meaning of Humanistic Astrology*, p. 3. http://www.stand.cz/astrologie/czech/texty/rez-ru-a/rez-ru-a.htm, consulted 25 Jan 2002.
39. See also Rudhyar, Dane, *The Lunation Cycle: A Key to the Understanding of Personality*, Santa Fe: Aurora Press 1967, pp. 9. 12, 13; Greene, Liz, *Relating: an astrological guide to living with others on a small planet*, London: Coventure 1977, pp. 7, 13; Hand, Robert, *Planets in Transit: Life Cycles for Living*, Atglen PA: Whitford Press 1976, pp. 5, 13.
40. Ptolemy, Claudius, *Tetrabiblos*, trans. F.E. Robbins, Cambridge Mass., London: Harvard University Press, 1940, I.3.
41. See for example, Pico della Mirandola's attack on astrology in the 1490s, as summarised in Thorndike, Lynn, *History of Magic and Experimental Science*, 8 Vols., New York: Columbia University Press, 1923 – 58. Vol. IV, pp. 529-543.
42. Ruggles, Clive and Nicholas Saunders, 'The Study of Cultural Astronomy' in Ruggles, Clive and Nicholas Saunders, *Astronomies and Cultures*, Niwot CA: University of Colorado Press 1993, p. 1.
43. Caird, Dale and Henry G. Law, 'Non-Conventional Beliefs: Their Structure and Measurement', *Journal for the Scientific Study of Religion*, 1982, Vol. 21 no 2, p. 153.
44. Husserl, Edmund, *Ideas: General Introduction to Pure Phenomenology*, London: Collier-MacMillan 1972 [1913, Eng. trns.1931], p. 7.
45. Smart, Ninian, *The Science Of Religion And The Sociology Of Knowledge: Some Methodological Questions*, Princeton: Princeton University Press 1973b, pp. 94, 108.
46. Smart, Ninian, *The Phenomenon of Religion*, London: MacMillan 1973a, p. 12.
47. Ruggles, Clive, *Astronomy in Prehistoric Britain and Ireland,* New Haven and London: Yale University Press 1999, pp. 151-2.

48. Ruggles, Clive, 'Megalithic astronomical sightlines', in D.C. Heggie (ed.), *Archaeoastronomy in the Old World*, Cambridge: Cambridge University Press 1982, p. 104.
49. Ruggles, Clive, *Astronomy in Prehistoric Britain and Ireland,* New Haven and London: Yale University Press 1999, p. 155.
50. Ruggles, Clive, *Astronomy in Prehistoric Britain and Ireland,* New Haven and London: Yale University Press 1999, p. 204.
51. http://ethel.as.arizona.edu/~white/insap/
52. The papers are published as Serio, Salvatore (ed.), *Proceedings of the INSAP III Conference, Memoire della Societa Astronomica Italiana*, 2002, Special number 1, Pisa: Istituti Editorialle Poligrafici Internazionale and the Societa Astronomica Italiana.
53. The papers are forthcoming as Campion, Nicholas (ed.), *Proceedings of the Fourth Conference on the Inspiration of Astronomical Phenomena*, Bristol: Canopus Press 2004.

From Allegory to Anagoge: The Question of Symbolic Perception in a Literal World

Angela Voss, University of Kent at Canterbury

This paper will discuss the relevance of the 'four levels of interpretation' of medieval theology – literal, allegorical, moral, anagogical – to the teaching of astrology at both undergraduate and postgraduate level. In an educational system increasingly bound to positivist assumptions a way is required to lead students to a deeper perception, and experience, of the symbolic. This system unlocks the door to a hermeneutic of divination and magic relevant and accessible to beginners in this field, yet grounded in philosophical and theological tradition.

We must surely all agree that the general movement of Western intellectual life since Descartes has been towards increasing detachment of observation, compartmentalised thinking and rational explanation. We no longer live in a world of mystery. Yet at the heart of astrological practice and teaching lies a process that defies the strivings of the mind and is itself profoundly mysterious: how to 'see' symbolically. How do we help clients to glimpse the underlying meaning of their concrete life-dilemmas, and how do we teach students to begin to move from fact-accumulation to an awareness of a different kind of knowledge, one which arises at the interface of their soul with the world? This is a challenge that we are encountering at both undergraduate and postgraduate levels in our Cosmology and Divination courses at the University of Kent, and today I want to present to you a model or image which in our experience facilitates a move away from the 'literal' thinking which pervades our society with its pragmatism towards a richer, deeper and more meaningful way of approaching the study of astrological symbolism and divinatory practices. It first arose in the context of looking at Botticelli's *Primavera*, a painting which lends itself to multiple levels of interpretation.[1] Central to the painting is the relationship between Venus and Mercury, whose conjunction marries imagination and intellect, love and reason. In the Platonic and Hermetic traditions which inspired Botticelli's work, the fusion of these two modes of perception has always been regarded as the basis for a human knowledge which is philosophical in the true sense, and which is stirred by the evocative power of a symbol. The *Primavera* also gives us the key to the means of attaining this knowledge, to which I shall return.

In discussing the model of the four levels of interpretation – literal, allegorical, moral and anagogical or mystical – I am locating astrology in a hermeneutic principle which enables us to articulate, and enter, the mystery of symbolic perception. This principle, explicit in early Christian and Medieval theology and the poetic theology of Dante, is implicit in the Platonic image of the Cosmos as ascending spheres from the material earth to the intelligible One; and it is all too tempting to take the very scheme of this model literally. But we are not talking here of a hierarchy of discrete levels where one jumps further and further away from the world to some sort of immutable abstract truth, which is a common criticism of Platonism, but of a process of deepening perception or unfolding consciousness, like the unpeeling of an onion, which gradually moves from the cause-and-effect, 'out there-in here' objectivity of our habitual mode of thinking to an increasing awareness of the unity of subject and object, until the kind of knowledge is reached which can only be described as spiritual in that it fully embraces both inner and outer, or psychic and material reality in a single act of perception. It is a model which allows something to be revealed as something we have always known – an innate knowledge of how we mirror the world, of an inner cosmos as vast and as awesome as the outer one. This kind of knowledge plays little or no part in the programmes of our schools and universities.

So what does it mean to see behind the literal? Let us begin by considering the words of St Augustine and Thomas Aquinas, who write specifically about allegorical and symbolic interpretation in relation to the reading of Scripture.[2] Augustine stresses at the outset that the intuition of deeper meaning in a text stimulates the student's own desire to learn, and that the penetration of this meaning is a pleasurable activity in that it leads towards the ultimate joy of union with God. We have certainly found that students respond to the 'opening' of astrological symbolism with some amazement, for nowhere else in their studies do they find this element of revelation. Of course the capacity of the text, image or symbol to disclose its meaning in this way is the very reason we consider it to be 'sacred' in the first place.

In defining the four levels, Augustine and Aquinas speak of the literality of a text as a material reality, the story taken at face value. Here we find the meaning or signification of the words themselves in their historical, linguistic and literary contexts; statements of fact, from which Aquinas does not exclude metaphor and analogy. An example he gives is the assertion that 'Christ sits on the Right Hand of God' which is a 'literal' statement of the power of God but given as a metaphor.[3] Both theologians make it clear that there is no 'spiritual' sense understood at this level, although this does not lessen its importance, and we may note that Augustine explicitly warns of the dangers of disbelieving in the reality of an underlying historical and factual truth.[4] We may perhaps define the literal as a 'horizontal' discourse, expanding the medieval understanding to a quantitative weighing and measuring, comparing, arguing, clarifying, conceptualising and rationalising, which of course has its value. But still it remains a demonstration of a reality from a position that is not yet participating in that reality, that is not engaged in it but stands apart; it is what we call 'knowing; it is how we have all been taught to think, to evaluate. Starting here, however, with the separation and clarification of things – the *episteme* of the philosophers – the foundation stone is laid for further meaning, for the process of discovering what the things signified by the words *themselves* signify. Aquinas tells us:

> that signification whereby things signified by words have themselves also a signification is called the spiritual sense, which is based on the literal, and presupposes it. Now this spiritual sense has a three-fold division.[5]

This moves us on to the territory of allegory, the 'speaking otherwise' (from the Greek, *allegoria*) or, in the case of the fables of the poets, truth 'disguised' by poetic metaphor. For Aquinas, allegory is the first stage of the discernment of 'divine' meaning in scripture, for example, the 'thing signified' by words may be Christ. Traditional academic thought has no problem with allegory as a literary device, because it does not yet demand that we enter into the process of knowing, or are changed by it. As Henri Corbin explains:

> The difference between "symbol" and what nowadays is commonly called "allegory" is simple to grasp. An allegory remains on the same level of evidence and perception, whereas a symbol guarantees the correspondence between two universes belonging to different ontological levels: it is the means, and the

> only one, of penetrating into the invisible, into the world of mystery, into the esoteric dimension.[6]

Allegory is the way we usually explain astrology, the symbol 'standing for' the emotion, or person, or event. But when we move to the two further stages of interpretation, we can no longer keep our distance. There begins a process of 'seeing through' the literal or allegorical which stirs self-reflection; Corbin describes this movement from sensible to symbolic perception as a "transmutation of the immediate data (the sensible and literal data) [which] renders them transparent".[7] It is this very transparency which enables the transition to take place, and paradoxically, allows the literal and spiritual senses to be understood simultaneously.

The third stage is called the moral or tropological, which derives from the word *tropos* or turning, and does indeed form a turning point for students. It demands a turning back to *oneself* in order to understand, and thus has implications and effects which are moral in that they influence how we act. At this point, we enter into a mode of knowledge which is commonly called esoteric. In Christian contexts, this is the interpretation which leads to a greater imitation of Christ. In an astrological context, it brings into play the relationship of the astrologer to the client and his or her participation in the particular circumstance within which a symbol 'manifests'. It can arise at that moment when you realise that your client's chart mirrors your own current preoccupation, when you utter words you do not intend which shock you with their truth, or when you are moved by the meaningfulness of a synchronistic event which calls you to action. It is experienced as a revelation which arises in the moment and spontaneously connects your inner life to the outer event or image, beyond your conscious intention. This is not knowledge which is accrued through human effort. Marsilio Ficino calls it a 'gift of the soul' which is dependent on Grace.[8] Now the astrologer is no longer the detached observer of God's creation but is challenged to acknowledge the 'secret mutual connivance' as Jung put it, between himself and the world he perceives.[9] It is not comfortable, because it involves a breaking down of our assumptions about the nature of reality; and it is very hard to stay with. Not all students are able to have a sense of this *tropos*, but the beauty of the model as a whole is that it allows everyone to enter the world of symbolic interpretation at their own level, even if it is to just make the first step from fact to metaphor.

For those rare souls who can penetrate further than moral perception, the *anagogic* or mystical dimension lies in wait. For Aquinas, this level, the 'sense beyond', can only mean the ultimate glory of redemption, life with Christ in heaven.[10] It is about union, union of the act of perception with what is perceived, union of literal and symbolic, world and psyche. The world no longer *imitates* the divine word, as in allegory, but *becomes* the divine word. At this stage all divisions are transcended and embraced, as all four levels become contained in one. The Platonist Iamblichus says that this is the mode of knowledge which is truly that of divination, "suspended from the Gods, spontaneous and inseparable from them".[11]

In looking at knowledge in this way, it becomes clear that there is no disembodied 'truth' that stands apart from the vision of the reader or student. The degree of engagement of the person with the symbol or text or image IS the 'truth' revealed to that person at that moment, yet it is always possible to go deeper. We begin to realise that, if we are to take our authorities seriously, the very process of developing symbolic perception has profound spiritual implications. Aquinas says "it must be said that Sacred Scripture is divinely ordered to this: that through it, the truth necessary for salvation may be made known to us";[12] and Ficino stresses that when one penetrates to the deepest meaning of a text, it is the word of God that one hears. He likens the nature and quality of the 'signification' apprehended through the actual words to the presence of the soul in the human body:

> The human soul therefore will be immortal and introduced by God into our body, like the signification introduced into the air by God. If one pays attention to this signification, it is the thought of God who speaks that one comprehends.[13]

This is why we can legitimately locate astrology in Religious Studies, and even, I would suggest, understand it as a practice of initiation.

I would like now to consider the nature of symbolic knowledge in relation to Platonism, for in the works of Plato and his followers we find myths and allegories which speak clearly to students of the differences between literal and metaphorical thinking. The most direct and powerful of these must be the allegory of the Cave in the *Republic*.[14] Here Plato makes the distinction between the literal world of the region of shadows and the spiritual or intelligible world of true knowledge. The people in the cave do not have freedom of movement. They are fettered and can only see shadows of objects carried behind them, projected by the light of a fire onto the back wall of the cave. When they are released and are able to turn round, they then see representations of real objects being carried along a walled path. This stage we might compare to allegorical interpretation, and it is the first step towards seeing things 'as they really are'. Platonically, the fire is an image of the Sun, whose light fosters understanding; but it is also something else. Fire is passion, desire, longing; it is the stirring power of the imagination. In Platonic and Sufi traditions, one is not led to anagogic perception through intellectual striving but is led there because one *desires* union. Engagement through love leads to changed perception, as we all know when we are 'in love', and this is why Cupid or Eros hovers over Venus in the *Primavera* and is about to wound the Grace Chastity with a burning love for Mercury, who has penetrated with his caduceus every level of reality. Eros – the child of Mercury and Venus[15] – draws one from the literal world through love and points to the kind of knowledge Plato calls intelligible, which for Socrates includes the contemplation of the stars and the Sun as the cause of all things. That is, the contemplation of the 'real' heavens, standing under the stars in awe of their majesty. The stars are supreme symbols precisely because their life-giving powers so evidently manifest on all levels.

Modern positivist thought now takes the shadows of Plato's cave to be the 'real' world and reduces his Ideas to mere abstractions. The world beyond the literal becomes shadowy, superstitious mumbo-jumbo, inevitably, as it cannot reveal its meaning in the harsh light of scientific experiment or rational analysis. If we are to teach astrology in universities, we will have to reclaim our ground, the middle ground in which we delight in mystery with the 'divine enthusiasm' of the neoplatonic *magi*. At the anagogic or intellectual level of perception there may be no distinction between our thought and the thought of the Cosmos; but, at the symbolic we are entering into the life in between, whether through the use of an image or an act of divination. The language of astrology, poetry, art and music *is* the language of this middle realm, balanced between pure intellect and sensory perception yet encompassing both; drawing in the anagogic reality and displaying it to the senses through the beauty of its many forms. The 'poetic metaphor' of astrology, as Ficino would say, is not to be confused with 'reason or knowledge'.[16] When we are teaching astrology we are surely activating what Henry Corbin terms the 'cognitive imagination' an organ of true perception which mirrors the Images of the archetypal world.[17] This realisation helps students begin to free themselves from the tendency of our society to drag astrology, screaming, into a literal world in which it does not belong, a world in which vision is opaque, where the imaginal is reduced to the mere imaginary.

Perhaps most importantly, the four levels model gives students a framework within which to address the huge themes of Fate and Destiny which must be raised in any study of astrology, cosmology or magic. I have already emphasised the essential premise of Platonism – and of alchemy – that the human soul has the innate capacity to develop a way of knowledge which progresses from a clear separation of the knower from the thing known to an experience of the world and self as a unity, and that this is a spiritual quest. It was understood that when the depths of anagogic perception had been reached, the soul achieved the immortality of the gods. From this perspective, an attitude towards, or practice of ,divination which remains on the 'literal' level of cause and effect will inevitably give rise to the limitations of fated pronouncements, and the fulfilment of these pronouncements by the world 'out there'. Astrologers who give judgements purely from rational inference and the rule book are the 'petty ogres' Ficino despised, because they merely deal with the shadows in the cave and therefore keep the prisoners shackled.[18] It is possible to live in this world, and operate by its laws, but it will not free you.

The Ptolemaic model of astrology is literal and allegorical but goes no further, as it attempts to take on the mantle of Aristotelian natural science. The Platonic model can go further precisely because it takes on board the mystery of the symbolic image, and the possibility that something may be revealed to human beings from another order of reality. On the level of moral understanding, astrological prediction approaches prophecy and fate becomes destiny as the astrologer is moved by the symbol and the client recognises her own desire and freedom of choice. Ultimately, anagogically, linear time ceases to hold sway and the prophetic soul perceives past, present and future as one. Pseudo-Ptolemy, Ficino and William Lilly all tell us that true astrological judgement comes from a fusion of the 'divine chance' of the soul's 'turning' to its own wisdom with diligent study and practice, and Lilly himself points out that 'the more holy thou art.. the purer judgement thou shalt give'.[19] Our literal world does not recognise the 'divine chance' because it depends on the seizing of the meaning of a sign, the 'mere coincidence', the dream, the moment when our desire is revealed. But the very word desire – *desidere* (from the star) – takes us back to the stars, and if we can begin to evoke this desire in the hearts of our students then we can really begin to study astrology with them.[20] Plotinus talks of the divinity present in the literal, concrete material world as a 'lure' or 'bait' to enchant and draw people to a spiritual perception. 'The world is full of signs' he says, and 'the wise man is the man who in any one thing reads another'.[21] I would suggest that astrology itself can act as such a bait for students who are hungry for a deeper meaning in their studies, precisely because the planets literally exist and can be perceived through the sense of sight. From there they can begin, and the four levels hermeneutic enables them to move in a process of interiorisation so that they can enter into, rather than simply learn about, the meaning of a symbol. This surely has profound implications, for it may just begin to revolutionise the assumptions of an academic method which separates knowledge from knower, thought from being, conception of reality from its experience.

Endnotes

1. On the four levels of interpretation in relation to the *Primavera*, see Joanne Snow-Smith, *The 'Primavera' of Sandro Botticelli: a Neoplatonic interpretation* (Peter Lang, 1993).
2. See Aquinas, *Summa theologiae*, I.9-10; Augustine, *On Christian Doctrine* 2.6.7-8. Augustine on allegory is discussed in D.W. Robertson, *A Preface to Chaucer: Studies in medieval perspective* (Princeton, 1963), ch.2. See also John F. Boyle, 'St Thomas Aquinas and Sacred Scripture' at www.nd.edu/~afreddos/papers/Taqandss.htm
3. Aquinas, *Super epistolam ad Galatos lectura,*ch..4, lect.7, in *Super epistolas s.Pauli lectura,* ed. R. Cai (Turin, 1953), vol. 1, p.620. Reference from J. Boyle, op.cit.
4. See Augustine, *City of God*, XIII, ch.22: 'The spiritual interpretation of the paradise of Eden does not conflict with its historical truth.'
5. Aquinas, *ST* I.10.
6. Henri Corbin, 'Mysticism and Humour', in *Spring* (1973), p. 27, quoted in S. Wasserstrom, *Religion After Religion: Gershom Scholem,Mircea Eliade, and Henry Corbin at Eranos* (Princeton 1999), p.93.
7. Henry Corbin, *History of Islamic Philosophy*, trans. L.Sherrard (London, 1993), p.13, quoted in S. Wasserstrom, op.cit., p.95.
8. Marsilio Ficino, 'Commentary on Plotinus' in *Opera omnia,* (Basle, 1576, repr. Phénix Editions 2000), p.1626.
9. C.G. Jung, *Synchronicity: An Acausal Connecting Principle* (London 1972), p.85.
10. Aquinas, *In Galatos*, ch.4, lect.7, p.621.
11. Iamblichus, *On the mysteries*, I.III, trans. T.Taylor (Frome, Somerset 1999), p.23.

12. Aquinas, *Quaestiones quodlibetales,* 7.6.1., ed. R.Spiazzi, (Turin, 1956), p.146.
13. Marsilio Ficino, *Theologia Platonica*, 10.7, in P.Moffit Watts, 'Pseudo-Dionysius the Areopagite and Three Renaissance Platonists, Cusanus, Ficino & Pico on Mind and Cosmos' *Supplementum Festivum, Studies in Honour of P.O.Kristeller* ed. J. Hankins, (Binghamton 1987), p. 297.
14. Plato, *Republic* VII.
15. See Robert Graves *The Greek Myths*, vol.1 (Harmondsworth 1997), p.58, for reference to this version of the myth.
16. See M. Ficino, 'Disputatio contra iudicium astrologorum' in *Supplementum Ficinianum*, ed. P.O. Kristeller (Florence, 1949), vol.2, p.43.
17. Henri Corbin, *Celestial Body and Spiritual Earth*, trans. N. Pearson, (Princeton N.J. 1977), p.11.
18. M. Ficino, 'A Disputation against the pronouncements of the astrologers' in *The Letters of Marsilio Ficino* vol.3, (London 1981), p.77.
19. William Lilly, 'To the Student in Astrology' in *Christian Astrology* (1647, repr.Regulus 1985).
20. On the etymology of *desidere*, see Darby Costello, 'Desire and the Stars' in *the Astrological Journal,* vol.45, no.4, July/August 2003, pp.5-12.
21. Plotinus, *Enneads* II.3.7, trans. S. MacKenna (London 1962).

Astral Magic: The Acceptable Face of Paganism

Professor Ronald Hutton, University of Bristol

This paper will look at a topic hitherto equally neglected by classicists and medieval historians: the manner in which medieval scholars (including many churchmen) found a way of fitting the classical pagan deities back into Christianity through the medium of planetary magic. This enterprise lasted from the twelfth to the eighteenth century, and is one of the lost themes of the history of European religion

I am going to commence this essay by outlining four theoretical positions. First, that the visible planets have some influence over earthly affairs. Second, that they are animate, being homes or bodies for divine beings who empower them. Third, that humans can work with these beings to exert some control over those affairs. Fourth, that those beings can be identified with the Graeco-Roman deities whose names the planets concerned traditionally bear in Europe.

Anybody accepting the first of those positions is endorsing astrology. Anybody accepting the first and second of them is endorsing a form of astrology allied to religion. Anybody accepting the first, second and third of them is endorsing the practice of astral magic. Anybody accepting all four of them is endorsing both astral magic and a form of pagan religion, by according to the traditional deities of classical paganism an important role in governing the material world.

The importance of that assertion, and of this subject, is that such a role was found within western Christian culture for about eight hundred years, spanning the whole of the high middle ages and the early modern period. The story of it is fairly well known to historians of astrology and ritual magic, but it has been almost completely neglected by those of what has conventionally been termed religion. Because the latter have been central to the study of European history during these periods, while astrology and magic have been marginalised, this theme of European culture has been virtually ignored by mainstream historians of the middle ages, Renaissance, Reformation and Enlightenment. Where it has been noted at all, it has tended to be in different contexts, such as the history of art or of science. I would suggest that, because of this neglect, an important dimension to European intellectual and cultural history has been lost.[1]

First, it may be helpful to prove my point by looking at the views of a set of prominent western European thinkers in the years between 1120 and 1160, a period of exceptional ferment in European thought and art. It has been traditionally regarded with admiration, as defining the major preoccupations of high medieval culture, and has often been given the name 'the twelfth-century Renaissance'. Here we find Peter Abelard declaring that heavenly bodies could certainly control earthly phenomena and that they could be linked to certain forces hidden in plants and stones. He was not certain whether they were animated by divine beings, though he respected those who believed this.[2] William of Conches had fewer reservations. He argued that the Christian god had made the human soul but entrusted the forming of the body to planets and stars. He believed that the deities of Graeco-Roman mythology inhabited the planets and had power over particular aspects of the material world, and human life.[3] Bernard Silvester calmly called the planets 'gods who serve God in person', and who controlled the world of matter while enjoying a beatific vision of the supreme deity. He also believed that they revealed the future and that pious humans could ascend to them after death, in the manner of ancient pagan heroes, and become celestial bodies in turn.[4]

These, it must be emphasised, were all respectable and accepted thinkers, members of the public world of twelfth-century scholarship. There are also traces of a flourishing intellectual underground in which such ideas were given uninhibited practical application. Some of the best evidence comes from the rantings of the French archbishop William of Auvergne, recalling his mis-spent youth in the last decades of the twelfth century. During that period he had read many books of ritual magic, among which were some that prescribed the drawing down of the power of the planets for human purposes.[5] One of those that he named, and called *Tot Grecus*, has actually survived, more usually called the *Liber Veneris*, or *De Lapidus Veneris*, and teaches how to draw the influence of the planet Venus, conceived as the classical goddess, into a magical object.[6] This process of fumigation, invocation and inscription of signs could then be repeated with the other planets, until the object was imbued with the potency of all, and could function as an all-round transmitter of magical energy.

So, having illustrated the vitality of this complex of beliefs in the thoroughly Christian culture of the twelfth century, I need to ask two obvious questions: where did it come from, and where did it go? The immediate answer to the first of these is easy and plain. It came from the Muslim world, as soon as the latter was opened up by the crusading expansion of Latin Christianity at the end of the eleventh century, into the formerly Muslim-controlled areas of Spain, Sicily, Syria and Palestine. One consequence of this was the systematic rendering of Arabic manuscripts into Latin for the use of Christian scholars. Over a hundred of them were translated or paraphrased in the course of the twelfth century, and more followed in the thirteenth.[7] At times the process of transmission is very clear, and linked to the remarkable physical mobility of European humanity around the year 1100.

Adelard of Bath was born in Somerset in the late eleventh century, although his parents may have come from Lorraine. He commenced his teaching career at Bath Abbey and then went on to study at Tours and Laon. He followed this with travels that certainly took him to Italy and Sicily, and probably to Syria and Asia Minor as well. On his return, equipped with a knowledge of Greek and Arabic and a haul of texts, he seems to have worked at Bath, Hereford, Malvern, Worcester, Bayeux and Chartres.[8] Petrus Alfonsi was born a Jew, in the Spanish Muslim kingdom of Saragossa, where he grew up reading Arabic. In 1106, as Christian armies closed in on Saragossa, he converted opportunely to Christianity. He then began travels across western Europe, giving lessons in Arabic and translating manuscripts. One of the places where he taught was Worcester, where he seems to have encountered Adelard.[9]

The main interest of the documents that were rendered into Latin was what we would now call scientific, especially in the fields of astronomy, medicine and mathematics. These were also, however, heavily populated, in the manner of the time, by works that we would now label as concerned with astrology and astral magic. One of the texts translated by Adelard was the *De Imaginibus* credited to Thabit ibn Qurrah, which described how to make magical statuettes by using rings, seals and conjurations in harmony with the movements of heavenly bodies. Once empowered, these figures could be used for a range of purposes, from keeping away snakes and finding missing objects to destroying cities.[10] That was only one of a number of Arabic works that were rendered into Latin between 1120 and 1260, and which embraced the four postulates that I listed at the opening of this essay. Collectively, they taught a philosophical system by which a supreme god had entrusted the main pagan deities with the management of the world, operating out of the planets. They also taught a set of rituals by which humans could tap into the power of those deities for their own ends. Initially, the philosophical aspect of those teachings provoked remarkably little concern, and the practical magic only slightly more so. This was because, on those issues, the Church Fathers had actually left the door open.

Most of the key antique texts on which medieval Christians relied for their concept of the universe taught that the heavenly bodies were animate beings. Plato argued for the divinity of the planets and stars.[11] Aristotle described them as intermediaries between the One Mover and inferior entities, directly responsible for all life and action in the material world.[12] Cicero declared that they were divinities.[13] Some Christians had no difficulty in digesting this concept. One was the Roman, Julius Firmicus Maternus, who in the early fourth century wrote a ferocious attack on paganism as false religion.[14] He also published a book in which he referred to the planets as deities, serving the supreme god and carrying out his will, and recommended astrology as a means of discovering that will.[15] This text was rediscovered in the eleventh century, and much copied and discussed thereafter.[16]

Augustine, famously, condemned astrology with other forms of divination, but admitted that he could not himself answer the question of whether the planets were divine beings serving his god.[17] When the greatest of all the Latin Church Fathers implied that a view could be permitted, there was little to stop anybody else from holding it. This pattern seems to have signalled to some of the common people, at least, that pagan deities associated with planets were immune from Christian censure. In the 440s citizens of the devoutly Christian imperial capital of Ravenna were celebrating the New Year with parades of people costumed as the planetary gods and goddesses.[18]

Thus far the equation is simple: Arabic astral magic falls on medieval Christian soil that is already predisposed to accept it, because the fathers of the western Church had left open a place for pagan deities in the Christian system as planetary spirits. It is also clear that the great contribution of the early medieval Muslim world to the history of magic is the concept that the power of celestial bodies could be drawn down ritually into material objects, fashioned of suitable materials and inscribed with appropriate signs. We still preserve the distinctive Arabic word for these objects: 'talismans'. What is tougher is to work out where Arabic magic using talismans came from in the first place.

On face value it bears little relationship with the two classic bodies of evidence for magic in the late antique Mediterranean and Near Eastern worlds: the Graeco-Roman curse tablets and the Graeco-Egyptian magical papyri. The curse tablets are simply irrelevant to the subject.[19] The papyri, with their vast store of recipes for complex ritual magic, do not contain a single one for the making of talismans using invocations of celestial power.[20] It is tempting, therefore, to look to Mesopotamia, the birthplace of astrology, where from the second millennium BCE, if not before, deities were strongly identified with heavenly bodies in a way that was not yet found further west. It was in Mesopotamia, also, that observation of the exact movement of the moon and stars had developed into an important form of divination by the fifth century BCE.[21]

It is true that none of the surviving ancient Mesopotamian magical texts, including the large trove from the royal libraries of Assyria, contain rites for astral magic using talismans, any more than the Graeco-Egyptian papyri do.[22] Nonetheless, Arabic astral magic could represent a direct medieval development of native Mesopotamian tradition. This is made especially likely by the fact that the development apparently occurred in the heart of Mesopotamia itself, at Baghdad. One of its key texts, preserved in twelfth-century Latin translation, is the *De Radiis* of al-Kindi, the greatest scholar of mid ninth-century Baghdad. It suggested that all earthly affairs are influenced by rays from heavenly bodies, which interact with mundane materials and sounds. It went on to suggest that magicians could manipulate the world by directing such interactions themselves.[23] If al-Kindi provided the theory, then one of the most notable scholars of the next generation at Baghdad, Thabit ibn Qurrah, is said to have provided the practice. This is in the spells recommended in the work cited above, the *De Imaginibus*, which is attributed to him. During the following two hundred years, astral magic using talismans became the main practice of Muslim sorcerers. It is the central theme in the prototype for H. P. Lovecraft's *Necronomicon*, a wicked book written by a mad Arab. This is the wonderfully amoral *Ghayat al-Hakim*, 'the aim of the wise one', written in Arab Spain in the eleventh century and representing a digest of most of what was written about ritual magic in the Arab-speaking world up to that time.[24]

At this point, however, the plot thickens further, for claims have been advanced for a provincial city, rather than Baghdad, as the place where the ancient stellar traditions of Mesopotamia were transformed into the medieval tradition of astral magic. This is Harran, situated in the borderland where Mesopotamia and Syria meet. During the ninth to eleventh centuries it became famed among Arab authors as the home of a unique religious sect known as Sabians, who seemed to base their ideas on a mixture of native Mesopotamian religion and Hellenistic philosophy. They acquired a special reputation as magicians, and for venerating planetary deities. David Pingree has therefore argued that it was the

Sabians of Harran who developed the medieval system of astral magic, and passed it on to the Muslim world in general.[25] The logic of this argument, strong enough in itself, is reinforced by the fact that al-Kindi is known to have been influenced by books from Harran, while Thabit himself was a Sabian from that city.

There are, however, two separate problems with it. One is that the Mesopotamian emphasis on planetary deities and star lore was only one component of the late antique interest in magic and divination focused on the heavens. By the early part of the Common Era, that interest was firmly based on Hellenised Egypt. There we find all the ingredients of medieval astral magic already formed. It was there that the zodiac was put into its enduring framework. It was there that particular stones, metals, plants and animals became associated with specific planets.[26] The texts of ritual magic produced there between the second and fourth centuries include invocations to planetary deities and many procedures for the charging of material objects with divine power.[27] Although the seven planets are not prominent in the papyri, they play a major part in the Hermetic texts produced in Egypt at the same time, functioning as the immediate agents of a creator deity.[28] Other Hermetic writings teach how to make amulets from substances associated with particular planets, into which the power of the latter will descend: very clear proto-talismans.[29] It can therefore be suggested that, by the end of the ancient world, Alexandria had more of the components of the future astral magic than Mesopotamia; indeed it had all of them, ready to be assembled.

That does not, however, invalidate Harran as the point of assembly, because it is certain that some of the schools of Alexandria were moved to that city by early Arab caliphs. The doctrines imputed to the Sabians, furthermore, show signs of strong Egyptian influence. Here we encounter the second problem, that we have no firm idea of what the Sabians themselves actually believed. We can be sure that Harran became a major centre of the study of ancient Greek learning during the early middle ages, but it was only one of several places to have that distinction. We can be sure that the Sabians actually existed there, as a unique religious sect drawing at least partly on Hellenistic philosophy. As no writings have survived that are definitely by Sabians themselves, however, that is all we can say with certainty. What we do know is what Muslim, Christian and Jewish writers believed about them, and those beliefs may have been wholly or partly myths, constructed for the polemical purposes of authors from those other religions.[30] It compounds the problem that the texts of astral magic attributed to al-Kindi and Thabit may never have been written by those individuals but, like those attributed to Hermes Trismegistus, be the work of later authors using a famous name.

The quest for the origins of astral magic, which seemed for a moment to be reaching a successful conclusion in time and space, must therefore be left indeterminate. It can be said with confidence that it was developed by people in the Arab world during the early middle ages, using ideas current in Greek-speaking Egypt by the end of antiquity, but that is all. The time has come to reverse the flow of investigation, and see what happens to it in Christian Europe after it arrived there in the twelfth century.

Clearly the spectrum of views visible when it first became fashionable was reproduced constantly until the end of the thirteenth century. One author on the subject was Michael Scot, who subsequently acquired a great name as a wizard because of his interest in magic. In his own time he was a trusted clerical diplomat whom one Pope tried to make an archbishop. He declared that wise spirits ruled the planets in obedience to the creator and would respond to human wishes if invoked by name. His compromise was to substitute the names of Hebrew angels for the pagan deities associated with them.[31] Thomas de Cantimpre made another qualification. He opined both that planetary spirits controlled human behaviour in accordance with the will of the Christian god and that they could be given their pagan names. He thought it possible that all things on earth were generated by the power of Venus. Where he scrupled was to duck the question of whether humans could tap into that power themselves.[32] A similar course was taken by Robert Grosseteste, bishop of Lincoln. He thought that the heavenly bodies were animate, and that scarcely any human operation should be embarked on without taking their influence into account. While approving astrology, however, he did not take the further step of approving astral magic.[33]

That was taken by Albertus Magnus, probably the most prominent theologian of science in the high middle ages. He openly endorsed the idea that marvels could be worked by carving the images of planetary and stellar spirits on metals at the correct moment.[34] The same line was followed by the proto-scientist Roger Bacon, who honoured the spirits of the planets as classical deities and held that they ruled human affairs. Above all, he honoured Mercury as lord of wisdom and eloquence, and associated him with Christ.[35] Against them was pitted the anonymous *Speculum Astronomiae,* which denied that heavenly bodies were animate, and condemned the making of images of them as talismans, explicitly in the form of icons of ancient gods. This work still, however, recommended the use of talismans if they were empowered only by astrological conjunctions, and not by direct invocations.[36] The debate continued at full pelt into the early years of the fourteenth century. Then Arnald of Villanova tried to steer another middle path. He argued that humans should observe how the planets influenced the earth, and try to work with those influences, but not to gain power over the ruling spirits of the planets themselves. He gave the latter their classical pagan names.[37] His contemporary Peter of Abano repeated the argument of Michael Scot, almost a hundred years before, that humans could indeed invoke the power of the planets directly, but by the names of Hebrew angels.[38]

What must be clear from this was that by 1320 western European intellectuals had been accustomed for about two centuries to accept the argument that the planets were living beings, appointed by the Christian god to govern earthly affairs. What divided them was the issue of what they could do about it. Some argued that the divine beings concerned were the ancient deities, and that humans should observe and react to their workings but not manipulate them. Some believed that it was permissible to invoke them, but in the sanitised form of angels with Hebrew names. Others both accepted them as the ancient deities and believed in the right of Christians to work with their power ritually. It must be emphasised that each of these three different points of view was articulated by churchmen who were equally high-ranking, orthodox and reputable. Furthermore, the complaints of the first two groups and the survival of relevant manuscripts prove that the third position – effectively a revival of rituals dedicated to pagan deities within a Christian cosmology – was very commonly held and acted upon by less celebrated figures.

In the 1320s, however, this third position struck a very sharp rock, in the shape of an all-out attack on ritual magic mounted by Pope John XXII. He launched it in 1322, and within five years it had claimed a spectacular victim, a professor at Bologna called Cecco d'Ascoli. He was first sacked from his chair and then actually burned at the stake by a regional inquisition. Scholars of the case have agreed that Cecco's opinions were not particularly extreme; he had defended the use of planetary magic using talismans in a way that had provoked no such reactions during the previous two centuries. It seems that he was just unlucky enough to make some unusually determined local enemies.[39] Nonetheless, his fate does seem to have had a dramatic effect on the debate, for public discussion of astral magic halted abruptly. Over the following 150 years, the typical position was that advocated by the famous early fifteenth-century French theologian Jean Gerson: that the planets were ruled by angels accountable to the Christian god, and could be invoked only by devout prayer, making no use of talismans or invocations.[40]

It is possible to make three qualifications to this picture. One is that astral magic certainly continued to be practised in private, because the texts prescribing rites for it continued to be copied and recopied. The second is that a very occasional intellectual still published a defence of it. The clearest case is that of another professor at Bologna, half a century after the unfortunate Cecco. This was Antonio de Monte Ulmi, who advocated planetary magic with talismans in both theory and practice. His own favourite working was with Mercury, drawing its power into an icon of the Graeco-Roman god, and his only sop to opponents was to insist that a priest should bless the image beforehand.[41] He got away with it. My third qualification is that to some extent such practices had permeated at least well-heeled lay culture. One piece of evidence for this is a tray made as a wedding gift for merchants' children at Florence in the 1420s. It is painted with a nude Venus, floating in the sky and shedding her radiance over happy humans on the earth below.[42] This neatly conflates the classical image of the goddess with the planet, and is effectively a talisman in itself, presented to bless the nuptial union.

Still, the profile of astral magic in the later middle ages is still relatively low, until it comes roaring back up again in the Florentine Renaissance. Thanks to D. P. Walker and Frances Yates, this has become one of the few well-studied episodes in the history of European magic. It resulted from the convergence of three forces, brought together by the Renaissance project of a renewed and increased effort to recover ancient knowledge. One is the medieval Latin tradition, with which I have been dealing. Another was an infusion of Greek manuscripts brought by refugees from the dying Byzantine empire, especially Hermetic texts. The third was a fresh dispersal of translated Arabic books, especially the *Ghayat al-Hakim* itself, translated into Latin under the name of *Picatrix*.

The individual who launched the new effort was of course Marsilio Ficino, seconded by his friend Giovanni Pico della Mirandola. They attempted in general to reassert the place of the classical pagan deities in religion, as embodiments or symbols of cosmic forces such as love, creativity and wisdom: above all, Mercury, Apollo and Venus. They also, however, explicitly defended astral magic, especially in the context of healing. Their basic argument was that the animation of talismans was the result of the manipulation of celestial influences decreed by God Almighty, and not the conjuration of demons. The talismans themselves were not to be worshipped but used in magical operations, and the latter were designed to make humans more receptive to the natural power of the planetary divinities.[43] Their arguments inspired a large number of friends and followers. Some indeed went further, such as the poet Pontano, who depicted God the Father as entrusting the seven planetary spirits with the work of creating the material world.[44]

They also aroused much opposition, but it is interesting to note how qualified this was. The newly restated case for astral magic was formally condemned by Pope Innocent VIII, but absolved with equal formality by a new Pope, Alexander VI, six years later.[45] At the time of the initial papal condemnation a Spanish bishop, Pedro Garcia, set to work to provide a semi-official refutation of the arguments of Pico in particular. He agreed that the Christian god had entrusted the planets to good spirits, and that the latter controlled earthly phenomena. He even supported the idea that humans could work with them reverently, and admitted that great medieval thinkers had endorsed the use of astral talismans. His only qualification was the traditional fear that to invoke celestial power into material images ran the risk of calling in demons instead.[46] The ruling of Alexander VI, therefore, represented a direct snub to even Garcia's moderately expressed doubts. Three years after Alexander pronounced, the physician to the queen of Naples tried to make his name with a further reasoned defence of the making of images of planetary deities to utilise their influence.[47]

It was only in the middle of the sixteenth century that learned opinion began to turn back against it. This was mainly because of that hardening and narrowing of attitudes that was a general feature of the contest between Reformation and Counter-Reformation. In particular, since it had been Italians who had been most prominent in rehabilitating astral magic, the new intolerance and suspicion of Tridentine Catholicism was a major factor. The papal index of forbidden books issued in 1559 included works on talismans, and in 1586 Sixtus V prohibited astrology. In 1570 the local inquisitors arrested Giorolamo Cardano, a professor at that old stronghold of planetary magic, Bologna. He had tried to compromise by calling the planetary powers angels, and suggesting that talismans might be fashioned to absorb their influence if no invocations were used. He still lost his job and his books were banned. In the same decades attacks on this form of magic, by both Protestant and Catholic theologians, greatly increased.[48] It is also true that it suffered from the taint of keeping bad company, most obviously that of the author of the first full survey of Renaissance magic, Cornelius Agrippa. His underground classic, *De occulta philosophia,* published in 1533, trampled all over the subtleties and cautions of the apologists for planetary talismans. It emphasised that the spirits of the planets were the deities of ancient paganism and revelled in the fact, and in the details of the incantations and fumigations that were needed to draw down the power of each. To those who had feared such operations he returned the robust reply that any Christian magician worth the name should be able to control demons.[49]

Nonetheless, the open practice of it continued among avant-garde intellectuals, three of whom achieved considerable distinction, or notoriety. Their differing fates illustrate the hazards now attending these rites, and the potential open to those who used them. One was the Welshman, John Dee, better known as a mathematical genius with a habit of trying to talk to angels. He believed in the efficacy of astral magic, and has left a gorgeous manuscript now in the Warburg Institute that gives precise directions on how to draw down the power of Venus, portrayed as the classical goddess.[50] Dee, famously, died in his bed, although he died poor and after a few attempts by the papal authorities to capture him on his travels. The second was Giordano Bruno. Frances Yates has drawn attention to the works that he published in the 1580s, recommending rites to the planets, whom he characterised as 'the sacred gods'. They were based on those by Agrippa, and involved the same material correspondences. Bruno was, of course, arrested by the Venetian inquisition when he was stupid enough to get himself into its territory in 1591. He was sent to Rome for final judgement, where, after eight years in which he refused to admit the error of his call for a religion mixing Christianity and Hermetic paganism, he was finally burned. He was the only martyr of the Renaissance love affair with antiquity.[51]

The third celebrated intellectual was Tommaso Campanella, who has traditionally been called the last of the Italian Renaissance philosophers. Like Bruno he was a rogue Dominican friar from southern Italy, but one who embarked on political revolution, trying to overthrow Spanish rule and to reform the Church in Calabria. After his capture he only apparently escaped execution by feigning madness. He officially regained his sanity after a few years in prison, and obtained his freedom after many more by reversing his politics while retaining his ideals. He still called for a reformed Christianity, but this time one led by the Pope and the king of Spain. This was clearly the right answer, and gave him a chance to promote his vision of an ideal state based on a combination of

Christian and solar religion, with temples to the planetary deities. His reputed expertise in the powers of the latter led in 1628 to one of the most remarkable episodes in the history of the Counter-Reformation papacy. It was brought about when Pope Urban VIII felt himself to be personally threatened by the malevolent influence of some impending solar eclipses. He asked Campanella to devise a way of protecting him, and the Pope duly found himself talked into participating in a rite of planetary magic at the Vatican. The two of them sealed themselves into a room which was then sprinkled and censed with appropriate aromatics, hung with appropriate decorations, and stocked with a sympathetic combination of musical instruments, gems, odours, colours and flavours. The object of all this was to draw down the power of Venus and Jupiter to protect the Pope. Needless to say, it worked.[52]

It was, however, a Pyrrhic victory for Campanella and those with his interests and beliefs. For one thing Pope Urban was so impressed that he proceeded to impose a new and more savagely worded ban on astrology, feeling that if the heavenly bodies were so powerful, then humans should not try to pre-empt the divine will by reading it in them. For another, Campanella's own defence of planetary magic, published in 1638, seems to be the last to be produced by a leading intellectual figure.[53] By contrast, the number of works condemning it increased still further in the course of the seventeenth century. Significantly, those that held the practice to be impious were now reinforced by a new kind, of those that held it to be contrary to the laws of physics. The new science was starting to reject astral magic and astrology together.[54]

This said, the power of the planetary deities did not disappear in the course of that century; they just ceased to interest prominent members of the intelligentsia. The quantity of works written against their invocation suggests in itself that there were plenty of people around who still needed persuading. In the early eighteenth century it was still believed by some scholars that the planets were animate beings, and a hundred years later doctors could still be found who were confident that they influenced human health.[55] While it was getting hard, if not impossible, to find reputable people who practised invocation of them, one of the most exuberantly disreputable personalities of the eighteenth century certainly did. This was Casanova, who was imprisoned by the Venetian inquisition in 1755, not for his amorous escapades, nor for his tendency to confidence trickery, but for his possession of various works of ritual magic, including *Picatrix*, the Latin version of the *Ghayat al-Hakim*. Having made his escape, Casanova proceeded to work absolutely classic rites of planetary magic using talismans for the benefit of French aristocrats.[56] The tradition survived, of course, to enter workings of the magicians of the Golden Dawn and to have a lingering presence in modern ritual magic.

Nonetheless, by 1700 it had retired to the margins of acceptability and visibility, after six centuries in which it had represented one of the major ways in which western Christianity had absorbed and revitalised classical pagan ideas. Indeed, it was *the* way in which Christian thought had come closest to finding an orthodox manner of perpetuating belief in, and reverence for, the old deities. As such, it throws down a challenge to anybody concerned with the limitations of conventional academic perspectives. The problem is not merely one of the neglect of the study of magic and divination in general, but of the dichotomy that has commonly been drawn between Europe's classical heritage and its Christian heritage. With the (arguable) blessings of the planetary deities that represent communication, generosity and compassion, both barriers may at last be starting to dissolve, and this collection of essays is one sign of such a development.

Endnotes

1. This argument may be found elaborated, and better contextualised, in Ronald Hutton, *Witches, Druids and King Arthur: Studies in Paganism, Myth and Magic* (London, 2003) [hereafter Hutton, *Witches*], pp. 136-92.
2. *Opera hactenus seorsim edita* (Paris, 1849), ii. 647-9.
3. William of Conches, *Philosophia* (Basle, 1531), pp. 24-37.
4. Bernard Silvester, *De mundi universitate sive Megacosmus et Microcosmus*, ed. in Bibliotheca Philosophorum Mediae Aetatis Vol. 1 (Innsbruck, 1976), lines 1.36-7, 1.3.33, 2.4.49-50, 2.6.47.
5. William of Auvergne, *Opera Omnia*, edited by Damian Zenaro (Venice, 1591), p. 895.
6. David Pingree, 'The Diffusion of Arabic Magical Texts in Western Europe' in *La Diffusione delle Scienze Islamiche nel Medio Evo Europeo* (Rome, 1987), pp. 76-7.
7. Charles Burnett, *The Introduction of Arabic Learning into England* (London, 1997) [hereafter Burnett, *Introduction*], pp. 2-39.
8. Adelard of Bath, *Conversations with his Nephew*, ed. and trans. Charles Burnett (Cambridge, 1998), pp. xi-xix.
9. Burnett, *Introduction*, pp. 11-39.
10. *The Astronomical Works of Thabit b. Qurra*, ed. Frank Carmody (Berkeley, 1960), pp. 167-97.
11. Cited in S. J. Tester, *A History of Western Astrology* (hereafter Tester, *Astrology*], p. 17.
12. In the *Metaphysics*, book 12.

13. In *On the Nature of the Gods*, book 2, section 15.
14. *De errore profanarum religionum*, ed. K. Ziegler (Leipzig, 1907)
15. *Mathesis*, ed. W. Kroll and F. Skutsch (Leipzig, 1896).
16. Tester, *Astrology*, pp. 132-42.
17. Lynn Thorndike, *A History of Magic and Experimental Science. Volume Two* (London, 1923) [hereafter Thorndike, *Magic*], p. 5.
18. Peter Brown, *Authority and the Sacred* (Cambridge, 1995), p. 15.
19. *Curse Tablets and Binding Spells from the Ancient World*, ed, John G. Gager (Oxford, 1992).
20. *The Greek Magical Papyri in Translation*, ed. Hans Dieter Betz (Chicago, 1986).
21. Tester, *Astrology*, pp. 11-14.
22. R. Campbell Thompson, *The Devils and Evil Spirits of Babylonia* (London, 1903); F. A. M. Wiggerman, *Mesopotamian Protective Spirits* (Groningen, 1992).
23. Al-Kindi, *De Radiis*, ed. M. T. D'Alverny and F. Hudry, *Archives d'Histoire Doctrinale et Litteraire du Moyen Age*, 41 (1974), pp. 139-260.
24. *Picatrix: Das Ziel des Wissen von Pseudo-Magriti*, ed. Hellmut Ritter and Martin Plessner (London, 1962).
25. David Pingree, 'Some of the Sources of the *Ghayat al-Hakim*', *Journal of the Warburg and Courtauld Institutes*, 43 (1980), pp. 2-15 [hereafter Pingree, 'Sources'}; and 'Indian Planetary Images and the Tradition of Astral Magic', *Ibid.*, 52 (1989), pp. 8-11.
26. Tester, *Astrology*, pp. 11-29.
27. *The Greek Magical Papyri in Translation*, passim.
28. *Corpus Hermeticum II and XVI*, and *Ascelpius* I, ch. 3, ed. Walter Scott in *Hermetica*, (Oxford, 1924).
29. Pingree, 'Sources', pp. 5-6; Frances A. Yates, *Giordano Bruno and the Hermetic Tradition* (London, 1964) [hereafter Yates, *Bruno*], pp. 47-9; Henry and Renee Kahane and Angelina Pietrangeli, 'Picatrix and the Talismans', *Romance Philology*, 19 (1966), pp. 574-93; Lynn Thorndike, *A History of Magic and Experimental Science. Volume One.* (London, 1923), pp. 582-7.
30. Argued at length in Hutton, *Witches*, pp. 137-58.
31. Bodleian Library, MS 266, fols. 28. 68, 150-8.
32. British Library, Egerton MS 1984, fos. 1-98.
33. Ludwig Baur, *Die Philosophischen Werke des Robert Grosseteste* (Munster, 1912), pp. 1-7.
34. Albertus Magnus, *De Causis*, ed. A. Borgnet (Paris, 1899), Book II.iii.3-5.
35. *The Opus Maius of Roger Bacon*, ed. J. H. Bridges (Oxford, 1897), i. 138-9, 381-99.
36. *Speculum Astronomiae*, chs. 6-12, in *Albertus Magnus, Opera Omnia*, ed. A. Borgnet (Paris, 1899), x. 629-73.
37. Bibliotheque Nationale, MS 6971, fos. 65-82.

38. Thorndike, *Magic. Volume Two*, pp. 900-1.
39. Knowledge of the affair does not seem to have progressed beyond the debate summarised in Thorndike, *Magic. Volume Two*, pp. 948-68.
40. Thorndike, *Magic. Volume Four*, pp. 117-23.
41. Bibliotheque Nationale, MS 7337, pp. 1-9, 26.
42. Reproduced in Kenneth Clark, *The Nude: A Study of Ideal Art* (London, 1956), p. 91.
43. D. P. Walker, *Spiritual and Demonic Magic from Ficino to Campanella* (London, 1958) [hereafter Walker, *Magic*], pp. 35-51; Yates, *Bruno*, pp. 56-107; Nesca A. Robb, *Neoplatonism of the Italian Renaissance* (London, 1935), pp. 47-104; Edgar Wind, *Pagan Mysteries in the Renaissance* (London, 1967, pp. 81-123; Marsilio Ficino, *Opera Omnia* (2nd ed., Basle, 1576), pp. 532-72, 1326-27.
44. Jean Seznec, *The Survival of the Pagan Gods: The Mythological Tradition and its Place in Humanism and Art* (New York, 1961), pp. 80-3.
45. Yates, *Bruno*, pp. 112-115.
46. Petrus Garsia, *Ad sanctissimum patrem et dominum Innocentium papam VIII* (Rome, 1489).
47. Girolamo Torrella, *Opus praeclarum de imaginibus astrologicis* (Valencia, 1496).
48. Lynn Thorndike, *A Histoy of Magic and Experimental Science. Volume Five* (New York, 1941), pp. 569-73; and *Volume Six* (New York, 1941), pp. 147-71.
49. Cornelius Agrippa, *De occulta philosophia*, ed. Donald Tyson (St Paul, MN, 2000).
50. Warburg Institute, London, *Tuba Veneris*.
51. Yates, *Bruno*, pp. 190-355.
52. Ibid., pp. 360-75; Walker, *Magic*, pp. 207-36.
53. *Metaphysica* (Paris, 1638).
54. Lynn Thorndike, *A History of Magic and Experimental Science. Volume Seven* (New York, 1958).
55. E.g. David Boyd Haycock, *William Stukeley* (Woodbridge, 2002), pp. 57, 97-8.
56. S. Guy Endore, *Casanova: His Known and Unknown Life* (London, 1930), pp. 78, 119-25, 208-19, where the accounts in Casanova's *Memoirs* are checked against contemporary records.

'Aspects' of Deity

Prudence Jones

The Triple Moon Goddess of contemporary New Age thought has much deeper roots than is commonly believed. This paper demonstrates how Akkadian astrological tradition appears to have been incorporated in the development of a triple Moon goddess during the Hellenistic era. It offers an example of the way that astrological knowledge can be important in the practice of historical research.

Current literature

Contemporary commentators on ancient and modern Paganism freely discuss individual deities as 'aspects' of a more general or perhaps ontologically prior divine being. The paradigm case of this is modern religious witchcraft or Wicca, which venerates a triple Moon goddess who is seen as the archetype of all goddesses. Thus Janet and Stewart Farrar, in their seminal book *The Witches' Way* (1984),[1] tell us: "All Goddesses are one Goddess – but she shows herself in many aspects, all of which relate to the three fundamental aspects of the Maid [...] the Mother [...] and the Crone [...] every Goddess-form contains all three [...]". 'Aspects' of other lunar and non-lunar deities are also described in non-Wiccan contexts. Jungian analyst Esther Harding reported in 1955 that: "[the ancient Babylonian Moon god Sinn] has two aspects or phases, one lived in the upper world and the other, during the dark of the Moon, in the underworld".[2] In 1948, Robert Graves in *The White Goddess* observed that "Apollo [...] adopted the titles and emblems of a Pelasgian "Averter" or "Destroyer", in one aspect (as his title Smintheus proves) a Cretan Mouse-demon".[3] And Mme Blavatsky's vast and polemical survey of Asian and European spirituality, *The Secret Doctrine* (1888), states: "All the lunar goddesses had a dual aspect – one divine, the other infernal".[4] In present-day academe too, Walther Burkert uses the same term in both the German and English versions of his 1985 textbook *Greek Religion*, referring to "[Persephone's] two aspects, girl-like daughter of the Corn Goddess and Mistress of the Dead".[5]

Multiple deities in the ancient world, however, are not described as 'aspects' of one another. Pausanias for example (VIII.22.3) tells us how at Stymphalus the goddess Hera had three sanctuaries, where she respectively had the bynames or surnames of child, mature woman, and widow. He also tells us (IX.16.3) of the three images of Aphrodite in Thebes, one of them called Heavenly, another called Of-the-People, and the third being the Turner-Away. These titles are perhaps simply epithets, different roles of one goddess shown simultaneously rather than three different goddesses. Around 400 CE, Macrobius reports many examples of deities being called by the names of others or being the same as other deities, such as the oracular saying "One are Zeus, Hades, Helios and Dionysos" (*Saturnalia* I.18.18). Here his explanation, from the oracle of Apollo at Didymus, describes the supreme god Iao undergoing seasonal transformations (*ibid.* I.18.20) "In winter [he is] Hades; Zeus, at the beginning of spring; the Sun in summer; in late autumn, delicate Dionysos".[6] In this case one god is identified with four hitherto separate and independent ones who are revealed as different stages of his yearly life-cycle. This is a stronger case of identification than the mere epithets of Hera or roles of Aphrodite, as it involves equating one deity with others who are otherwise ontologically independent. For our purposes, however, it is enough to note that the four gods are not called 'aspects' of Iao but are said to be identical with him at different seasons.

Syncretism occurred in imperial times as well. One deity could have several names, especially in inscriptions from the provinces where a name in the local language would be linked with that of a deity from the imperial culture: Sulis Minerva at Bath, Zeus Chrysaoraeus at Stratonikeia,[7] for example. One deity may simply be called by different names, often beginning as epithets, as Dionysos is called Bacchos or Iacchos (Shouter) and Bromios (Roarer). These names are not always epithets; the *interpretatio romana* and *interpretatio graeca* simply call native deities by the names of deities from the imperial culture without the dual names of the inscriptions, as when Caesar tells us that the Gauls worship Mercury (*DBG*.6.17). Such equivalences raise metaphysical questions concerning identity which are not our direct concern here. What is relevant is that they are expressed simply by the copula or by a verb of naming rather than by any equivalent of our modern term 'aspect'.

The ancient world also gave us indistinctly individuated collective deities such as the Dioscuroi (Castor and Pollux), the nine Muses and three Graces of classical mythology, as well as the three Matres, the Veteres and the genii Cucullati etc. in northern Europe. These are siblings or companion deities rather than a single deity with three personae. However some of these, like the Christian trinity of three persons in one godhead, will prove to be implicated in the linguistic and ontological developments which follow.

Linguistic clues

So which deities are called aspectual in the ancient world? In English, the word 'aspect' can mean simply 'appearance', as also in Latin. The aspects of a single deity then would be its appearances at different stages in life or in different roles, depicted simultaneously. Intriguingly, however, the OED begins its discussion by stating that the earliest use of the word in English is astrological (Chaucer, 1386) and that it "often coloured the others". This technical meaning (from the Latin *aspicere*, i.e. to look at) refers to the angular relationships between celestial objects as seen from earth. Latin texts refer to astrological aspects by a variety of terms, and planets/signs are sometimes said to *behold* each other (*conspicere*...etc). The word *aspectus* however is not used in the astrological sense until mediaeval times, e.g. 1233 in Britain. In Greek an astrological aspect is consistently rendered *skhema*.[8]

Here a new line of enquiry opens. One text from the middle of the first century CE links two, or perhaps three, deities by astrological aspect. The commentator Cornutus identifies the goddesses Hecate and Artemis with the Moon. He asserts (*in schol. Theocr.* 2.12, p. 208, Osann) that Artemis is "none other than three-formed Hecate, because the Moon completes three related aspects (*genikotata skhemata*)". Now the Moon's aspects to the sun (the Moon is called a planet by astrologers), are her phases. This terminology was also used in the ancient world.[9] A preliminary survey of Greek and Roman passages concerning Artemis and Hecate, helpfully listed by Farnell in *Cults of the Greek States* vol. 2 (see no.14), reveals many passages of apparently astrological origin. The significance of the aspects or phases of the Moon, and the nature of the goddesses Artemis and Hecate, opens long perspectives both on the past and towards the present.

Lunar deities: the astrological perspective

Esther Harding introduces an extremely ancient group of phasal deities when she refers to a Babylonian cuneiform text from the earliest records of astrology, the second millennium BCE. Here, she tells us, "the time of [the Moon's] brightness is now divided into three phases, each of which is ruled over by a separate aspect of the god. Sinn has become a triune god, composed of three persons".[10] The actual text makes it clear that only the first half, the Moon's waxing phase, is divided into three five-day or sixty-degree (sextile) divisions. This is not our contemporary triple division into waxing, full and waning phases of the whole monthly cycle.

"The Moon is during the period of his visibility, in the first five days, the god Anu; from the sixth to the tenth day, the god Ea; from the eleventh to the fifteenth day, the god Enlil". The Babylonian Epic of Creation, the *Enuma Elish*, in one of its versions expands:

> From the first day to the fifth, five days, (it is called) the sickle. It belongs to Anu. From the sixth day to the tenth, five days, (it is called) the kidney. It belongs to Ea. From the 11th day to the 15th, five days, (with a) crown of brilliance he is clad. It belongs to Enlil.

Thus the Moon god Sin (as the name is more usually spelt), himself the father of the gods, is like Macrobius" fourfold Iao, a multiple being, identical with three different gods during different phases of his planet's waxing cycle.[11]

Astonishingly, these same five-degree phases are repeated by no fewer than three astrological commentators perhaps 1500 years later, in late antiquity. The scholiast to Euripedes' *Medea* 396 (referring to "my chosen helper Hecate") remarks of the Moon: "Sometimes she is called on the third day Selene, on the sixth, Artemis, and on the fifteenth, Hecate". These appear to be the same phases as in ancient Babylon but are allotted to different deities, this time as the names of a Moon goddess rather than a god. Here again it is verbs of naming which are used, not the word 'aspect'. In the second century CE, according to Eusebius (*Praep. Evang.* III.11.32) the astrologer Porphyry in his essay *On the Statues in the Temples* could describe images of Hecate as the Moon, which he thought represented what appear to be the same three phases as those identified in the *Enuma Elish*. In Porphyry's version there are the new Moon and the full Moon, but the 'kidney' or quarter-Moon phase of the Babylonian text has become a 'basket':

> In addition, Hecate is the Moon, the power within and because of the changes of aspect (*metaskhematismoi*) which surround her. Therefore her power is triple, that of the new Moon is the white-robed and gold-sandalled one with torches; the basket which she bears in heaven represents the cultivation of fruits, which she nourishes with the increase of the light; the symbol of the full Moon is the [figure] with sandals of bronze [...with] a laurel branch [...and] a poppy.

At about the same time as Porphyry the commentator Cleomedes also described the same phases but called their visible markers unnamed 'faces', masks or personae of a single goddess rather than different identities: "For the ancients said that there are three aspects (*skhemata*) about the Moon: the crescent, the half Moon, the full Moon. For this reason it is customary to depict Artemis with three faces (*prosopa*)". (*Meteor.* II.5.111).

Thus deities associated with three 'aspects' or phases of the Moon appear in practice before the first millennium BCE, and are named as such by the mid-second century CE. The deities themselves are not called 'aspects' but are associated either with verbs of identity or, in one case here and more to follow, with one of several words meaning a mask or a face. The word in question, *prosopon,* is not peculiar to astrology. It is used to describe the Hebrew 'faces of God' and so has an association with divinity independent of astrology. Relevantly for our purposes however it is also used throughout the astrological literature to refer to the ruling planets of the three ten-degree subdivisions of the signs (originally marked by stars or constellations called 'decans') which are nowadays called 'faces' or 'decanates'.

Prosopon generally means a face, countenance, expression or theatrical mask, hence persona or role, delegated power or office, and it was also used of the three persons of the Christian Trinity. The decan star 'wears the face' of its ruling planet.[12] One decanate, ten degrees of the zodiac, is ten days of the sun's travel, and since both solar and lunar months last thirty days, ten days is also the length of each of the trine phases or aspects of the soli-lunar cycle, the waxing, full and waning phases of the Moon. But Porphyry's and Cleomedes' 'faces' are not ten-day periods, equal to the decanates of the solar and lunar months; merely the ancient five-day divisions of the waxing half-month. However they share their name with the astrological decans: the Hellenistic Moon goddess 'wears the face' of the deity associated with each of her three waxing five-day phases or aspects.

The second association that arises from this ancient tablet concerns the three Babylonian gods identified with the Moon god in his waxing phases. They are already well known as the three ruling gods who in the second millennium BCE were associated with the three zones of the sky known in Babylon as the three 'Ways'. These were defined by declination (distance above or below the celestial equator) and very roughly corresponded with our three tropical and equatorial regions. Enlil was the god of storms and the atmosphere, ruling the northern zone; Anu ruled the heavens and the central zone; and Ea, sometimes known as the 'antelope of the Southern Ocean', ruled the waters and the southern zone.[13] These were the three cosmos-measuring gods, high in the order of celestial hierarchy.

Astronomically, to equate the three phases of the Moon's waxing half with the three gods of the celestial circles is bizarre. The phases of the Moon's synodic period are not correlated regularly every month with its distance above or below the celestial equator in the three 'ways' of Ea, Anu and Enlil. The place of the new Moon and following lunar phases in the three zones depends on the season, moving north then south with the sun over the course of a year. A literal meaning cannot be assigned to this equation, but a symbolic meaning also seems forced. The period of least light is here linked with the sky and the central zone of the heavens, the period of middling light with water and the southern heavens, and that of most light with storms and the northern heavens. There is no obvious rationale for this, yet clearly some kind of identification did take place. Furthermore, the identification of the waxing sub-phases with the celestial zones also persisted into late antiquity, in the same way as the identification of the third, sixth and fifteenth days with phasal deities did. The commentator Servius, glossing Virgil's *Aeneid* IV.511 in the fourth century of our era, observes:

> The three faces [*ora*] of the virgin Diana: [...] Luna, Diana and Proserpina. When she is above the earth she is believed to be Luna; when on earth, Diana; when below the earth, Proserpina. Therefore triplicity pleases these people, because Luna has three shapes [*figuras*], first the crescent, following which is the quarter Moon, and on the 15th the full Moon.

Luna and Diana are the Roman equivalents to the Greek Selene and Artemis, whom we have seen already identified with the third and sixth days. Proserpina can be linked with Hecate because the latter, seen throughout antiquity as a goddess of the dead (among other rulerships) was the constant attendant of Proserpina the underworld queen.[14] The word translated 'faces', *ora*, is one standard Latin version of the Greek *prosopa*, the word for the astrological faces or decans which we have already seen. Yet here once more the passage does not describe three ten-day divisions but the old three five-day divisions and, as in Babylon, the height of the Moon relative to the earth, whether this means the line of the actual horizon or the celestial 'earth', the equator.

The association of the Moon deity with three levels of the universe is reinforced when we remember that one of the goddesses mentioned by Cornutus and Porphyry, Hecate, is said in the earliest written account we have of her, Hesiod's *Theogony*, written around 700 BCE, to have been so honoured by Zeus that she was allotted 'a share' (*moira*, the word later used for a degree of the zodiac) in all three levels of the universe, "in earth, in starry heaven and in the unharvested sea" (*Theog.* 412-15). Here is early evidence of her threefold nature. Hesiod's father came from western Asia Minor, and at Lagina in Caria (near Milas in south-west Turkey), the inscriptions from the late second century BCE in Hecate's temple identify her as *megiste thea*, the Greatest Goddess, as they do in the sanctuary of the 'Greatest God' Zeus in the city of Stratonikeia at the end of the processional route to the south. Hecate was known as 'She of the Ways' (*Enodia, Trioditis*) in classical times and given rulership over crossroads, or rather the forks in mountain paths, the junctions of three ways, which are typical of Greece. It is thought to be the three masks hung for her at these three-ways which gave rise to the triple images which became typical of her.[15] She also became associated with magic and the dead, perhaps through her access to the underworld and companionship of its queen, as well as being seen as a fiery being (Porphyry, for example, explains the laurel as a token of her fiery nature). Hecate's rulership of the triple paths or ways, her presence in all three zones of the universe (whose names however do not include 'ways' in Greek; indeed *hodos* means astronomical longitude rather than either latitude or declination[16]) and the description of one of those three zones as the sea rather than the underworld, may prove to be no more than coincidence, or they may eventually reveal her as a descendant of the Babylonian Sin, whose characteristics these also are. If so, this would include a lunar aspect in Hecate's earliest nature, contrary to the current consensus of opinion on the subject which links her with the solar goddesses of the Near East.

We know that the astrological corpus was transmitted from Mesopotamia to Greece and Egypt and thence to Rome. Nevertheless the exact similarity of this lunar iconography is striking: in two of the oldest Mesopotamian astrological documents, written some time between the fall of Crete and the fall of Troy, as well as in the philosophical religion of late antiquity, the Moon's waxing half only is divided into three equal periods which are ruled by deities who are also rulers of the three levels of the universe. In both these sets of documents, the three phasal deities are said to be identical with the Moon deity during their particular phase.

This transmission would be remarkable enough without our further seeking a precursor to the modern threefold division of the whole month, were it not that we already know that in both ancient Babylon and ancient Greece the whole calendar month was in fact divided into three. We are surely entitled to ask whether the whole month too had three ruling deities.

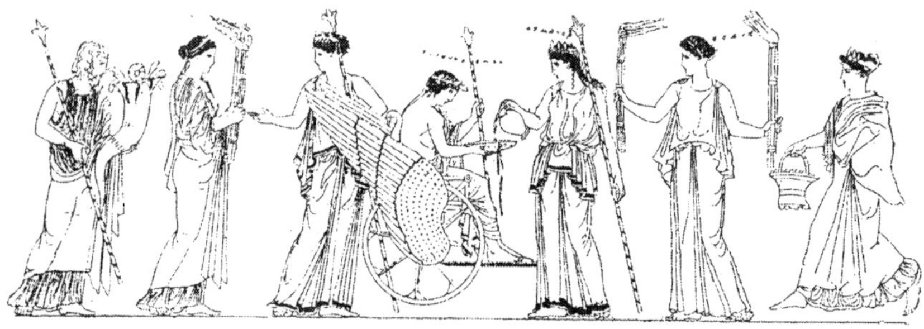

Drinking cup showing deities of the underworld.
From Left: Plouton, Artemis (?), Demeter, Triptolemus, Persephone, Hecate, unknown nymph. From Harrison, *Mythology and Monuments of Ancient Athens*, (1980), p. iii.

The triple month

At this point it is important to distinguish between the months of the solar/sidereal year of the seasons and those of the so-called lunar month, the soli-lunar cycle of the new and full moons. The solar year is timed either by the sun's position against the fixed stars, e.g. the solstices and equinoxes, or by that of the earth, e.g. the first rising of a certain star or constellation. The lunar month lasts 29 or 30 days; the solar year can also be arbitrarily divided into 'months' of this length, or indeed into any other periods. The sun also remains in each of the astrological signs for approximately 30 days (they extend for 30° of celestial longitude), but the starting dates of the signs are not those of the modern solar months. As we shall see, the months within each of these three types seem to have been subdivided into three periods: the solar month in the earliest Mesopotamian records; the astrological month or sign (at latest by the first century BCE in Mesopotamia and, by means of the three decanates, throughout later astrological practice); and finally the lunar month in Greece.

The Babylonian creation epic of the second millennium BCE, the *Enuma Elish* (V.3.4), tells us that the great god Marduk, who remodelled the universe after overthrowing the primal parents, 'fixed the year' and "for the twelve months [...] placed three stars each".[17] These twelve solar months, needed for the agricultural cycle, were roughly co-ordinated each year with the lunar months, based on the first sight of the new Moon, which timed the civic festivals, so that each year began respectively at or around the springtime rising of the star Dilgan in Cetus. In this way the calendar months kept in line with the 365¼ day true solar year and the seasons.

The earliest lists of the 'three stars each' per month do not as we might expect mark dates five or ten days apart, dividing either the first half or the whole solar month into three as in the lunar traditions already described. These earliest lists, the 'astrolabes', composed at the beginning of the first millennium BCE, name the three stars (or constellations) associated with each of the months, and assign each star to one of the three gods of the celestial zones, Ea, Anu or Enlil. A later text, the *Mul Apin* of around 700 BCE, which lists the dates on which these (and other) stars rise with the sun, reveals intervals of 5, 10, 19, 20, 25, 30 and 35 days, with 20 days as the most frequent interval. A cursory comparison of the star names from the astrolabes with those of *Mul Apin* also shows only one month (the seventh) being marked unambiguously by stars from each of the three zones. The 'three stars each' thus divided the solar months irregularly, and certainly not into neat intervals of five or ten days mapped onto the three zones as in the lunar months already described.

Within 100 years of the composition of *Mul Apin*, the zodiac or sun's path had begun to replace the equator and its parallel zones of Ea, Anu and Enlil as the reference system of choice for locating the stars and planets. Yet far from disappearing, a set of 'three stars each' in the solar and astrological months is reported by Diodorus Siculus (II.30-31) midway through the first century BCE. 'Chaldean' astrologers described stars within, above and below the zodiac which rose and set at intervals of ten days. Twelve of these were chief, owning "a month and one of the signs of the zodiac", twelve were situated in the northern sky beyond the zodiac, and a further twelve similarly in the southern sky. B.L. van der Waerden seems to have been the first to point out that if the astronomical problems with Diodorus' account (30 stars rather than 36; the visibility of each of them for six months; the calendrical incorporation of the 5¼ days remaining at the end of the year) are disposed of as misunderstandings, what we seem to have here is a calendar system similar to the Egyptian one, which was (subdivided without reference to months by the decan stars which rise every ten days, but here linked with the months and signs of the zodiac as well as with a zodiacal equivalent of the three equatorial zones.[18] If any star rose on the first day of any month, each month would then be divided into three equal periods. Unfortunately Diodorus does not tell us the dates on which these decan stars rose and so the date divisions remain unspecified.

By the time of the Roman Republic then we see a threefold solar (astrological) month in use among 'Chaldean' astrologers. Whatever the details of its composition and origin, as yet unknown, it is similar to and, as van der Waerden argues, possibly adapted from the earlier Mesopotamian calendar systems of *Mul Apin*, the astrolabes and perhaps the 'three stars each' of *Enuma Elish.* Although the astrological months or signs calculated from the spring equinox have continued to be divided into three decanates until the present day, there is no hint of a ten-day triple division of the solar month in the civil calendar of Rome, whatever may have been the case in the civil calendars of Sumer and Assyria.

The ancient world did however possess a lunar month of three ten-day periods, which was that of ancient Greece. (There was an Egyptian lunar calendar but this contained 30-day months divided by the half and quarter Moons rather than by three decanates.[19]) These periods were called 'waxing' (*histamenos*), 'middle' (*meson*) and 'waning' (*phthinon*). In alternate months the last decanate was only nine days long. They are mentioned for example in the *Works and Days* of Hesiod, e.g lines 819-21 which give all three instances of the fourth day of each decanate. Hesiod describes the traditional attributes of each day of the month, its lucky and unlucky days and the deities who preside over these. This calendar was modified slightly during the classical era but fell out of use following the Roman conquest in the early second century BCE, to be replaced by the Roman solar month (which retained its own lunar terminology of the Kalends, Nones and Ides), and then in the early Common Era by the seven-day week.[20] Coordinating the dates of the visible month, the month 'according to the Moon', with those of the civil month ('according to the archon') and again with the solar year proved to be a hit-and-miss business. Aristophanes, in the *Clouds* 615-16, has Selene the Moon complaining that the calculation has gone wrong and dates are not being kept according to her phases, so that the gods are missing the banquets that humans hold in their honour.

Were the three decanates also ruled by three goddesses, or perhaps by one goddess of three aspects or 'faces'? From the calendar, as also from cultus, it seems not. The Moon was certainly personified as Selene, the 'shining one', but this divine being was not portrayed in art as threefold and did not have a temple or a priesthood during the classical era. The association of Artemis and Hecate with the Moon, mentioned in our philosophical texts above, also came late. The earliest textual evidence I have found for Artemis as a Moon goddess is from Chrysippus (fl. 232 BCE), slightly before Diogenes of Babylon (c.240-150), mentioned by Sarah Iles Johnston in her detailed study of Hecate. Johnston finds that goddess identified with the Moon only as late as the writings of the Roman Stoic, Seneca, at about the same time as Cornutus in the first century CE.[21] Cleomedes, whom we have already seen (p.4 above) in the second century CE describing the three Babylonian aspects of the waxing Moon, might seem to offer further assistance, as he continues: "modern people add to these three [aspects] the so-called 'gibbous' Moon", which in modern astrology and for later astrologers in the ancient world such as Paul of Alexandria and Heliodorus (see no.9), marks the first third of the Moon's travel, 120°, thus indicating an awareness of the triple division of the whole lunar period. Cleomedes, however, appears confused about the gibbous Moon. For him it lay "midway between the quarter Moon and the full Moon", not the 120° trine but the sesquiquadrate aspect or 135°. In any case Cleomedes does not link this phase with any particular deity or face. For him the three faces of Artemis remain those of the waxing disc only.

In the Hellenistic age, after Alexander, astronomy and calendar-making continued their advance, laying the foundations for the division of astrological signs, the astrological months, into three. The foundation of the great library at Alexandria in about 300 BCE provided an enormous resource for the scholars of the ancient world. By the second century Egyptian astrological papyri began to appear, as well as others dealing with the calendar and with astronomical calculations such as the exact date of new Moon and the planetary aspects.[22] We know from a passage in Diodorus of Sicily (II.30.6,7; II.31.4,5) that by the first century BCE the tradition of the decan stars, which divided the solar months into three, being identified by their position relative to the celestial equator had been replaced by their identification relative to the sun's path, the ecliptic. Solar months and lunar months could now be measured on the same scale. Indeed, the decanate rulers of the zodiac (rather than the calendar month) had appeared earlier, in the writings of Teucros of Babylon in or before the early second century BCE, and they were soon known as 'faces', *prosopa*.[23]

Religious and philosophical speculation were also fuelled by the documents available in Alexandria. It may be no coincidence that Stoicism, a philosophical school which taught the providence and orderliness of a harmonious universe manifested in the movements of the celestial bodies, was founded (in 310) and flourished at about this time. Astrology, astronomy and religion were fused in the Stoic outlook, many of whose masters, including Zeno himself, Diogenes of Babylon, Posidonius of Apamea and others, were from the East, and this philosophy became acceptable to educated and otherwise sceptical people of the time. As Frances Yates observed, for the religious gnostics of late antiquity, the laws of nature were in fact astrological laws.[24] The astronomical cosmology of philosophically minded people was essentially astrological, ensouled by the intelligences of the celestial bodies. Thus astrological considerations can seldom be ignored in theological writings from this era.

The Moon goddess appears

A radically new development in religious imagery seems to have come about at the beginning of the second century BCE. In 196 BCE in Athens the calendar Moon began to be described as a goddess: dates were no longer listed 'according to the Moon' but 'according to the goddess'.[25] The early second century was also the time when the crescent Moon first appeared on the denarii of Rome, as well as the image of the Moon goddess Luna herself in her two-horse chariot.[26] In fact, according to Livy (XL.2.2) by 182 BCE Luna had acquired a temple in Rome. Provisionally, then, this may point towards a growing interpretation of the Moon as a divine being at the time. But curiously, none of these images is triple.

However by 43 BCE at Aricia, south of Rome, coins were minted presenting the image of Diana Nemorensis in her grove as three goddesses standing side by side: one with a bow, one with a poppy, and one with a pomegranite.[27] Diana (whose name means 'the shining one', 'the goddess', *dea*) was a Latin goddess whose temple in Aricia was the headquarters of the Latin league of city-states, conquered by Rome in the sixth century BCE. Diana was then adopted into the Roman pantheon with her own temple on the Aventine Hill and was later (or had already been: see below) assimilated to the Greek Artemis.[28] Her temple in Aricia remained and by the time the coins were minted, the goddess was known to the Roman poets, including Horace, Ovid and Statius, as Trivia, 'she of the three ways', a direct equivalent to Hecate's Greek epithet *trioditis*.[29]

Another contemporary, Virgil, referred in the *Aeneid* IV.511 to "triple Hecate, the three faces of the virgin Diana", giving rise to the later commentary by Servius which has already been quoted.

It is therefore tempting to interpret these figures as portraying the three goddesses of Servius' three celestial zones in his comment on Virgil's line: the poppy identifying Luna, mistress of the sky, the bow Diana, mistress of the earth, and the pomegranite Proserpina, mistress of the underworld.[30] The Arician coin would then be the first visual image of the trio of goddesses identified with the Moon by the commentators of late antiquity. Their position side by side, rather than like the Hekateia of the three-ways, back to back forming a complete circle, would argue in favour of this. Against it we should however remember that the poppy is not necessarily of the Moon. Porphyry for example describes both the poppy and the pomegranite as attributes of Hecate, with whom Artemis/Diana was often identified from classical Greece onwards. Two hundred years before Porphyry the coin might merely have shown Diana, Hecate and Proserpina together, three bloodthirsty goddesses who would suit the bloodthirsty nature of the Arician cult. Diana Trivia was identified with Artemis Tauropolis, who demanded human sacrifice, and her priest was the notorious *rex nemorensis*, gaining his office only by winning a fight to the death against the existing incumbent. The association of Artemis, Hecate and Persephone goes back to Greek vase paintings of the classical era, where they are portrayed, together with other underworld deities such as Hermes, Hades, Demeter etc., in underworld scenes. Persephone, like Artemis in a different context, is as we have seen closely associated with Hecate, the original Trivia. Thus the three might easily be grouped together by an enterprising artist.

It has also, more radically, been suggested that the image on the coin is not simply an invention or reconstruction of the first century coiner, but an accurate representation of the original cult statue from the fifth century. Commentators agree that the figures portrayed are in an archaic style typical of that period (see no.29). If so however, a connection with the Moon would be even less likely as the links between Artemis, Hecate and the Moon are extremely dubious at that time and no threefold statue of Selene has ever been identified. The threefold imagery of Hekate had however spread to Artemis by that time in Greece, to the extent that the triple image which stood outside a gateway or at a crossroads was sometimes called an Artemision rather than a Hecateion. We have no certain images of these triple statues of the three-ways unfortunately, but the earliest triple statues of Hecate (e.g. that from Ægina, dated around

350 BCE) took the form of three identical figures, usually standing back to back, sometimes carrying torches, sometimes offering plates or jugs, but not pomegranites or poppies. Later images might carry a key (for the gate of Hades) or a whip (likewise for Hades). The image of a goddess with a bow, however, a true Artemis, is unknown in this context, and incontrovertibly lunar symbols, such as a crescent moon on the forehead of one of the figures, only appear during the Roman empire[31] It has been suggested that Artemis became seen as a Moon goddess under the influence of her brother Apollo's incorporation of the sun god Helios as early as the fifth century.[32] Thus the triple Hecateia of the three ways could well have been reinterpreted at the time as personifications of the triple lunar month, a triple-faced or triple-bodied Artemis/Hecate who was the Moon. Unfortunately for this theory, however, no such interpretation seems to have been expressed in the visual arts or poetry for several hundred years thereafter.

Thus a fifth century temple image including Luna with Diana and Hecate/Proserpina would be a new development in iconography, peculiar to the grove of Trivia at Aricia. The creation of such an image in the first century would be more easily explained by the astrological developments described in the previous sections above. The easiest explanation of all would be that the poets and intellectuals of the early Empire reinterpreted an existing triple image of the Artemision type, whether of the fifth or the first century, in accordance with then current philosophical, i.e. astro-cosmological, theories. By catching the imagination of the Roman poets, it nevertheless seems that Diana Trivia formed a significant link in the chain of development of the ancient triple Moon goddess.

The three personae of Diana Trivia, indeed, seem to have constituted a challenge to early Christianity. Around the year 300 the new Christian convert Arnobius could complain:

> Some of your learned men […] say that [each of] Diana, Ceres and Luna is the head of a single triple goddess (*caput esse unius deae triviali*) and that there are not three distinct persons (*personarum*) as there are three distinct names; and that Luna is named by all of these and that the rest of the series are bynames (*cognominum)* added to hers. But if this is […] true then Ceres and Diana are empty names. [*Adversus Nationes* III.34]

(Here, rather than Proserpina, Arnobius sees that goddess's mother Ceres.) His objection seems to be about the distinction between separate persons and the beings corresponding to mere bynames, or as we should nowadays say, 'aspects' of a triple goddess. Rival religious schools would naturally attempt to distinguish the ways in which their deities could be three in one, and here a technical terminology of non-astrological origin seems to be developing. To investigate the relationship between the threefold goddess and Christianity would however overexpand the present investigation.

The Arician Diana herself does not seem to be of astrological origin, though the interpretations made of her may have been. Nor does her appearance lead us any nearer to a triple goddess who ruled the ten-day periods of the triple month.

Deities of the triple month

So far then we have uncovered two groupings of lunar deities, both astrological in the sense of personifications of astronomical phenomena. These are: a god or goddess who is identified both in ancient Babylon and in late Graeco-Roman antiquity with three other deities during the three phases of the waxing Moon; and god/s or goddess/es who are identified similarly with the three zones of the heavens as seen from earth (and sometimes with the phases of the Moon as well). During late antiquity they are named as the goddesses Selene/Luna/Mene, the Moon; Artemis/Diana, goddess of the hunt; Hecate, a complex triple goddess; and Persephone/Proserpina, mistress of the underworld. The reason for choosing these goddesses is unknown, but we may speculate that it stems from their independently arising mythological dominance of the heavens, of the wild untamed earth and of the underworld, or in Hecate's case of all three. (The later development of Hecate into a goddess who communicates between all three celestial/conceptual zones, presented in the Chaldean Oracles but perhaps going back to Xenocrates' tripartite division as reported by Plutarch, *de fac.* 943f, is investigated by Johnston and Ronan but is outside my scope here.) Triple imagery in art came long before the Common Era but is not explicitly of the Moon. Hecate's triple statues from the fifth century onwards, not lunar statues but guardians of the three-ways, seem to have shaped the imagery of Artemis, with whom she is associated, in particular in the latter's Latinised form as Diana Trivia at Aricia, and later texts interpret these triple images as depictions of three of the goddesses listed above, described as 'faces' of the Moon or of Artemis/Diana.

It is to an entirely different set of goddesses that we must turn to get any hint of the hoped-for ruling deities of the ancient triple month, the major lunar phases. Amazingly these go back, at least in the interpretations of philosophers, as early as the third century BCE. Clement of Alexandria, a second century Christian writer (*Stromata*: Abel, frg. 253) quotes the grammarian Epigenes, active in the third century BCE at the library of Alexandria, as reporting that Orpheus "said the Fates are [...] divisions of the Moon [*selene*]: the thirtieth and the fifteenth and the first [literally 'the new Moon']". That is, the Fates, the Spinner, Measurer and Cutter of the thread of life, are likened to the days of the New Moon, Full Moon and Dark Moon in the 30-day lunar month. Here then finally is a division of the full course of the lunar month into three phasal decanates marked respectively by their end point (last decanate), midpoint (middle decanate) and beginning (first decanate). These phases are associated not with the familiar Artemis-Selene-Hecate triad, but with one of the teams of semi-differentiated personalities mentioned briefly in the introduction. How credible is this?

It seems to be a theologian's interpretation rather than a report of actual worship. The words 'Orpheus said' generally refer to an interpretation of mystical philosophy, usually Neoplatonic or Pythagorean and often with some astrological content. What is not normally meant is that the Hellenistic Greeks sacrificed (in this case) to Atropos, the final Fate, during the waning Moon, that they called the waning Moon by the name 'Atropos', or any other detail of public cult. Calendar records reveal nothing about ceremonies for the ten-day 'weeks', the calendar decanates, merely for individual days. Here however it is perhaps significant that the typical ceremony for the 30th of the month was for Hecate, the deposition of 'Hecate's suppers' at the three-ways after the ritual monthly cleansing of the house, and that on the 16th, like the 15th the approximate time of the full moon, cakes were taken to sanctuaries of Artemis and to the three-ways. The first of the month was a time of no religious festivities at all, but it was said in the second century CE by Plutarch (*Moralia* 828A) to be 'the holiest of days', and from earliest records it was called after the moon, not as Selene but as Mene, by the name 'new moon' (*noumenia*).[33] Here then we have ceremonies for two of our three goddesses on their appropriate days and a mention of the third on the relevant day, reinforcing Epigenes' choice of these days rather than others to characterise their particular decanates. Three dates of the month are of course three degrees of the Zodiac, which in Greek are *moirai*, the same term used for the portions or lots of Hecate in the three celestial zones by Hesiod.

A corroborative statement comes from Porphyry, some four hundred years later in his continuation of the quotation already given (in Eusebius: *Praep. Evang.* III.11.34): "The Fates by contrast are related to [the Moon's] powers: Clotho to generation, Lachesis to nourishment, Atropos to the rapacity of the goddess". Servius, six hundred years after Epigenes, in a further comment on *Aeneid* IV.511, uses a similar metaphor, embodied not in the Fates but the familiar triad of independent goddesses:

> Some people call Lucina ["Light", said to be the Moon by Varro, *d.l.l.* V.69], Diana and Hecate the same, because to the one goddess they assign the powers of birth, health and death, and some call Lucina the goddess of birth, Diana the goddess of health, and Hecate the goddess of death, because of which triple power they depict her as triple and therefore build temples to her at the three-ways.

Servius is of course wrong about the reason for temples at the three-ways, but his reference to birth, health and death describes the provinces of the three Fates as well as the visible changes of the Moon's light during her three ten-day phases.

The Moon is also linked with similar triads of collective goddesses in at least two other mystical hymns. One, a prayer to Selene (*PGM* IV 2785-2870), is translated by Stephen Ronan in his 1992 book *The Goddess Hecate*. (Unfortunately we have no date more precise for it than before the fourth century CE.) It combines much of the imagery we have already seen, invoking 'Three-faced Selene', and most gloriously it explicitly refers to the calendar (or astrological) decanates. The relevant lines are:

> You dance with the triple forms of the triple Graces
> [...] You are Justice and the thread of the Fates,
> Clotho, Lachesis and Atropos,
> O Three-headed One you are
> Persephone, Megaira and Allecto [the three Furies]
> [...] Hecate, Many-named, Mene,
> Cleaving the air like arrow-shooting Artemis,
> Thrice-resounding, Triple-voiced, Three-headed, Thrice-named
> Selene,
> O Trident-bearing One of Three-faces, Three-necks, Three ways,

Who holds undying flaming fire in triple baskets.
You frequent the Three-ways and are Mistress of the
Three Decads.[34]

Here is a trove of relevant imagery: a triple goddess, 'Mistress of the Decads', called Selene and Hecate and Mene (Moon), likened to Artemis, carrying fire in baskets, and also connected not only with the triad of the Fates but with that of the Furies (evil fates?) and that of the Graces (good fates?). On a similar point the magical hymn no. 5, *To Selene*, includes the line: "You who shape the triple dance of the triple Graces". Thus although we do not know of any triple statues from the classical age of Selene the Moon, it seems that for mystical initiates there were plenty, for every statue of the Graces, Fates, Furies or, as we shall see, the Seasons could be interpreted as expressing the three phases of the Moon's complete cycle, and any complete cycle, according to the Pythagoreans as reported by Aristotle in *de caelo* 268.11-14, is contained in the triple form of beginning, middle and end. Thus we see how the triple statues of Hecate and later Artemis, three statues back to back making a complete circle, could also plausibly be interpreted in the same way, as representations of the Moon's ten-day phases rather than as the guardians of the three-ways that they originally were.

An archaeological argument for believing that this imagery was widely recognised in the ancient world was offered by the nineteenth-century lexicographer W. Roscher, in his *Lexikon* col. 1904. The influential Cambridge classicist Jane Ellen Harrison repeated the argument in three of her books. *Themis* (1912), from which the texts of the quotation from Epigenes and the line from the prayer to Selene are taken, includes a condensed and difficult passage explaining that the seasons of the year were triple in Greece because they are proportions (*moirai*, allotments, the word used for the Fates as well as for astrological degrees), "and the Moirae, as Orpheus tells us, are but the three moirae or divisions (*mere*) of the Moon herself, the three divisions of the old Year [*annus*, circuit, here = lunar month]. And these three Moirae or Horae are also Charites".[35]

The Charities around Hecate (Prague).
From Harrison, *Mythology and Monuments of Ancient Athens*, (1980), p. 379.

Why should the Seasons, who are Fates, also be the Charites (Graces, givers of good things)? The reasons are given in Harrison's first book, *Mythology and Monuments of Ancient Athens* (1890). Here she discusses the second-century (CE) traveller Pausanias' account of the worship of the Graces on the Acropolis and the statue of Hecate on the Tower, also at the Acropolis, mentioned in his account of the island of Aegina. Hecate on the Tower, says Pausanias, was the first triple statue of that goddess, three bodies in one, made by Alcamenes c. 430 BCE. (This is presumably not including the existing triple masks and crude Hekataia of the three-ways.) From a nearby inscription which assigns the Graces to the same priesthood as that of Artemis on the Tower, Harrison proposes that the three Graces and Hecate (already linked with Artemis in cult and iconography) received joint worship at the gate of the Acropolis. On vase paintings also the Graces and/or the Seasons, carrying flowers and fruits, are often shown together with Artemis and/or Hecate. Thus it seems likely that the three female figures seen dancing around some statues of Hecate portray the three Graces, bringers of abundance. A similar argument, interpreting the three female figures forming the Hecateion in the museum at Prague as the three Graces or the Seasons, seen as Moirae (apportionments) of the Moon, appears on page 408 of the 1908 edition of her book *Prolegomena to the Study of Greek Religion*.[36]

In this way Jane Harrison argues that the Seasons, the Fates and the Graces (Charities) were seen by mystics at least as the ruling goddesses of the ancient calendar decanates, the phases of the Moon. This argument depends on seeing Artemis and Hecate as lunar goddesses, which is not of course the standard interpretation today and is one which was hotly debated in Harrison's day. It is not surprising that Roscher, one of the proponents of Hecate's lunar origin, actually explains the triple imagery of that goddess as deriving from "the triple appearance of the Moon as waxing, full and waning [...] which also corresponds to the ancient division of the month into decades" (*Lexikon* col. 1890). On the contrary, it seems, the calendar interpretation of Hecate's three faces appears to have come from the speculations of Hellenistic philosophers, initially embodied in that goddess's companions the Graces, but later attributed to the three deities who had become associated with an independent astrological tradition, that of the three equal phases of the waxing Moon.

Conclusion

Astrological knowledge has allowed us, in this preliminary investigation of aspectual deity, to distinguish separate strands in the development of a threefold lunar goddess in the Graeco-Roman world. Triads of lunar deities from the ancient world have been shown to be related by aspect in both the theological and the astrological senses, although no clear differentiation of terminology appears to have taken place. Deities who are explicitly said to personify three phases of the waxing moon are found in both ancient Babylon and Hellenistic antiquity. In both systems, some of the deities are also credited with some power over the three universal zones measured from the celestial equator, although this seems less than integrated with their lunar rulership. Two separate traditions may be involved here.

These deities are not called 'aspects' of one another (or 'persons') but in the Graeco-Roman world 'faces' (*prosopa, ora*) or 'images' (*figurae*), or they are simply said to be or to be called one another in specific circumstances.

Finally, some commentators and theologians, one as early as the third century BCE, interpreted the waxing, full and waning phases of the Moon to signify birth, life and death, or the three Fates or the three Seasons or possibly Charites, with whom Hecate and Artemis were often depicted from fifth-century vase paintings onwards. Triple goddesses and triple groups of goddesses could therefore be interpreted in this way, and triple statues portraying one of the goddesses with a lunar crescent appeared from Imperial times onwards, but it is not clear how much popular currency this interpretation had. This version of the aspectual Moon deity has however gained wide currency in the twentieth century.

Many further questions remain to be asked. The exact relationship between the 'faces' of the Moon goddess and the 'faces' of the decan deities who rule the decanates of the astrological signs has not been investigated here. A thorough examination of the corpus of ancient astrological and mystical texts remains a massive investigation, which the sketchy examination of literary sources above suggests would yield much useful information. A more detailed investigation of ancient iconography would add further nuances to what is currently a more text-based approach. Nor has this paper investigated how the concept of aspectual deity, the triple Moon in particular, was transmitted to the modern age. The Renaissance Neoplatonists, who avidly read the mystic writings of late antiquity and who were also interested in the doctrine of the Christian Trinity, are a likely place to start: their heirs are certainly among the precursors of Jane Harrison in the nineteenth century.[37]

Nevertheless, the overriding purpose of this paper is to show how astrological knowledge can help historical research. Astrology alerts us to the technical meaning of 'aspects' and reveals the relevance of the triple Moon deity. It allows us to find our way easily around the structure of ancient cosmology and to unpick ambiguous definitions. It allows us to see the specialised meaning of terms such as 'face' and indeed 'aspect' which otherwise seem merely picturesque. Without insider knowledge we are lost when dealing with the astrological worldview of Hellenistic (and much earlier) philosophy. With it we can begin to make sense of otherwise baffling imagery.

Endnotes

1. J. & S. Farrar, *The Witches' Way* (London, 1984), pp. 71-2.
2. Esther Harding, *Women's Mysteries, Ancient and Modern* (London, 1971, 1st ed. New York, 1955) [hereafter Harding, *Mysteries*] p. 90.
3. Robert Graves, *The White Goddess*, (1948; London 1984) ch 22, p. 390.
4. H.P. Blavatsky, *The Secret Doctrine* (1888; Point Loma, California, 1909) vol. I, p. 400.
5. W. Burkert, *Greek Religion* (Stuttgart 1977; tr. Oxford 1985), III.2.9.
6. Macrobius glosses 'Liber Pater', i.e. Dionysus, as the final 'Iao' on the authority of Cornelius Labeo.
7. Strabo XIV.2, 25, 660 and commentary in A. Laumonier, *Les Cultes Indigènes en Carie* (Paris, 1958).
8. The OED has no entry for the so-called 'aspects' of a deity. In Latin the words used for the astrological sense vary, including *conspicere* (to catch sight of, Manilius II 280, 291 etc), *linea* (line; *ibid.* 274), *angulus* (angle: *ibid.* 277), *mathematicum* (calculation: Firmicus II xxii), *radiatio* (ray or radius: *ibid.*), and *forma* (shape: Manileus I.60; II.317, 333, 664; III.178 etc.; Pliny, *N.H.*, II.77). In Greek the word is consistently *skhema* (figure, diagram, posture or attitude, evoking the image of a planetary dance). See the summary in the *Thesaurus Linguae Latinae*; for mediaeval Latin, R.E. Latham, *Mediaeval British Latin*, OUP 1965; for Greek: Liddell and Scott.
9. Paul of Alexandria in the third century CE, (*Eisagogika*, ch. 16, ed. AE Boer, Leipzig 1958) and his fifth-century commentator Heliodorus (*In Paulum commentarium*, ch. 15, ed. AE Boer, Leipzig, 1962), list 'the aspects (*skhemata*) of the Moon which are called phases (*phaseis*)', i.e. its aspects to the sun.
10. Harding, *Mysteries* p. 89.
11. Harding's reference is given as H.C. Rawlinson, *The Cuneiform Inscriptions of Western Asia* (London, 1861) III.55, 3. I have access only to the companion volume of facsimile drawings published in 1866, for which the relevant caption supports Harding's text, reading: '55 no. 3 is a Fragment in which the first half of a Lunation is divided into three parts of 5 days each, called by distinctive names'. The *Enuma Elish* text is K13774, quoted in S. Langdon, *The Babylonian Epic of Creation*, (Oxford, 1923) [hereafter Langdon, *Babylonian Epic*] pp. 160-1 n.3.
12. For *prosopa* as astrological decanate rulers see W. Gundel, *Dekane und Dekansternbilder* (Hamburg, 1936) [hereinafter Gundel, *Dekane*], p. 32. General uses: B.A. Sophocles, *Greek Lexicon of the Roman and Byzantine Periods*. The compiler criticises the use of *prosopon* within the Trinity as 'a gross Latinism'.
13. M. Jastrow, *Aspects of Religious Belief and Practice in Babylonia and Assyria* (London, 1911) pp. 37-7.
14. Hecate appears as goddess of dead souls, sorcerers and the underworld at least as early as Euripedes' *Medea* in the fifth century BCE. Her attendance on Persephone is introduced even earlier, in the *Homeric Hymn to Demeter* 438 ff., and she consistently figures with the underworld queen in vase paintings. See the

discussion of both points in Sarah Iles Johnston, *Hecate Soteira*, Atlanta, Georgia, 1990; also L.R. Farnell, *The Cults of the Greek States* vol. 2 (Oxford, 1896) [hereafter Farnell, *Cults*, 2], pp. 512 ff.

15. According to H. Evelyn-White in his introduction to Hesiod in the Loeb Classical Library, the poet's father came from Cyme on the coast of Lydia, the province to the north of Caria. For Hecate's apparent origin in Caria, see Burkert *Greek Religion* III.3.1, p. 171. For Hecate as a Great Goddess and her connection with the local Zeus: inscriptions 11.l.6; 22 ll.4-5 and others in J. Hatzfeld, "Inscriptions de Lagina en Carie", *Bulletin de Correspondence Hellenique* 44 (1920), 70-100. Masks at crossroads: Burkert, *ibid.* The observation that 'crossroads' are triple in much of Greece is from personal communication by Bernard Eccles. Their name, after all, is *triodoi*, 'three-ways'.

16. *Hodos* as celestial longitude: O. Neugebauer, "Studies in Byzantine astrological terminology", *Trans. Am. Phil. Soc.* new series 50, pt 2, Philadelphia 1960. *Hodos* is used generally for the 'paths' of the heavenly bodies, whether of the planets seen against the fixed stars or of the fixed stars themselves against the horizon.

17. Translation and date from Langdon, *Babylonian Epic*, p. 153, and no. 4.

18. For the star lists and discussion of how the 'three stars each' may have developed into the decans of Greek astrology, see B.L. van der Waerden's article in the *Journal of Near Eastern Studies* VIII, 1949, 6-26.

19. R.A. Parker, *The Calendars of Ancient Egypt* (University of Chicago 1950), pp. 11-12.

20. See Bischoff, "Kalendar", in W. Roscher, *Lexikon der klassischen Altertumswissenschaft* [hereafter Roscher, *Lexikon*], (Leipzig, 1919); W.K. Pritchett & O. Neugebauer, *The Calendars of Athens* [hereafter Pritchett, *Calendars*], Harvard U.P. 1947, pp. 25, 30.

21. Selene never threefold: Farnell, *ibid.* p. 552. Chrysippus is reported in the *Scholia Genevensia* I p. 210, (Nicole) to have demonstrated in his *Physics* that the Moon is Artemis (*Stoicorum veterum fragmenta*, ed. J. von Arnim, (Leipzig, 1903): II, §748). Johnston refers to Diogenes of Babylon, *Doxographia* 549 b 7, for Artemis; Seneca, *Medea* 790, for Hecate: see Iles Johnston, *Hecate Soteira* p. 31 notes 7,8. The consensus of earlier opinion, e.g. Farnell *Cults* 2, pp. 509-12, is based on details of worship which could be interpreted differently, as indeed Farnell points out.

22. O. Neugebauer *The Exact Sciences in Antiquity* (1952), pp. 84-5.

23. Teucros first: *CCAG* VII.195.11; see also Gundel, *Dekane*, pp. 28, 31.

24. F. Yates, *Giordano Bruno and the Hermetic Tradition* (London, 1964), p.22.

25. Pritchett, *Calendars*, pp. 37-8, and table p. 15.

26. M.S. Crawford *Roman Republican Coinage*, (Cambridge, 1974): p. 720, and plates pp. 31-4

27. A. Alföldi "Diana Nemorensis", in *AJA* 64 (1960), pp. 137-44: p. 140 *et passim*; F.-H. Pairault, "Diana Nemorensis", in *Mélanges d'Archéologie et d'Histoire* 2 (1969), pp. 425-71.
28. For history of Diana see G. Wissowa *Religion und Kultus der Römer*, 2nd edition, Munich 1912; brief account in M. Beard *et al. Religions of Rome*, Cambridge, 1998, I, p.3; II, 1.5d. It may be that her etymological association with light also assisted her association with the Moon, if this took place at the earlier period.
29. Golden Age poets mentioning Trivia include Catullus (34, 15), Horace (3, 22, 4ff.) and Propertius (2, 32, 9f.). A fuller list is in Alföldi "Diana Nemorensis" p. 140.
30. Alföldi "Diana Nemorensis", p. 140; Pairault "Diana Nemorensis", p. 457 ff.
31. No triple Selene: Farnell, *Cults 2*, p. 552. Artemision, *ibid,* p. 517. Lunar symbols late: Farnell *Cults 2,* p. 531; Roscher *Lexikon* §§ 1904-6.
32. Artemis and Helios: Farnell, *Cults* p. 461; see also F. Cumont, *Astrology and Religion among the Greeks and Romans* (1912; New York, 1960), p. 27, concerning the replacement of the Greek names for the five planets (but not mentioning the luminaries) by those of Olympian gods.
33. J.D. Mikalson, *The Sacred and Civil Calendar of the Athenian Year* (Princeton U.P., 1975). 30th: Apollodorus in *Ath.* VII 325A (Jacoby *Fr. Gr. Hist.* 244F 109) and Schol. Arist. *Plut.* 594. 16th: Philochorus, *Peri Hemeron* (*Fr. Gr. Hist.* 328 f 86), a late source, from the fourth-fifth century.
34. Translation by S. Ronan, *The Goddess Hecate* (Hastings, 1992), pp. 75-6.
35. J.E. Harrison, *Themis* (Cambridge, 1912), pp. 189-90, interpolations in square brackets mine. Her argument from the inscription was essentially foreshadowed by W. Roscher, *Lexikon* §.1904. On p. 38 of *Mythology and Monuments* she credits a different German encyclopaedist, Dr Robert, for insights on the role of Artemis as leader of the Graces.
36. *Mythology and Monuments of Ancient Athens*, London, 1890, p. 379; *Prolegomena to the Study of Greek Religion*, 2nd edition, Cambridge, 1908, p. 408.
37. See my forthcoming paper, "Origins of the New Age Triple Moon Goddess" (2004).

Astrology and Science: Two Worldviews Searching for a Synthesis

Jesús Navarro, University of Zaragoza, Spain

The astrological worldview takes for granted an interrelated wholeness to which humanity belongs, a systemic totality having harmony, resonance and tuning as primal characteristics. On the contrary, modern science assumes a paradigm in which separateness, reductionism and empirical positivism implies the strangeness between human (the observer-knower) and universe (the observed reality). This thesis-antithesis antagonism is searching for a synthesis capable of solving its contradiction into complimentarity, giving rise to a new paradigm rooted in a human-cosmos integrated vision without losing the explicative success of modern science. Twentieth century research, both in science and astrology, has begun to pave the way towards such an emergent worldview. This paper offers a glimpse at all of this.

Introduction

Astrology, having a history several thousand years old, was a reputed science in the past, being academically accepted, studied in university and visibly present in western culture. The arrival of modern science forbade its teaching and practice, removing it from universities and leaving no academic room for astrological knowledge. Two confronting paradigms about humanity and universe were at the root of that historical break.

As discussed in the first section of this paper, astrology implies relatedness, mutual implication, global perspective, a harmony between humanity and cosmos. The universe is seen as an animated whole, giving rise to a worldview characterised by harmony and sympathy, a paradigm which was blown away with the arrival of modern science.

Classical physics, based on Newtonian principles, presents us on the contrary with a human, the observer, alien to the universe, the observed reality, a mechanical cosmos, an automaton made of inert parts and devoid of life, mind and intelligence, a paradigm to which the second section of this work will be devoted.

But the twentieth-century revolution in physics, with Einstein, and Planck's quantum theory, opened the door to a new scientific worldview. It is commonly held that this new paradigm is founded in Einstein's relativity, that is, relatedness, and Heisenberg's uncertainty, which implies there is no possibility of describing the universe without taking into account the whole of it – as present cosmology is beginning to clarify. Thus we return to some philosophical ideas which are deeply rooted in the traditional astrological paradigm, a point which will be stressed in the third section.

Certainly, today, scientific epistemological treatises continue to set aside astrology as having nothing to do with science, an opinion shared by some astrologers; but a different tendency has developed, which points towards a synthesis of these two antagonistic paradigms. The postmodern criticism of classical rationalism has, of course, helped that conceptual evolution, but twentieth-century astrology has also taken certain steps to accept some scientific research tools and methodologies, opening a growing dialogue with science and scientists and facilitating the discussion of traditional ideas, as will be shown in the fourth section.

The development of a new scientific paradigm synthesising actual and traditional postulates is a desirable possibility, although there is still a long way to go. There are several factors which may, and could, help to catalyse this process. Sections five and six will briefly consider these issues.

Finally, this paper will conclude by summarising the main aspects of this discussion.

The astrological worldview

The traditional paradigm to which astrology belongs postulates an interrelated universe, where the whole is present in its parts and the parts reflect the totality to which they pertain. The parts are harmonically interrelated, and have a mutual resonance which suggests a kind of universal holographic principle. Truly, astrology was the leader of such a systemic worldview, becoming the greatest tentative of a constructive and systemic conception of the universe ever conceived by human spirit (Knappich 1988).

This conceptual view, rooted in the Chaldean culture, was rationally developed by the Greeks to such a degree that O. Neugebauer, the great science historian, referring to the Hellenistic period, tells us that, compared with religion, magic and mysticism, Hellenistic astrology should be seen as a science (Neugebauer 1957). Ptolemy's *Tetrabiblos* (1980) is a classic example of the scientific attitude from the second-century CE. But Ptolemy also points out the non-deterministic character of astrology, stating (*Tetrabiblos* I.3) that "we must not think the effects of heavenly bodies upon human destiny as fatal things that cannot be avoided". In fact he only brings to our consideration the pure concepts of the old astrological lore. In its Chaldean origins, astrology was a divine language informing humans of the gods' will, not a corpus of ironclad rules enslaving human will.

As we can read in the texts of *Enuma Elish*, the Babylonian creation myth, with the aim of allowing the gods to rest, humanity was created as a substitute for the gods, to do their works. The gods delegated their control of destiny and gave humanity heavenly messages through astrology so that humanity might know their divine wills. So, humanity is responsible for maintaining a harmonic universe and following its correct destiny, being guided, not enslaved, by astrology in order to be successful in these tasks.

It was only stoicism which brought into astrology a deterministic doctrine, in contrast to the best thinkers of Greek, Middle-Ages or Renaissance science and/or philosophy (Pérez 1994). In fact, the traditional Ptolemaic concept of astrology was easily integrated into Aristotle's model of the universe, rooted in biology, not in mechanics. Joined to this philosophical worldview, astrology retained its scientific status throughout the Middle Ages and Renaissance and was only deprived of it with the advent of rationalism, which relieved astrology of its privileged position. Even though it has been catalogued since then as 'irrational', 'superstitious', or a 'pseudo-scientific' subject, Neugebauer reminds us that we should not dismiss the astrology of the ancient world, because it heralded the beginning of an orderly methodology as a means of formulating a theory within which all phenomena could be explained (Neugebauer 1957). Really, this is the true aim of science. One consideration, however, is the philosophical difficulty of ascertaining precisely what is and what is not a science (Chalmers 1982), a subject to which we will return in the following section.

Why has astrology lost that recognition? One answer that can be put forward in the light of Kuhn's works (Kuhn 1996) is that a new scientific paradigm appeared that confronted and displaced the Aristotelian one. So astrology, having a much older history than the Aristotelian worldview, was not capable of academic survival once its adoptive paradigm lost its conceptual and scientific appeal. Notwithstanding, the traditional worldview found a refuge in hermetic doctrines, and these doctrines fed the deep and powerful thoughts of Leibniz (Orio 2002), whose philosophy profits from the old ideas embedded in such doctrines. Confronted with Descartes' and Newton's positions, Leibniz was capable of rationally developing a bunch of new concepts and proposals rooted in the ancient thoughts present in traditional doctrines (mainly alchemy and astrology), leaving an invaluable legacy to both the philosophy and the science of the future (Smolin 1997, Orio 2002), as we shall see in the following sections.

The paradigm of modern science

To speak of 'modern science' calls for a double definition of what is 'modern' and what is 'science'? It is simple to define what we mean by the former: 'modern', in this context, means from the seventeenth and eighteenth centuries until the present day. But, as previously mentioned, it is difficult to define science. As stated in the prologue of *What Science Is and How it Works* (Derry 1999), "debates and contrasting perspectives among scientists and philosophers concerning the true nature of science" are common, while Chalmers (1982) noted the absence of definitive criteria for most definitions of science.

This absence of precise definition allows assertions such as the following tautological statement (Derry 1999: 3): "science is what is taught in science books". It is also admitted that "we can't have a valid science with an inbred worldview isolated from the scientific community as a whole" (Derry 1999: 185). In addition, in order to do science, "one must at least have faith in the integrity of one's overall worldview" (Derry 1999: 128).

But what about this 'overall worldview'? It is based on the existence of absolute space and absolute time, two abstract – not empirical – concepts, but supposedly containing in them an atomised, mechanistic reality, observed by an individual aside from it, estranged from it. Smolin (1997: 14) stated that:

> The fundamental principles in the Newtonian picture of the world included the idea that the universe is eternal, that everything is made out of particles which obey absolute and unchanging laws, and that everything in the world can be reduced ultimately to the action of these absolute laws. If this view is correct, then the only truly fundamental science must be the study of what these particles are, and how they move and interact with each other. Everything else, whether it is biology or astronomy, is to be understood ultimately in terms of these fundamental particles and the laws they obey.

Against a traditional worldview, the new one of modern science rendered the universe devoid of intelligence, in-animated, eternally determined and, once entropy was discovered, damned to a disordered death. Bearing that in mind, the restrictive use of the word 'science' by a great number of modern scientists and authors to mean 'natural science' comes as no surprise, forgetting that the understanding of human nature, as well as of the human condition within nature, is one of the central themes of science (Bronowski 1978).

But this aim of true science is, obviously, wholly contradictory to the modern science paradigm, the classical physics paradigm: there is no room for humanity in it, nor for its mind, its emotions, its creativity, its life time, its history, its evolution – relegating these subjects to the so-called 'soft', second rank, sciences (Altman 1986).

'Time' was only taken into account, philosophically and scientifically, since the nineteenth century (Guzón 2002), and this interest paved the way for the greatest breakthrough in physics, science and philosophy since Copernicus, to be fuelled by Einstein and Planck at the beginning of the twentieth century. It opened the door to a new and more comprehensive worldview (Smolin 1997), to which we will return in the next section.

At this stage, let us comment further on the so-called *scientific method*. As we have been told, "science demands that its standardised procedures be adhered to", namely empirical, positivist and reductionist procedures; but we are also told that this *scientific method* "does not force itself upon human mind either logically necessary nor inevitable. Therefore, it would be fair to call it a convention" (Newton 2000: 10). Historically, the *scientific method* "was not initially regarded as crucial to obtain knowledge of nature. In fact, Boyle's promotion of this methodology gave rise to vigorous controversy, and [...] Boyle himself explicitly stated that his refutation of Hobbes' physical theories was intended to undermine his religious and political views" (Barnes 1996 *et al*., 1996: 142, 143), and "before this time the experimental method was associated traditionally with alchemists, and more recently with various 'new' philosophers who used specially designed experimental demonstrations to prove the truth of their preconceived hypothesis" (Barnes *et al*. 1996: 143)

On the other hand, many twentieth-century philosophers agree with Feyerabend when he asserts that "there is no one 'scientific method', but there is a great deal of opportunism" defending also that "the fictitious unity of 'science' (namely, modern science) that is supposed to exclude everything else simply does not exist" (Feyarabend 1996: 36). He states firmly: "we may conclude that there exists no scientific argument against using or reviving non-scientific views or scientific views that have been tested and found wanting" (Feyerabend 1996: 36; see also 1975). Moreover, it is clear to many that "what science has been doing for the last 400 or so years is giving a description, not of the universe as a whole, but of small parts of it" (Smolin 1997). In fact, "Newton's physics was a great achievement, but it relied heavily on the use of a fixed background and, for this reason, it could never have stood as a theory of a whole universe" (Smolin 1997: 14).

Towards a new paradigm

To quote Smolin once more, "we live in the ruins left by the overthrow of Newtonian science, trying to make sense of many new discoveries that have grown up suddenly like a lush forest among the scattered stones of an ancient temple" (Smolin 1997: 14) and:

> a picture is emerging of what this new universe will look like [...] the evidence for this new picture of cosmology comes from several different directions and sources [...] beyond the simple fact that the universe is evolving and changing, we are finding we live in a world that is much more dynamical, much more intricately structured, much more interesting than the previously imagined (Smolin 1997: 12).

And he follows:

> [The Newtonian point of view] has often been opposed because it seems to cheapen life, to make our existence meaningless, to make beauty irrelevant. Of course, these kind of arguments have not mattered much to science, because this view was seemed a necessary underpinning of its momentous progress. But now, at this moment of crisis, it seems that it is exactly this view of things that must be challenged. It is not a question of ethics, or what makes us feel comfortable, this view is no longer working as a science (Smolin 1997: 15).

In relation to that, he writes:

> the most basic properties we may imagine an object to possess are its position in space and its existence in time. After the triumph of Einstein' theory of general relativity, these must be seen as meaningful only in the context of the relations of that body to the rest. It can no longer be maintained that the properties of anything in the universe are independent of the existence or non-existence of everything else (Smolin 1997: 239).

To which we can add the non-local characteristics of the universe at quantum level, as stated by Aspect's experimental verification of Bell's theorem but, at the same time,

> while the overthrow of Newtonian physics is certainly irreversible, we should avoid the temptation to take quantum mechanics, in its present formulation, too seriously (...) when we speak of the quantum we must be very careful to separate talk of quantum phenomena from talk of quantum theory. Quantum phenomena are real, and are genuinely puzzling. But not all of the idealisations and postulates of the quantum theory may actually correspond to nature. (Smolin 1997: 243)

On the other hand,

> if we keep the focus on the attempt of unify relativity and quantum theory, then we are continually impressed by the fact that each of these are transitional theories. Each radically challenges the Newtonian conception of the universe, but only in part. Each holds unchanged a certain but different part of the classical picture. So the situation is genuinely confused. However, underlying both theories is clearly the move from an absolute, Newtonian picture of nature to a relational, Leibnizian conception. As I will try to argue here, this is the ground on which we may hope to find their ultimate reconciliation and unification. (Smolin 1997: 243-4)

Alas, science has, as has our culture, the opportunity to return, through Leibniz's thinking, to its traditional roots. This opportunity is increased by the growing state of opinion about the most probable foundations of that new scientific paradigm: biology. Aristotle's model is also biologically based, a characteristic valued by Prigogine, one of the twentieth century's greatest scientists and thinkers (Guzón 2002). There are also authors who, accounting for the parallelisms and similarities between biological, social and cultural evolutions, defend them as being different aspects of a single and fundamental process: the evolution of nature (Laszlo 1977). Moreover, Smolin's cosmological theory is also rooted in such an evolutionary thinking (Smolin 1997). Time, dynamical aspects of reality – like non-equilibrium thermodynamics, self-structured systems, evolution theories and so on – are at the roots of this emergent scientific paradigm (de Duve 1995, Grand 2000, Kauffman 1993, 1995, Prigogine 1984, 1997, 1998, Smolin 1997).

A past with future

Time is a key element of astrology, the old science of universal cycles. But a common explanation of the astrological concept of time in a mythical context of unendingly repeated cycles in an eternal unchangeable universe is not so acceptable to my mind, if we are to be faithful to the conceptual seeds offered by the oldest known roots of astrology. As previously mentioned, *Enuma Elish*, the Old Babylonian poem of creation, describes the Chaldean gods giving a hard task to humanity because they were so tired of creating that they needed someone to control the universe and destiny for them.

So mankind takes charge of destiny and does not become a slave to it, and the key question is 'what for?' The *Enuma Elish*'s answer is immediate: to guarantee cosmic harmony and to maintain the dynamics of the universe according to "its right rules". But these right rules are not that of mythical time but that of real time, evolving and creative time, as *actual science* (Guzón 2002, Prigogine 1979, 1984, 1997, Smolin 1997) and *actual astrology* (Arroyo 1979, Ruperti 1978) is constantly reminding us.

This is an evolutionary perspective also present, explicitly or implicitly, in Ptolemy's *Tetrabiblos* (I.2), where we can read about the similarities, but not the identical nature, of astrological figures and aspects over time. On the other hand, this 'opening' of time cycles is an exact understanding of what astronomical cycles are: three-dimensional curves never completely closed. Indeed, they are more or less geocentrically 'almost' closed, thus showing continuity gaps that open up chances of diversity, newness and creativity – the very job of gods for whom mankind, according to *Enuma Elish*, are substituting.

From this deepened, dynamical and evolutionary comprehension, astrology has a great many contributions to make in a historical period in which science and western culture are searching for a new paradigm, a new worldview centred in the dynamic characteristics of time, cosmos and mankind in the evolutionary signature of reality. This evolutionary perspective, along with the ecological one (mankind both in narrow interdependence and interaction with its universal surroundings), is inherent in astrology, but wrongly interpreted by mythical misconceptions of it.

Actually, the primary roots of astrological concepts are those of the individual and mankind being the pinnacle of evolution, the final element of the gods' creative effort towering the whole of the universe, having to take charge of its dynamic reality, maintaining its right evolution through our own responsible actuation – namely correct evolution – and being guided to do that by the celestial messages conveying the privileged information offered by heavenly gods to assist human success.[1]

Right now it is clear to science that information is not only an essential ingredient to life ("no definition of life could suffice that ignored the role that information and control play in the workings of a living cell", Smolin 1997: 156) but also an evolutionary advantage when linked to our inhabited environment: "a sensitivity to our environment that has doubtless saved us from extinction many times in the past" (Grand 2000: 130). That is why there is a growing number of researchers who are not surprised by the suggestion that our behaviour is linked to environmental influences, and which take into account the reality of biological phased-locked loops "which can be influenced by quite subtle external influences and will really fall into step with any similar periodic changes in its environment" (Grand 2000: 129), and accepting that "such a sensitivity to the moods of the planet or of others is something to be astounded rather than offended by" (Grand 2000: 130). Obviously, this is a convergent approach which can (and must) give a chance to astrology, opening it to a future which classical science had stubbornly tried to bury in the past.

But there are more clues to consider information as a promissory nexus between present day science and astrology – information is being associated with space-time structure and order (Stonier 1990, de Vree 1996) and it is beginning to be considered (besides mass and energy) as the third fundamental magnitude of the universe (Gitt 1989, Stonier 1990), and accepted as a physical magnitude (Smolin 1997).

A quantitative equivalence between information unity – the 'bit' – and the energy unity – the Joule – has also been proposed (Stonier 1990), and today there are authors who speak about information as a third-order ontology capable of bridging (apparently) disjointed ontological systems (Goppold 1998). Moreover, present day science is trying to include 'time's arrow', the irreversibility of real time, in its theoretical formulations. But this dynamic arrow is an essential characteristic of our evolving universe, so essential that some scientists are beginning to assign time an undeniable ontological meaning (Guzón 2002). However, physically speaking, this time irreversibility emerges from entropy, a physical magnitude that, not surprisingly, is directly linked with information (Abrahamson 1966, Stonier 1990) and is also opening the doors to the emerging new science (Prigogine 1979).

In parallel, there has been a growing interest among twentieth-century astrologers in taking advantage of scientific tools and methodologies to advance their astrological research. To name briefly just a small sample of relevant examples, we can remember the great impact of Gauquelin's work (see among many other references, Gauquelin 1978, 1979a, 1979b) or the new mathematical approach proposed by Addey (Addey 1976), without forgetting more collective initiatives (Pottenger 1995). In fact, Gauquelin's research has been taken as a solid reference point by different scientists and astrologers as a convenient way to value astrological assertions and to open the door to a scientific treatment of them (Eysenck *et al.* 1982, Seymour 1990, West 1992) – a way clearly followed, among others, by Seymour and Fuzeau-Braesch (Elko 1998, Fuzeau-Braesch 1992a, Fuzeau-Braesch 1992b, Fuzeau-Braesch 1996, Seymour 1990).

The necessary synthesis

The last decades of the twentieth century have seen a progressive approach by some scientists to astrology and by some astrologers to science. The historical wall separating modern science and astrology is gradually being eroded by the increasing conceptual contacts between experts from both sides. This convergent dynamism ought to lead to a positive re-encounter between astrology and science, giving birth to a recast overall paradigm, taking into account the most valuable traditional and modern concepts in a newly synthesised worldview. To my mind, we astrologers and scientists have a number of issues to keep in mind in accepting this challenge. Some of these are as follows.

First, let me remind you of a phrase previously quoted: “It can no longer be maintained that the properties of anything in the universe are independent of the existence or non-existence of everything else” (Smolin 1997: 239). Then, let us consider the symbolic value of astrology (Eysenck *et al.* 1982: 211): “astrology is not worse than some psychological techniques such as inkblots, which are widely used although no one pretends that inkblots contain real meaning. In fact astrology can be superior because its concepts have undeniable beauty and appeal, and because taken one at a time are attractively simple”, and also to state that therapists “are finding that astrological concepts can provide a useful framework for exploring and describing persons and situations in understandable and very human terms”. These benefits “would of course apply whether astrology was objectively true or not” (Eysenck *et al.* 1982: 211), but it is necessary to point out the convergence of astrology, taking into account the different events through their space-time characteristics, as in the following statements from Smolin: “the most basic properties we may imagine an object to possess are its position in space and its existence in time” and “all properties that have to do with space and time must be constructed from relations between things in the world” (Smolin 1997: 239).

Moreover, modern cosmology tells us that “there is a limit to how much information may be contained inside a given region of space [... and it] is proportional to the area of its boundary” (Smolin 1997: 239, 241). We are also told that, after quantum mechanics, if we observe some part of the world, a complete description of ourselves is impossible without incorporating the description of that observed part (Smolin 1997: 274).

Strikingly enough, astrology relates the relevant space-time information to a closed surface, a sphere surrounding our planet, and uses the information related to the outer observed part of the universe to base its descriptions of the observer, without forgetting to also take into account some complementary (genetic, social, cultural, an so on) information, as the astrologers in history remind us (Ptolemy 1980, ben Ragel 1997). In fact, in spite of its holistic perspective, astrology does not look at the whole universe, mainly limiting its considerations to our solar system and its cycles. But we must remember that “long-range order can be exhibited in an infinite system in which components only interact with their nearest neighbours” (Longair 1999: 165), and take into account the existence of both macroscopic, that is, astronomic (Seymour 1990)[2], and microscopic, that is, quantum entanglement (Smolin 1997)[3], criteria supporting these restricted considerations.

Another point to be considered is the growing scientific will to integrate time, biology and mind – namely humanity – in the overall paradigm of the universe, as clearly shown by the following quotes:

> We come to a world with an open future, where time plays a constructive role. (Prigogine 1998: 28, 98)

> The existence of a microscopic formulation which makes explicit the role of irreversible processes and gives an unified image relating many of our observations on physical and biological systems. (Prigogine 1980: xiii-xiv)

> We are observing the birth of a science that is no longer limited to idealised and simplified situations but reflects the complexity of the real world, a science that views us and our creativity as part of a fundamental trend present at all levels of nature. (Prigogine 1997: 7)

> In Roger's (Penrose) theory of mind is the idea of mentality as something ontologically fundamental in the Universe. (Longair 1999: 153)

In addition, it is worth mentioning the growing academic interest in promoting interdisciplinary activities, opening up, little by little, to new perspectives about rationality and irrationality, as stated by E. Klein:

> Because there is a gap between things and the images we build of them, we have to be cautious in our use of *rational* and *irrational*. The word *reason* has become as magical as a quality label, investing everything it is attached to with an aura of excellence. Yet the idea that reason is absolute and inmutable is merely a doctrine, an obsolete doctrine [...] What seems to us rational today once had to fight for recognition: it was not instantly recognized as such [...] Rationality is a construct [...] rationality can, paradoxically, be built upon the irrationalities that it was first responsible for producing. (Klein 1996: 9. 10, 11)

It is also pertinent to stress here the great growth of both chronobiology and the many aspects of natural cycles study offers us the success of a historical vindication: almost two centuries late, the assertions of Herschel about the relationship between the evolution of the climate, the prices of wheat and the sun spots cycles is being scientifically accepted (Nesme-Ribes 1996).

Certainly, there are no small handicaps to be overcome, inside science and also inside astrology, to reach the necessary synthesis of paradigms. We are reminded of this by, among others, some opposing astrologers (Nègre 1994) and Barnes, Bloor and Henry (Barnes et al. 1996): "Michel Gauquelin's statistical evidence in support of astrology would perhaps be a serious embarrassment to scientists if they were not so good at ignoring it. But one day it could conceivably come to be accommodated as a triumph of the scientific method". Nobody told us the task was easy. Notwithstanding, it is not only valuable and exciting but also credible and workable.

The catalytic factors

There are different factors, both cultural and academic, which could help the serious study of astrology and the advent of the new overall paradigm to which I have dedicated the last paragraph. Of course, they must counteract other factors which strengthen the well-ingrained and conservative habits of both the scientific and the academic community.

One of them, probably the most negative and also the most folkloric, is the omnipresent media interest in a trivialised and caricatured astrology, to be properly called pseudo-astrology, whose contents are the main target of anti-astrological scientists' and scholars' criticisms (see Feynman 2000, for example).

These media practises try to cover, but mislead, the popular interest in astrological knowledge – an interest that, if rigorously taken into account, should, in my opinion, open the door to approaching astrology from different sociological and psycho-sociological perspectives. In fact, our western contemporaries (astrology is a much more ingrained reality in eastern culture), regardless of their school degrees, social status, or economic rank, know generally the signs of the zodiac and also their associated astrological basic typologies much better than any other psychological, or equivalent, classification.

The search for the roots of these facts, centred in the present, ought to be expanded to the past, converging with the undeniable interest and significance of astrology in our history, our philosophy, our science, our culture, in the whole western civilisation over many millennia. We should have here a number of reasons, or catalytic factors, to thoroughly explore astrology and its far and wide implications in our past and our present and, implicitly or explicitly, also in our future. If we intend to understand ourselves, we need to study not only the historical perspective of astrology but also all its remaining facets, and especially its conceptual and methodological contents.

It is undeniable that our architecture, our painting, our literature, our philosophy and so on are permeated by a vigorous astrological element which is waiting for an attentive group to bring it into the light: an impossible task to be undergone without thoroughly and deeply knowing the evolution of astrology and that of its concepts and techniques throughout the centuries. We should also mention the impact of astrology on scientific and practical knowledge: namely astronomy, mathematics, navigation, medicine and so on. In fact, Christian churches have always saved the applied benefits of astrological knowledge, mainly in medicine and navigation, from their anathema. In my opinion, the universities, and we who integrate them, have the great opportunity, privilege and responsibility, to lead the necessary, unavoidable academic approach to astrology.

The search for the roots of our own being, namely the deepest passion of western mind (Tarnas 1991), and also the characteristic searching for unity and integration of humanism, the most nuclear tradition of European culture (Guzón 2002), are claiming for it, and we are in the right place, and just at the right time, to proceed.

Moreover, as it is well known, one of the universities' fundamental goals and responsibilities is to promote critical thinking. Another one is to dig in our past to offer its treasures to our present. A third one is to lead the progress of knowledge. The procurement of each and every one of these goals are very good candidates, perhaps the best ones, to be included in our list of catalytic factors. From my own perspective, it is possible to cover all of them giving a serious academic coverage to astrology.

Fortunately, this scholarly interest in astrological knowledge has already started. We can see evidence of this in the activities of the Sophia Centre at Bath Spa University College (http://www.bathspa.ac.uk/sophia/), under the umbrella of a much more ambitious project, the Sophia Project (http://www.sophia-project.org.uk/), supported by the Sophia Trust. Among the universities funded by the Sophia Project are the University of London (Warburg Institute), the University of

Southampton, the University of Kent at Canterbury, Leicester University and Bath Spa University College. Also, Kepler College began to offer BA degrees in 'Astrology and the Liberal Arts' in July 2000 (http://www.kepler.edu/), and we should also mention a number of doctoral thesis related to astrology and held at different western universities (Guinard 2000). It is also worth mentioning the University of Amsterdam which has set up a department for the study of western esotericism (www.amsterdamhermetica.com), and the University of Málaga (www.webdeptos.uma.es/dep_griego/ASTROLOGIA.htm) where a program for recovering old astrological bibliography has been initiated.

There are also professors, or small groups of them, actively working in different universities. The present author, as professor of the University of Zaragoza, is active in one of these groups together with three colleagues. I can also witness about three other Spanish colleagues, all of them holding professorships at different universities (two of them from Barcelona and the third one from Valencia) regularly working on astrology and lecturing, as I have done, at different astrological conferences.

Conclusions

There are a growing number of universities around the western world showing an increasing interest in the serious study of astrology. This fact ought to be, probably, the most important catalyst to recover this traditional knowledge, to understand it in a new light, devoid of misconceptions and prejudices, and to better perceive the historical evolution of our culture, obtaining new perspectives about its past and present dynamics and also about the potentialities of its future.

The potential benefits this approach can offer us are varied. These include gaining a renewed comprehension of both the universe and the place of mankind in it, taking some new perceptions about its evolutionary processes and about how they are pushing us towards our own future. These new thoughts would help to construct the emerging overall scientific paradigm having its roots deeply steeped in human reality and giving it the holistic consistency associated with human-cosmos interdependence. This constructive, systemic and evolutionary approach would lead to an organic integration of physics, biology, psychology and sociology, taking advantage of symbolic, that is, informational, capabilities of astrology.

An astrological knowledge to be actualised, modernised and returned to its roots, eliminating from it the debasements, distortions and deformities caused by past centuries of scientific and academic dispraise and scorn, religious anathema and cultural abandon. The old-time princess and modern Cinderella is claiming a new role in our culture, perhaps the role of our wiser counsellor, capable of giving us the companion of the whole universe in its pushing of our personal and collective developments and, at the same time, its own thorough evolution. Perhaps the most important lesson to be learned by us human beings from astrology is our common future with the cosmos, our inextricable solidarity, interdependence, history with it (maybe he/she) and to accept its almost cyclical remarks to remind us the right dynamics of our common evolution.

In my opinion it is time to give way to those old ideas about humanity damned to be enslaved by an ironclad universe, or on the contrary to our proud pretension of becoming the uncompromised and unconditioned masters of our universe. Commonality, solidarity, interdependence – this is, in my opinion, the most valuable teaching of that old wise knowledge called astrology.

Endnotes

1. A perspective today also detectable through the etymology of words like 'disaster'.
2. The existing nexus between planetary cycles, sun magneto-dynamics, solar wind and earth magnetism.
3. The numerous and intense interactions among particles present in the cloud of gas from which our solar system evolved gave rise to, I suggest, privileged and more direct connections among solar system objects.

Bibliography

Abramson, N. (1996) *Information Theory and Coding*, New York: Mc Graw - Hill.

Addey, J. M (1976) *Harmonics in Astrology,* Romford: Fowler

Altman, H. (1986) *À Tort et à Raison: Intercritique de la Science et du Mythe*, Paris: Le Seuil.

Anon (translated 1994) *Enuma Elish,* Madrid: Trotta.

Arroyo, S. (1979) *Astrology, Psychology and the Four Elements*.Vancouver: CRCS.

Barnes, B., D. Bloor & J. Henry. (1996) *Scientific Knowledge. A Sociological Analysis*, London: Athlone.

ben Ragel, A. (1997) *El Libro Conplido en los Iudizios de las Estrellas*, Valencia: Gracentro.

Bronowski, J. (1978) *A Sense of the Future*, Boston: MIT Press.

Chalmers, A. F. (1982) *What is this Thing called Science?* St Lucia: University of Queensland Press.
Derry, G. N. (1999) *What Science is and How it Works*, Princeton: Princeton University Press.
de Duve, C. (1995) *Vital Dust. Life as a Cosmic Imperative*, New York: Basic Books.
de Vree, J. K. (1996) "A Note on Information, Order, Stability and Adaptability", *BioSystems*, no. 38, pp. 221-227.
Elko, B. (Aug./Sept. 1998) "The Magus of Magnetism: An Interview with Dr. Percy Seymour". *The Mountain Astrologuer*, no. 80.
Eysenck, H. J. & D. K. B. Nias (1982) *Astrology: Science or Superstition?* London: Temple Smith.
Feyerabend, P. K. (1975) *Against Method,* London: New Left Books.
Feyerabend, P. K. (1996) *Farewell to Reason*. London: Verso.
Fuzeau-Braesch, S. (1992a) "An Empirical Study of an Astrological Hypothesis in a Twin Population". *Person. Individ. Diff.*, vol. 13, no. 10, pp. 1135-1144.
Fuzeau-Braesch, S. (1992b) *Astrologie: la Preuve par Deux*, Paris: Laffont.
Fuzeau-Braesch, S. (1996) *Pour l'Astrologie. Réflections d'une Scientifique*, Paris: Michel.
Feynman, R. P. (2000) *The Pleasure of Finding Things Out*, London: The Penguin Press.
Gauquelin, M. (1978) *Cosmic Influences in Human Behaviour*, New York: ASI.
Gauquelin, M., & F. Gauquelin (1979a) "Star US Sportmen display Mars Effects". *Skeptical Inquirer*, Winter.
Gauquelin, M., F. Gauquelin & S. B. G. Eysenck (1979b) "Personality and Position of the Planets at Birth: an Empirical Study". *British Journal of Social and Clinical Psychology*, no. 18, pp. 71-75.
Gitt, W. (1989) "Information: The Third Fundamental Quantity". *Siemens Review*, no. 6, pp. 36-41.
Goppold, A. (1998) "Information and Third Order Ontology". *BioSystems*, vol. 48, no. 1, 2, pp. 169-173.
Grand, S. (2000) *Creation. Life and how to Make it*, London: Weindenfeld & Nicholson.
Guinard, P. (2000) "L'astrologie (et l'épi-astrologie) à l'université: Un siècle de thèses doctorales", http://cura.free.fr/01authd.html
Guzón, J. L. (2002) *El Nuevo Estatuto del Tiempo: Introducción al estudio del concepto del tiempo en Ilya Prigogine*, Salamanca: Universidad Pontificia de Salamanca.
Kauffman, S. (1993) *Origins of Order: Self-Organization and Selection in Evolution*, Oxford: Oxford University Press.
Kauffman, S. (1995) *At Home in the Universe. The Search for Laws of Self-Organization and Complexity*, Oxford: Oxford University Press.

Klein, E. (1996) *Conversations with the Sphinx. Paradoxes in Physics*, London: Souvenir Press.
Knappich, W. (1988) *Geshichte der Astrologie*. Klostermann, Frankfurt.
Kuhn, T. S. (1996) *The Structure of Scientific Revolutions*, Chicago: The University of Chicago Press.
Laszlo, E. (1977) "Mankind in Transition: the Evolution of Global Society", in E. Laszlo & J. Biermann (eds.) Pergamon Press, as quoted in Guzón 2002.
Longair, M. (ed.) (1999) *The Large, the Small and the Human Mind*, Cambridge: Cambridge University Press.
Nègre, A. (1994) *Entre Science et Astrologie*, Paris: S. P. M.
Nesme-Ribes, E., S. L. Baliunas and D. Sokoloff (Oct 1996) "La Dinamo Estelar", *Investigación y Ciencia*, pp. 12-19.
Neugebauer (1957) *The Exact Sciencies in Antiquity*, Providence.
Newton, R. G. (2000) *The Truth of Science. Physical Theories and Reality*. Harvard: Harvard University Press.
Orio, B. (2002) *Leibniz y el Pensamiento Hermético* (2 vols.), Valencia: Universidad Politécnica de Valencia.
Pérez, A. (ed.) (1994) *Astronomía y Astrología. De los Orígenes al Renacimiento*, Madrid: Ediciones Clásicas.
Pottenger, M. (ed.) (1995) *Astrological Research Methods (2 vols.),* Los Angeles: ISAR.
Prigogine, I. (1979) *La Nouvelle Alliance*, Paris: Gallimard.
Prigogine, I. (1980) *From Being to Becoming: Time and Complexity in the Physical Sciences*. San Francisco: Freeman.
Prigogine, I. (1984) *Order out of Chaos: Man's New Dialogue with Nature*, New York: Bantam.
Prigogine, I. (1997) *The End of Certainty. Time, Chaos and the New Laws of Nature*, New York: The Free Press.
Prigogine, I. (1998) *El Nacimiento del Tiempo*, Barcelona: Tusquets, Barcelona.
Ptolomy, C. (1980) *Tetrabiblos*. Madrid: Barath.
Ruperti, A. (1978) *Cycles of Becoming. The Planetary Pattern of Growth*. Reno: CRCS.
Seymour, P. (1990) *Astrology: The Evidence of Science*, London: Arkana.
Smolin, L. (1997) *The Life of the Cosmos*, New York: Oxford University Press.
Stonier, T. (1990) *Information and The Internal Structure of the Universe. (An Exploration into Information Physics)*, London: Springer-Verlag.
Tarnas, R. (1991) *The Passion of the Western Mind*. New York: Harmony.
West, J. A. (1992) *The Case for Astrology*, London: Arkana Books.

Astrology and Science – A New Millennium

Maarit Laurento, Finland

The paper addresses the boundaries between astrology and science and concentrates on a demarcation problem. It will explore the criteria science poses for new sciences. In order to be a science one has to take into account for example the idea of a theory, methods and paradigms. An independent branch of science is known for its own methodology but in astrology's case usually statistics are introduced. However, qualitative methods will give new and fresh viewpoints to this issue. "Astrology and Science – A New Millennium" discusses the position of astrology in the academic world and the possible advantages and disadvantages that might arise along with that position.

Who would have believed some time ago that the third millennium would begin a new era in the relationship between astrology and science? Although attempts have long been made to restore astrology's position in the academic world (e.g., Kepler College started negotiations with members of the academic world back in the early 1990s), the positive academic response has been a surprise to many.

In September 2002, the Astrological Association of Great Britain (AA) held a conference at the University of Swansea in Wales. Academising astrology was rightly one of the conference's themes as, in October of the same year, twelve students were due to start their studies in *Cultural Astronomy and Astrology* at Bath Spa University College. This is a one-year course leading to an MA. Nicholas Campion represented the discipline at Swansea, and reported on the College's positive response to the new course. The news was well received by the audience, so used to being opposed and unnecessarily defamed by a vocal group of sceptics. It seemed that the relationship between astrology and science was being re-examined.

Why is there such a gap between astrology and science? We have to go back a few centuries to find some explanations. In the Copernican revolution of the sixteenth century and the scientific revolution of the seventeenth century, astrology suffered a series of setbacks. Practically speaking, astrology went underground and its relationship with science became a negative one. Now it seems, however, that this relationship is changing in many respects.

What is most interesting is that the change is happening concurrently in many places around the world. In 2000, Kepler College of Astrological Arts and Sciences in Seattle, USA, was the first western university to offer studies in astrology leading to a BA, with an MA in the planning stages. Simultaneously, the Minister of Education in India suggested that an astrological faculty be set up in thirty-five Indian universities. In Europe, the University of Zaragoza in Spain offered a course in the methodology, history and symbolism of astrology to over a hundred students, beginning in 2000. Astrology also caused global controversy when the French astrologer Elisabeth Teissier, President Francois Mitterand's astrologer, defended her doctoral thesis at the Sorbonne. Interestingly, hers was not the first doctoral thesis in astrology at the Sorbonne; Patrice Guinard had defended his thesis in astrology and semiotics in 1993 in the philosophy faculty. Furthermore, Angela Voss defended her thesis on Marsilio Ficino at City University of London in 1992, and Patrick Curry had defended his thesis on the decay of astrology in England at University of London College in 1987. Indeed, theses relating to history have been more easily accepted by the academia than studies on the contents of astrology.

According to the list of academic studies in astrology provided on the website of C.U.R.A. (Centre Universitaire de Recherce en Astrologie, http://cura.free.fr), run by Patrice Guinard, more than one hundred academic theses (MA and doctoral) have been conducted in the twentieth century. Although long, this list does not include for example Tamsyn Barton's doctoral thesis on the history of astrology (1994) nor Andreas Vladimirou's study (1996) on astrology and religion, on which he is basing his doctoral thesis. Thus, there is reason to believe that the list is much longer. The topics of the studies vary from history to personal traits and from the relationship of career and astrology to cosmological questions. Is astrology, therefore, science? What is the relationship between astrology and science? On what aspects do we focus when we talk about science and astrology?

What is science?

Science is the organised, planned and systematic gathering of data as well as the critical analysis of that data. Science aims at finding the truth – or to come as close to it as possible – and this can be achieved through critical analysis. Hence, science is not merely the gathering of data and information; the research method employed is of critical importance. The chosen methods can be employed to make justified arguments, generalisations and predictions.

Science is also self-correcting, which means that a previous theory can be replaced with a newer one; just as when the geocentric worldview was replaced with the Sun-centred one as a result of Copernicus' work. Development is not always rapid but, nowadays, we are used to the fact that truths change fairly swiftly. Technology progresses and new insights come along. Sometimes it is even quite difficult to differentiate between what is true and what is not, what is science and what is not. The demarcation between science and non-science is one of the key questions in the philosophy of science today.

There are various criteria depending on which type of science is being defined. Some basic criteria are as follows (e.g., Niiniluoto, 2001; Kaitaro, 1998):

1. Science is a public activity. Research has to be clearly reported and explained on all the methods and experiments used, enabling them to be replicated if necessary. Furthermore, all arguments must be documented and references to other researchers' texts and ideas must be presented, allowing anybody to check the researcher's conclusions.
2. One has to use valid methods. Rationality, empiricism and logic are guaranteed by applying a reliable methodology. Validity and reliability must also be checked. Quantitative and qualitative methods have their own validity checking methods requiring rigid documentation.
3. Data gathering has to be systematic. It is not enough that one gathers data merely on the basis of naïve inductivism. One should also be ready to test one's hypothesis with data which challenges the original results rather than only supporting it.
4. Criticism is essential in science. Research is – must be, in fact – subject to critical review, to searches for its weak points, allowing its validity and truth to be traced. Scientific criticism is also guaranteed in the form of referee proceeding by having scientific articles reviewed with an outside estimator, who points out the weaknesses of the research before its publication. In this way mistakes and false arguments can be eliminated before wider publicity.
5. Causality: the task of science is to show how things are causally related.
6. Science is self-correcting, a process which is guaranteed by the previously discussed critical process. False arguments and opinions will

not survive as they are removed at an early stage and replaced by a stronger theory.
7. Science is not personal. The researcher's own likings and preferences must not affect the results, instead they should be as objective as possible. On the other hand, nowadays the researcher's own voice is also acknowledged, albeit in a controlled manner.
8. Replication: it is essential that the results of scientific study can be recreated. Hence all material, methods and arguments should be well documented.
9. Science progresses: criticism also guarantees that nothing is believed before critical analysis. This leads to increasingly better and more realistic views of reality.

How does astrology respond to the criteria of science?

It has been argued that astrology is pseudo-scientific or unscientific as it does not take into account the criteria of science (e.g., Kaitaro, 1998). But one may legitimately ask: must astrology be science? This question will be addressed later. I will first concentrate on how astrology can make use of the criteria of science.

Astrology, like science, is a publicly scrutinised activity. Astrologers have their own forums where articles and ideas can be published, such as the *Astrological Journal*. In Finland, for example, *Astro Logos* is an example of such a journal, and countless equivalent journals worldwide offer such an arena. It is increasingly common for astrological writers to refer to other astrologers and give value to their ideas rather than writing solely on the basis of their own subjective assumptions. Astrological discussions that test existing viewpoints are thus more frequent. Referee proceedings are employed particularly in the research journal *Correlation*. In many journals, articles are also thoroughly edited before publication.

Research methods have always been a bone of contention in astrology. What astrological research methods can be considered reliable? A basic premise of independent research is that the research methods employed should be appropriate for the given field. Research methods are chosen according to the researchers' areas of interest and the viewpoint adopted; there are no neutral methods (Varto, 1996). Various methods have been connected with astrology, the statistical approach being by far the most common. However, many astrologers are unconvinced about the value of statistics (see the various contributions in Phillipson, 2000) on the grounds that an astrological chart is regarded as being an integrated whole. For example, statistical analyses of Sun sign correlations with given occupations are not considered appropriate if the astrological chart is considered to be much more than just the Sun sign.

Nevertheless, academic research offers other types of research methods besides the statistical approach. The biographical method, for example, could provide completely new viewpoints. All in all, various qualitative methods open up interesting channels for the study of astrology.

A theory is a scientific presumption which can be tested empirically. This has generally been the stumbling block of astrology as there is not a single accepted theoretical context. There are several different viewpoints about material effects on linguistic systems, for example, but no consensus on the matter. The demand for a single, overriding theory is partly misleading, and is usually imposed on astrology but not on other disciplines. Reality is studied in many different ways in the academic world. There are different theories and various competing ideas, whose view of what truth constitutes can be completely different, depending on the branch of science that is considering it. It is, for example, often required that astrology explain laws of material effects, i.e., that planets have a material influence over events on the Earth in a similar way that the Moon affects tides and menstruation. This idea appeals to a number of researchers (e.g., Seymour, 1988) and it does offer a logical basis for astrological analysis.

Causality is also a major consideration. It is often claimed in astrological discourse that the Moon has an *impact* on moods and that one is reserved in nature under the *influence* of Saturn. Are astrologers talking about material influences? Do planets' magnetic fields have a material impact on events on the Earth? Is it gravity or something else? There are astrologers who definitely think that astrology is a matter of physical influences. For example, transiting Uranus crossing the Sun affects the person so that she/he starts to behave in an unexpected and surprising manner. On the other hand, there are astrologers who maintain that events happen concurrently for no apparent causal reason. C.G. Jung described this as synchronicity, an acausal unifying principle. For example, transiting Uranus signifies/indicates, but does not cause, particular styles of behaviour. According to scientific standards, an explanation has to be provided in both approaches as to how the correlation occurs and how systematic or permanent it is. In other words, how accurately can one say that when Uranus crosses the Sun, such and such an event or mood is possible to a given degree of certainty? Positive evidence alone is not enough if we want to provide an explanation according to scientific rules.

We also have to take into account events and happenings that invalidate the theory, i.e., situations in which transiting Uranus crossing the Sun does not signify anything special, surprising or unpredicted.

Statistical methods have generally been suggested as a solution to the problem. However, astrologers usually reject them because they do not necessarily meet the special requirements of astrology. For example, Press (1993) and her research group carried out a statistical analysis of people who had committed suicide and compared the hour of death to various astrological ways of anticipating future events (transits, progressions, directions). The result was embarrassing from an astrological point of view: no connection was found. Suicide is, after all, a major event, so the researchers expected it to be evident in the chart. The underlying idea was that planets have a physical impact on a person's life.

Nevertheless, this result does not mean that astrology cannot be researched. The biographical approach is an example of a method whereby various situations and moods in a person's life can be analysed with the aim of "presenting a holistic picture of the research object in such a way that besides individual life experiences, the surrounding society and its changes are also described" (http://honeybee.helsinki.fi/users/niskanen/jkotu/elama.htm). This type of research procedure could be carried out as follows: a group of people are interviewed about their life without any preconceptions. The researcher pays particular attention to such events in the interviewees' lives when a surprising, extraordinary or peculiar (Uranus) event has happened. The subjects are then asked to elaborate on such events further, for example to describe the exact points in time when they occurred. Accounts of events affecting people collectively and simultaneously are collected from newspapers. Another alternative is to observe a pre-selected group of people who will all be under the influence of a strong Uranus transit and note what happens to them. The control group can be a randomly selected group of people whose life experiences are noted down in the same manner as those with a Uranus transit. These two groups are then compared with each other, thereby identifying how a Uranus transit can influence a person's life, or signify a change in his/her life.

The problem with astrological research is that positive results have not been received positively outside astrological circles even when they have been conducted according to the strictest scientific criteria. Anti-astrology groups go so far as to falsify their own studies (see Rawlins) in order to denigrate results that present astrology in a positive light. Needless to say this is in conflict with the ethics of science, but unfortunately it is all too common for astrology. It is true that a new field of research always constitutes a threat to the existing field and that the doors of scientific fora do not open easily to a new discipline that would rather be seen as integrating with a prevailing discipline. As far as astrology is concerned, however, there is more to it than the mere struggle for independence of a new discipline.

Sound replication of research results is often difficult in an astrological "experiment" due to the extreme rarity of given events reoccurring in an astrologically identical state. For example, if one wants to examine Neptune conjoining the natal Sun, it is often impossible to construct two astrologically identical Neptune-Sun transits, because it only takes place in one sign once every 165 years. Thus, it is impossible to repeat the transit during one lifetime. However, the repeatability criteria of qualitative research, which analyses unique events and processes is appropriate. Qualitative research employs action or ethnographic research methods, to mention but a few. Because identical replication of research events is impossible, qualitative research talks about the concept of *transferability*. The research process is documented and described in the greatest detail possible, allowing other researchers to conduct new research by constructing an environment which is as close to the previous one as possible. This kind of transferability is employed in astrology, too, particularly in the analysis of transits. Even though, for instance, Neptune conjoining the natal Sun is not similar for Gemini and Pisces, certain similarities can be identified.

Demarcation

Science is generally held in high social esteem and protects itself through the maintenance of various boundaries. Because many areas of research want to be part of science, within science there is an ongoing debate over demarcation criteria. In other words, why may a given field of study be regarded as a science and not as a form of art or therapy? Astrology is often the subject of this kind of critical examination. In the glossary of a philosophy book for Finnish sixth-formers (Lukion filosofian sanasto), astrology is separately mentioned under demarcation criteria. "Demarcation = criteria for separating science from non-science (e.g., quasi-scientific hogwash theories such as astrological theories of the 'position of stars' influencing peoples' lives and other theories that, for one reason or another, cannot be regarded as scientific theories)".

The question is often posed on how to distinguish science from pseudo-science? According to Kaitaro (1998), characteristic to pseudo-science is that "it is presented as verified, scientific knowledge even if it is not. Because of lack of scientific support, such theories are often false. They are often related to matters which would require explicit scientific evidence (physical interaction, causal relations, probabilities, statistical connections etc.)".

Kaitaro suggests that pseudo-science can be recognised by the choice of sources used to reinforce the weight of the statement. If one makes vague assertions such as "research findings incontrovertibly show" or "on the basis of experience dating back millennia", or if the sources include questionable gossip magazines rather than scientific journals, there is reason to doubt the scientific basis of the research. One should also look at the results with a critical eye if physical terms – such as energy – are used loosely. Unrealistic claims are also a telltale sign of pseudo-science. Kaitaro stresses that "the texts of those that defend pseudo-science contain complaints about 'materialistic science', which does not approve of pseudo-scientific theories because of their revolutionary nature" (Kaitaro, 1998). In contrast, Niiniluoto (2001) discusses the oneness of sciences and emphasises *ontological monism* (the entire world is made of the same basic material) and so-called *emergent materialism*:

> the cosmic and biological evolution which has progressed historically as a physical process has generated sensing and thinking beings, who have gained an awareness of themselves, thanks to the symbolic language developed by man. Thus, the human mind, complete with its subjective experiences and qualities, has emerged from the material state, in that it is an emergent phenomenon, whose characteristics and regularities can be of such kind that they cannot be restored to the physical state with explicit definitions. Even though there is nothing supernatural about the human mind, its research can still take one beyond what is possible to achieve with physics. The contents of the mind are in a complex interaction and interdependent relationship with the neurological states of the brain. Nevertheless, psychology cannot be logically derived from physics. In contrast, Enqvist's view, whereby emergence means 'coarsening' and the losing of information relating to the description of reality, in principle does allow this kind of reduction.

Similar ideas have been raised in evolutionary psychology, where the functions of the mind are restored to physiology. In this way the concept of a materialistic view of science is not very far removed. This is a topical theme for astrology. Some support the materialistic view, to which physical laws can be applied, while others are in favour of linguistic metaphors and analyse astrology on such a basis. The discussion follows the same lines as the debate in social sciences about the structure of reality. Can it be analysed with material methods or is it constructed, for example, with the help of language in social reality? Materialism is thus under critical analysis both within the scientific community and outside it.

Challenges for a new discipline

There are a number of pertinent questions relevant to astrology's relationship with science. What happens when a new line of study seeks to be part of science? What kind of demarcation lines does it have to surmount? How is science canonised? What tools can a new line of study use to be accepted by the existing disciplines? What does a new discipline have to be aware of within itself before it is regarded as an independent discipline? These are the questions astrology will have to face if it enters the academic world. Even if astrology were not to be considered science, as a new area of research and study it has to distinguish itself somehow in order to become an independent field, one which cannot be integrated with any existing discipline.

I came across an interesting article about the independence struggle of *caritas*, or lay-work, science. The article looks at the possible mechanisms involved in a new practice-oriented, empirical discipline coming into existence (Varto, 1996). Caritas science is an excellent example, because its world view and ideology are more or less in conflict with those of science, and it has also had to struggle with the demarcation problem.

"Every new discipline faces big problems. The beginning may seem almost impossible, especially if everything seems to be unresearched. The situation is not so desperate in any branch of science: researched information exists but just it has to be identified" (Varto, 1996). Varto goes on to assert that often a new discipline has to cope with exceptionally harsh critique on the part of the established sciences, because a new discipline is always a threat to the existing structure.

There is no denying the fact that astrology will always have to face criticism no matter what. In fact, it is axiomatic that astrologers should be used to criticism, scorn and impertinent slurs, because that has been going on for centuries. Despite this, criticism is not something to fear.

Subjecting oneself to criticism is, after all, a normal procedure in science, even though for some disciplines, such as astrology, this procedure often resembles harassment. At best, criticism can be beneficial. After all, the very idea of a new branch of science is that it offers something new. In so doing it exposes the established sciences to criticism and thus poses a threat to them. They also have to re-analyse their views if a new discipline is accepted as part of the established sciences. If a new branch of science cannot bear criticism but surrenders to being part of the existing sciences, it admits that it does not deserve to be considered an independent discipline.

A new branch of science must be based on a practice that is the driving force for research. "There must be a practice which stirs something within either ourselves or other people. It is this that becomes the stimulant for research" (Varto, 1996). Astrology is interested in practical situations. What is the significance of Saturn transiting the Descendant? What kind of a person is someone with Pluto and Sun in the same sign? How do share prices perform when Mercury is retrograde? These practical questions require an appropriate research method. That is why the idea of independence is important. These astrological questions cannot be analysed just by borrowing or copying a research method. The starting point is the practical situation and we must consider how that question can best be analysed from an astrological point of view. "Every research target calls for specific methodical procedures that stem from the research material. Universally applicable procedures that are like recipes do produce research, but not new knowledge, let alone new, organic knowledge specific to a given procedure" (Varto, 1996). Similar challenges were encountered in the social sciences in the 1980s and 1990s, when the statistical research method was perceived to be inadequate. It was considered, for example, that different interview methods produced more profound knowledge than multiple choice questionnaires. Likewise, if we only analyse astrology with statistical methods, we lose valuable information which originates from the concept of comprehensiveness. As Varto explains, caritas science adopted action research, a method which has been used in cases where the researcher takes an active part in the lives of the research subjects and, through his/her own actions, attempts to affect their lives. This method is perfect for the practical study of caritas science. Each new branch of science has to find "its own niche, which both presents its research questions and attempts to find answers to them in its *own unique way*. It does not use the answers provided by other research methods, and this exactly is how it generates research. Eventually, a new discipline is born" (Varto, 1996). That is why astrology cannot be analysed with borrowed methods. We must contemplate how existing research methods can be applied to astrology, and if they are inapplicable, we must come up with new methods. Accordingly, astrology actually benefits science if there is interaction both ways.

Is astrology science?

So, can astrology be considered science? And above all, must it be considered science? On what terms can it be considered science? Is there possibly a better way to look at astrology?

I have often argued that astrology is not science, so why am I reluctant to declare that astrology is science in its own right? I am under the impression that astrology is being pushed into being science simply because of the status associated with science, and that many are prepared to give up the unique nature of astrology in order to integrate it into mainstream science. In my opinion, astrology can benefit science by putting forward new kinds of questions and, most likely, by formulating new kinds of methodical ideas. When I interviewed astrologer Dr Liz Greene in 1995 about astrological research, she argued that astrologers should not withdraw into a "ghetto" of their own by arguing that no one understands them.[1] Pluto entered Sagittarius around the time when the interview was made, and Greene saw this as a possibility for the commencement of a new kind of dialogue between astrology and science. She considered it important that developments in both fields are followed in order for fruitful interaction to develop and to ensure that the dialogue uses correct concepts for the benefit of both fields, in other words that those involved in the dialogue have a common language.

It is my opinion that astrology must benefit from the insights already achieved in science and learn from its criteria. But without giving up its indifference and originality. Robert Hand (1987: 35) has aptly crystallised the central theme as follows: "For the foreseeable future, it would be well to keep the science and craft of astrology separate. The science can draw inspiration and ideas from the craft but it should not try to pass judgement or otherwise impinge too closely upon its practices."

Acknowledgement
I would like to thank Eija Tervonen for translating this paper from Finnish into English.

Endnotes

1. Interview with Liz Greene, Astrological Association of Great Britain conference, Cirencester, 1-3 September 1995.

References

Barton, T. (1994) *Ancient Astrology*, London: Routledge.
Greene, L. (1996) *The Astrological Neptune and the Quest for Redemption,* Samuel Weiser.
Hand, R. (1987) "Astrology as a Revolutionary Science", in A.T. Mann, *The Future of Astrology*, http://koti.mbnet.fi/neptunia/, pp. 23-39.
Kaitaro, T. (1998) "Miten erottaa tiede pseudotieteestä?" (How to distinguish science from pseudo science?), *Skeptikko* 4, pp. 11-15.
Lukion filosofian sanasto (philosophical glossary for sixth formers) http://www.edu.espoo.fi/~amrusane/sanasto/demarkaatiokriteerit.htm.
Mann, A.T. (1987) *The Future of Astrology*, London: Unwin Hyman Ltd.
Niiniluoto, I. (2001) "Tieteiden ykseys", Tieteellisen seurain valtuuskunnan vuosikokousesitelmä. ("Unity of sciences", Annual conference presentation at the Federation of Finnish Learned Societies.), http://www.tsv.fi/ttapaht/014/niiniluoto.htm
Phillipson, G. (2000) *Astrology in the Year Zero*, London: Flare Publications.
Press, N. G. (1993) *New Insights into Astrology*, San Diego: ACS Publications.
Rawlins, D., "Starbaby", http://cura.free.fr/xv/14starbb.html
Seymour, P. (1988) *Astrology: The Evidence of Science*, Arkana.
Sullivan, E. (1992) *Retrograde Planets. Traversing the Inner Landscape*, London: Arkana.
Varto, J. (1996) "Uuden tieteenalan ongelmat" ("The problems of a new branch of science"), N&N, *Filosofinen aikakauslehti*, 4/96. http://www.netn.fi/496/netn_496_varto.html
Vladimirou, A. (1996). Paper on "Astrology and religion", unpublished research for an MA, Kings College, London.

Astrology at Work in Social Science Research

From the paper originally titled 'Astrological Research in the Field of Psychology'

Pat Harris, Southampton University

This paper discusses the appropriateness of social science models and tests in research in astrology in the field of psychology, the validity or otherwise of the results of research in this area that has already taken place, and how effective astrological research in the field of social science, which is of value to astrology and academia alike, might be carried out in the future. A report is also presented on the exploratory findings to date of the author's research into possible links between psychological and astrological factors and fertility treatment outcome.

When I gave a teaching session to students on the Master's degree in Cultural Astronomy and Astrology at the Sophia Centre, Bath Spa University College, during May 2003, I said that I did not believe in astrology in the sense that it was some esoteric language that only a privileged few could understand and use, but that rather I believed in the value of investigating its applications to different fields of study in order to assess its potential as a viable, predictive tool. I explained that I was very interested in testing certain applications of astrology related to the reliability of astrological forecasts to match a specific outcome. My research approach focuses on what Sean Lovatt[1] has called the "utility" of astrology and what I think of as its practical potential in social science research, particularly in the field of health psychology. I am seeking to answer questions such as: "can a forecast using certain configurations of Jupiter help to pinpoint, with enhanced accuracy, successful times for carrying out embryo implants or intra uterine insemination, to increase the likelihood of a successful pregnancy resulting in a healthy baby?" It has been claimed that it is possible to identify beforehand the times in a woman's life when her children are going to be born. I wanted to test this claim to see if there were significant associations between "certain configurations of Jupiter" and fertility treatments that resulted in the birth of a healthy baby.

There continues to be much lengthy discussion and debate about the nature of astrology. As yet, a proper understanding of its mechanisms remains elusive. And we may, for the time being, have to content ourselves with an understanding of its presence or nature that is limited by the scope of our observational abilities – rather as is the case in quantum physics, where we can deduce that a "thing" is present by the way it appears to behave in a given environment relative to our observations of it, as with the wave-particle duality concept for example (Zohar, 1990). As we have gradually developed our understanding of this duality by continuing to explore its apparent paradoxes, so we can gradually develop our understanding of astrology. If we utilise the wisdom gained from the philosophy of this approach, we do not need a comprehensive account of how astrology might work in order to usefully explore it, as such carefully considered investigations will contribute towards the development of further understanding. It is worth adding here that, in my view, no research has been carried out to date that either proves or disproves astrological claims.

Speaking as an astrologer and scientist, I must say that we should always be conscious of the limits of our understanding of "the bigger astrological picture" when we are designing research to investigate astrological associations and their apparent effects. We should always be aware, for example, that we are limited in our conclusions about astrological phenomena by the very methods we choose to use to investigate it. We cannot, for example, make any irrevocable judgements about astrology if we design a study that sets out to test the competence of astrologers by measuring their abilities to match birth charts with natives (McGrew and McFall 1992) when such astrologers fail to produce a significant level of accuracy. This may simply be due to the fact that the astrologers concerned did not know their astrology well enough. A study design would have to take into account many factors in order to allow for this and other possibilities, and what implications these may have for the conclusions that may be drawn from it.

We would have to test for a specific hypothesis relating to established interpretive meanings in existing astrological literature, in order to draw any conclusions about these meanings. We can't just assume that because it is written in a book somewhere, it will be true. Even after testing a particular hypothesis about whether Jupiter is associated with fertility, for example, when drawing any conclusions about this association, the limitations of the experimental methods have to be taken into account.

We cannot conclude that "astrology doesn't work", as does Ivan Kelly (1998) in his article which includes that assertion in the title. He concludes this because – in his view – no piece of research into various aspects of astrology has produced significant results under positivistic scientific analysis. In fact, as scientists, we can conclude *only* that these specific tests have shown no significant results, and we must continue to refine and develop our methods while the underlying rationale of astrological phenomena remains unexplained, much as Paul Feyerabend (1975) observes in his book "Against Method". Therefore, Kelly's conclusion that "astrology doesn't work" is premature because many other ways of exploring it exist.

Why is it important that we should constantly refine and develop our methodological approach? What does it mean for us in terms of our pursuit of a better understanding of the thing we wish to investigate? In my view, Patrick Curry (1981: 5) put this succinctly when he wrote: "it [...] means not investigating the subject in such a way as to destroy the phenomenon being investigated – and then claim that it never existed." With appropriate methods and tests it is possible to address astrological phenomena and gain a better understanding of them.

Addressing this need for refinement and development of appropriate methodology – whatever phenomenon we wish to investigate – is our duty as seekers after knowledge. The proper use of the scientific method involves open-mindedness and objectivity – categorical statements being the exception rather than the rule. Those "scientists" who make absolute assumptions about the nature of a thing cannot be, in my opinion, rightly described as true scientists, who are concerned only with the pursuit of knowledge that will lead to a better understanding. If assumptions are to be made the scientists who make them must be prepared to continually check and revise such assumptions as the process of research and accumulation of knowledge continues.

An example of the problems that arise from categorical statements being made by scientists has been shown on the *BBC World News*, a television news service that is currently running a series of small video clips under the collective heading "Just a moment". One of these clips deals with the greenhouse effect and global warming. In it, Professor Reid Bryson of the University of Wisconsin confidently stated in 1974 that the earth would get cooler because of the drier climatic conditions in certain countries that resulted in increasing dust levels in the air, which would rise into the atmosphere and block out the Sun. This was known as The Cooling Theory.

In the years that followed, another climatic scientist and prolific writer on the subject, Dr. Stephen Schneider (Head of Interdisciplinary Climate Systems at the National Centre for Atmospheric Research in Boulder, Colorado, and author of the book *Global Warming*, published in 1990) observed that the cooling effect was only regional and that the assumptions made in the 1970s were wrong because they had neglected the stratosphere CO^2 – which gave rise to *the greenhouse effect* – and this neglect had the effect of making the calculations out by 50% at the time. Schneider's categorical statement in the 1990s therefore directly contradicts Bryson's in the 1970s.

There is also the matter of looking in the right place using the right tools. Another analogy: if you are searching for something in the dark, you will see far less if you use a candle rather than a high-powered torch. And if you have only a candle because the technology has not yet been developed to provide you with a torch, you may be very surprised when the technology finally arrives and you have to revise your assumptions based on what you had found using only candlelight. It is better to acknowledge the limits of the candlelight and express your observations with the appropriate degree of circumspection. So it should be with scientific research in and, indeed, into astrology. We should always express our observations not as confident assumptions but as circumspect observations, which may (in the future) be improved upon or, indeed, completely overturned by those who come after us. Karl Popper (1983) called this process of revision "refutation".

There are in existence some challenging theories and models for testing astrological applications. John Addey's theory of Harmonics (1976) is one example that has been around for many decades. Addey advocated that it was not so much the signs of the zodiac that should be researched but rather degree areas within signs, because more insight may be gained through apparent correspondences. Using the theory of Harmonics he apparently showed how particular degree areas might correspond to particular meanings. He provided an example using a small group of six eminent astrologers, and appeared to demonstrate how, using the Harmonic theory, the Sun, Moon, Ascendant and Jupiter in the astrologers' charts were distributed around certain areas in the 360-degree circle of the Zodiac. He then proposed that these degree areas were likely to be prominent in the charts of astrologers, but more so in the charts of eminent ones such as Charles Carter, and, as it later transpired, Charles Harvey (Addey 1996: 115). Most social science research into astrology has focused on studies utilising signs of the zodiac. I would suggest that research into degree areas – in the sense John Addey referred to them – might yield more information about apparent astrological correspondences.

Michel Gauquelin's research may be understood under the Harmonics theory microscope (Addey 1981). Gauquelin identified zones or areas in the diurnal cycle that corresponded with certain professions when specific planets were found there. These findings are consistent with his character trait hypothesis research (CTH), which is widely known (Gauquelin 1985). However, Dean (1997/98) concluded that the significant results of Gauquelin's CTH research were due largely to artefacts involving, among other things, selector bias and that when Addey's Harmonics theory was applied in analysis of the Gauquelin data there were problems such as ineffective criteria for selecting amplitudes, non-independence of traits and sector bias together with the sample size being too small and sampling errors too large, which he argued constitute fatal weaknesses to the theory, rendering the results effectively meaningless.

A tremendous amount of information was generated in the application of the Harmonics theory to Gauquelin's CTH data, and this presented a further problem because, Dean suggested, it would be impossible to recognise any valid patterns due to the vast amount of "noise" that was potentially present. Kevin Hawley (2000) proposes that it is possible to construct an approach using certain existing statistical tests that will take this problem into account and make the recognition of valid patterns in large amounts of data possible. Hence future studies involving the use of Harmonics applied to the analysis of Gauquelin data might usefully take this factor into account.

It must be noted that although most of Gauquelin's research results have been strongly and perhaps plausibly disputed over many years in many publications, "The Tenacious Mars effect" (Ertel and Irving 1996) remains to be explained. It may very well be that future research into degree areas of the ecliptic may provide us with a clearer insight into the origins of meaning associated with particular signs, although with our present state of knowledge on this it is a matter for conjecture and philosophy regarding the past history and development of such associations.

However, researchers such as Kevin Hawley may help shed further light on this area. Hawley[2] suggested that with a thousand, or even as few as a hundred, pieces of data from astrologers who had reliable knowledge of their own birth times, it might be possible to conduct a further study of the sample of six astrologers and the apparent phenomenon of the "astrologer's degree" cited by John Addey. Hawley suggests that the use of appropriate methodology and statistical tests may help us to better understand the validity or otherwise of what the association or pattern described by Addey might be.

Why did astrologers of the near-east and Hellenistic world associate a particular meaning with a particular sign? When did it all start? I cannot answer these questions. Nor could John Addey, but he provided food for thought by creating a mathematical model – Harmonics – that has enabled researchers in astrology to add to the empirical observations that traditionally exist, as shown in the example of astrologers and the "astrologers' degrees." He made an observation that could be tested in the positivistic scientific framework of critical realism advocated by Karl Popper (1983) by identifying a phenomenon in a small group of astrologers and hypothesising about its meaning.

To some extent, that is the approach I am taking in my research into empirical observation associating Jupiter with fertility and Saturn with barrenness. I took a sample of women who were undergoing fertility treatment, separated the treatments into successful and unsuccessful groups and looked for astrological factors present in one group that were not present in the other. From this I then developed a hypothesis based upon what I had found. This is a process of investigation called "analytic induction" (Robson 1993).

First, I looked for contacts of Jupiter at the time of successful and unsuccessful treatments. I chose Jupiter because of the claims made for it being associated with fertility in astrological literature dating back to the time of Ptolemy (1980) and beyond. Initially, I used an orb of six months each side of the date of exactitude of the progressed Jupiter contact, but narrowed this down to three months either side, as the analysis of the data in the two groups suggested that a tighter time margin than is more commonly used by some astrologers would be more appropriate in this particular study.

I did this also for Venus, the Sun, the Moon, the fifth house ruler in the fifth house natally, the Ascendant and the Midheaven. However, using the system of *progression* (a definition of *progression*, *transit* and the range of *aspects* used are given in the discussion following the Table presented below), I found no significant difference for contacts of the Ascendant to the Moon – as defined by traditional astrologers such as William Lilly, who wrote that with these contacts one "may enjoy a daughter that year" (1985: 664) – or by the progressed Sun and Moon to

Ascendant and/or Midheaven (Davison 1979: 42, 43) or to their own natal positions.

Significant differences between successful and unsuccessful treatments were found, however, using progressions with Venus contacting the Sun, Moon, fifth house ruler in the fifth house natally, Ascendant and/or Midheaven, or where progressed Venus made a contact to its natal position in the birth horoscope of the woman undergoing fertility treatment. Because of the correlations indicated by my exploration of the preliminary sample, I also included certain *transits* of Jupiter, i.e. when Jupiter transited by *conjunction*, *sextile* or *trine* the Sun, Moon, Venus, fifth house ruler in the natal fifth house, natal Jupiter, Asc., or MC during the two weeks before implantation of embryos.

I then refined and developed my original hypotheses for further testing. Only the positive series of aspects showed significant results for Venus and/or Jupiter. No significant results were obtained for the Sun or Moon. I have now reached a point where I feel able to test the refined hypothesis on another sample of women undergoing fertility treatment. The results drawn from this second study, carried out at an NHS fertility clinic, will be the ones that will, if the sample is large enough, enable me to draw some conclusions about Venus and Jupiter and their association with fertility; but, when considering possible correlations between these planets and fertility, I would emphasise again that the limitations of the experimental methods used would have to be taken into account.

The table below shows some results for Venus and Jupiter in the first sample – which is called the "preliminary analysis sample". These results are regarded as exploratory because I did not state my refined hypothesis before analysing the associations. I used the data drawn from the groups to guide me on how to develop and refine my original hypotheses – which I had based on existing astrological literature – and work out more particularly what it was that I should be looking for.

The range of aspects used for the above were conjunction (0 degrees), semi-sextile (30 degrees), sextile (60 degrees) and trine (120 degrees), and very tight orbs of time were applied. Full details of the model will be given in my doctoral thesis, which will be available to read in the second half of 2004.

Two probability values[3] (*p* values) are given, one for contacts involving the acutely time-dependent factors – the Ascendant and Midheaven – and one for contacts that exclude these angles. It is useful to consider the *p* values with and without angles (Ascendant and Midheaven) simply because they are critically time-dependent. For example, if the woman's birth time is out by five minutes of clock time, the rising and culminating points could be off by one degree which, in terms of real time, means out by about one year using the secondary progression forecasting system where each day after the birthday is taken to represent one year of one's life. This would mean that the angular relationships formed to the planetary positions in the natal chart from the planetary positions given, say, for the tenth day after the birthday would be interpreted as having expression in the tenth year of life. However, if it is possible to find some significance by leaving out the acutely time dependent factors, that is, the Ascendant and Midheaven, i.e., just by considering the planets alone. This might then be of help to people who are not absolutely sure of their time of birth. The term *transit* or *transiting* refers to the position of the planet on an actual date and the angular relationships it forms on that date to planets in the *natal* chart (the chart drawn for the moment of birth).

Table showing presence or absence of contacts to or by Venus and Jupiter in the natal charts of women undergoing fertility treatment. Total number of treatments $n = 102$

Type of Contact	**Planet**	**Asc/ Mc***	**Live births**		**No/failed pregnancy**		***P* value (Fisher's exact)**
			Present	Absent	Present	Absent	
By secondary progression and in beneficial aspect at time of implant/IUI	Venus	Inc. Excl.	9 7	7 9	19 12	67 74	0.006553 0.008732
	Jupiter	Inc. Excl.	4 3	12 13	9 6	77 80	0.089483 0.114951
By transit during 2 weeks prior to implant/IUI	Jupiter	Inc. Excl.	5 5	11 11	2 2	84 84	0.000864 0.000864
By secondary progression and Jupiter by transit during 2 weeks prior to implant/IUI	Venus and Jupiter	Inc. Excl.	14 13	02 03	27 16	59 70	0.000034 0.000002

* *Asc = Ascendant or rising degree in the natal chart*
MC = Midheaven or culminating degree in the natal chart

The data for a further 12 unsuccessful fertility treatments were obtained subsequent to the above analysis with Venus and Jupiter distributions as follows:

	New probability
Progressed Venus inc. Asc/MC = 2	0.005025
Progressed Venus excl. Asc/MC = 1	0.006393
Progressed Jupiter inc. Asc/MC = 1	0.069712
Progressed Jupiter excl. Asc/MC = 1	0.113832
Transits of Jupiter during 2 weeks prior to implant/IUI inc. Asc/MC = 2	0.002434
excl. Asc/MC = 1	0.001207

It is interesting to note the strong association between the Jupiter-Venus model and success of treatments. The table shows that 14 of the 16 successful births (88%) had contacts to or by Venus and/or Jupiter when including acutely time-dependent factors, compared with only 19 out of the 86 unsuccessful treatments (22%). Similarly when time-dependent factors are excluded, 13 (81%) of the live and healthy births and 16 (19%) unsuccessful treatments had such contacts. Further, the additional 12 unsuccessful fertility treatments gathered subsequent to the development of the model appear to reinforce it when the findings on these data are incorporated into it. The next stage of the research will attempt to validate the model against a new sample of women undergoing fertility treatment.

Conclusion

From my research[4] for a Master's degree in Health Psychology, and at doctorate level so far, I would suggest that astrology is not mythical in the sense that it is imagined and has no reality in a world that tests, measures and compares in order to understand. It has many successful practical applications and the results of these applications – either as an adjunct to counselling, for example, or as a forecasting model in potentially identifying the best times for fertility treatment – can be gainfully explored in order to add to the body of knowledge that is social science. We may not know why or how these phenomena exist but it is our duty as scientists to acknowledge that they should be explored and to use whatever means and methods are appropriate in order to broaden and deepen our understanding of them. In this way, and in due course, it is my view that we will then come to understand the nature of astrology itself, by which I mean what it is and the reasons for its apparent phenomena.

Acknowledgements

The author would like to thank the Faculty of Astrological Studies (FAS), the Astrological Association of Great Britain (AAGB) and the Research Group for the Critical Study of Astrology (RGCSA) at Southampton University for their sponsorship of this research.

Endnotes

1. Sean Lovatt is a British astrologer well-known for his application of astrology in financial and meteorological analysis.
2. Kevin Hawley proposed that he would undertake such a study if the data could be provided for him (personal communication, July 2003).
3. A probability value, or *p* value, is a statistical calculation that indicates to what extent a finding is likely to be the result of chance. For example, a *p* value for 0.008 would indicate that the result or correlation detected indicates a one-in-8000 likelihood of it occurring by chance. *P* values cannot give absolute certainties but the smaller the number the more likely it is that the result is not by chance.
4. A copy of the paper "Astrology and Individuality – the potential value of astrological contribution towards understanding the psychology of chronic pain patients" (1996) can be obtained on request from the author.

References

Addey, John M. (1976) *Harmonics in Astrology*, Essex: L. N. Fowler & Co. Ltd.
Addey, John M. (1981) "The True Principles of Astrology and their Bearing on Astrological Research", *Correlation* Vol.1 (1) pp. 26-35.
Curry, Patrick (1981) "Astrology and Philosophy of Science", *Correlation* Vol.1 (1) pp. 4–10.
Davison, R. C. 1979 *The Technique of Prediction,* Essex: L. N. Fowler & Co. Ltd.
Dean, G. (1997/98) "John Addey's Dream: Planetary Harmonics and the Character Trait Hypothesis", *Correlation,* Vol. 16(2), pp. 10-39.
Ertel, Suitbert and Irving, Kenneth (1996) *The Tenacious Mars Effect,* London: The Urania Trust.
Feyerabend, Paul (1975) *Against Method* (5th impression 1984) London: Verso.
Gauquelin, M. (1985) *Cosmic Influences on Human Behaviour,* (3rd Ed.), New York: Aurora Press.
Hawley, K. G. (2000) "Testing for Isotropy in Circular Distributions", *Correlation,*, Vol. 19(1), pp. 34-41.
Kelly, I. W. (1998) "Why Astrology Doesn't Work", *Psychological Reports*, Vol. 82, pp. 527-546.
Lilly, W. (1647/1985) *Christian Astrology,* London: Regulus Publishing Co. Ltd.
McGrew, John H. and McFall, Richard M (1992) "A Collaborative Vernon Clark Experiment", *Correlation*, Vol. 11(2), pp. 2-10.

Popper, Karl R. (1983) *Realism and the Aim of Science,* (paperback edition reprint 1994) London: Routledge.
Ptolemy (CE 100-170) (1980) *Tetrabiblos,* edited by F. E. Robbins, London: William Heinemann Ltd.
Robson, C. (1993) *Real World Research: a resource for social scientists and practitioner researchers*, Oxford: Blackwell Publishers.
Zohar, Danah (1990) *The Quantum Self,* London: Bloomsbury Publishing Ltd.

The Academy as an Archetypal Group Dynamic

Liz Greene, Centre for Psychological Astrology, London

An academy is defined as a higher or specialised school, or a society for the promotion of science or art. Rooted in Plato's Athens and continuing through the Renaissance to the present day, the academy has always conjured images of a select group of scholars devoted to the exploration of what Plato called "the eternal realities". But any such group constellates innate and archetypal tensions, not with the "outside world" but also with similar groups each of which may feel it has the "only" claim to knowledge, thus generating inevitable psychological repercussions, both problematic and creative.

Bodies of learning, dedicated to education and the setting of standards in their field, come under many names. We may have a school, a university, a college, an institute, a lodge, a faculty, a foundation, a centre, a society, a guild, an association, or, perhaps, an academy. Within the astrological community, for example, we can find the Astrological Association, the Company of Astrologers, the Astrological Lodge of London, the White Eagle Lodge, the London School of Astrology, the Centre for Psychological Astrology and the Faculty of Astrological Studies; and there are many others. Each of these terms carries subtle differences and unspoken implications, suggesting not only the manner in which learning is pursued, but also whether and what kind of hierarchy might underpin the structure of the organisation. Such names are usually consciously chosen by the group to promote a particular image and attract a particular kind of student. A lodge, for example, carries echoes of the long tradition of Masonry, conveying an aura of secret knowledge available only to the initiate after ritual tests which determine the applicant's fitness to belong. A centre implies that the organisation, like the Sun, lies at the heart of things, giving light to those orbiting around it. An association conveys a loose and democratic feel, while a guild suggests a shared craft or skill rooted in tradition, not accessible to untrained outsiders and requiring absolute dedication and commitment. An institute has an official sound, and implies order, respectability, structure, hierarchy and the reassuring promise of intellectual certainties.

Groups, whatever their nature, express certain basic psychological dynamics in the same way individuals do, and such dynamics operate in similar ways in every culture. On the most obvious level, individuals influence the groups to which they belong, and every group is vulnerable to the emotional conflicts and personal rivalries of individual members; this is the case with any body of learning as well as any corporation, club, religious edifice or political establishment. On a deeper level, family dynamics are inevitably constellated in any group, for the family is the first group we experience and the patterns we learn there will inevitably reappear in any group we become involved with later in life. The patterns of family dynamics are instinctive and unavoidable; emotional triangles, sibling rivalries and alliances, the family "black sheep" or scapegoat, conflicts with authority and the perception of the group as a surrogate family exist within all organisations, whatever their nature. Group leaders, teachers and lecturers always invoke parental projections, however humble or democratic they might appear. Yet there is a deeper level still, where group dynamics reflect the meaning, essence or "soul" of the group, and this is archetypal terrain. Behind any medical or psychotherapeutic training body, for example, lies the mythic image of the healer-god, and this archetypal figure presents in imaginal form the meaning, albeit unconscious, that lies behind the enormous effort and sacrifice involved in training and working in this field. To the extent that the individuals in the group identify unconsciously with this kind of archetypal group dynamic rather than expressing the myth through their own individual values, these deeper patterns will dominate the life of the group in compulsive ways. This is, in part, what makes a group become fanatical rather than remaining open to change and new ideas.

Educational bodies also have their mythic background. Every society, whether so-called primitive or so-called sophisticated, has its "elders": those who, through study, training or the experience which time and age bring, know more about life and can instruct and teach those who follow. From the tribal elder to the bard, storyteller and shaman, from the master craftsman and his or her apprentice to the college of priests and the philosopher-king, we have always sought guidance from those fellow humans who, we hope, have greater understanding of life than we ourselves do and can educate us in its mysteries. Because group dynamics at this most profound level are archetypal, existing in every culture in every epoch of history and arising without conscious design, the different ways in which educational bodies pursue an ideal of learning are all described by mythic images which express them in poetic and pictorial form.

Myths are a language portraying fundamental psychological patterns, and our aspirations toward knowledge are as mythic as the great sagas of the heroic quest. We need only look at those deities known as "culture-bringers" – gods who offer knowledge to humans – to recognise the archetypal background of our educational institutions. When a human impulse is portrayed as a god, it is recognised as compulsive, necessary, inevitable and eternal. Thoth-Hermes teaches humans the alphabet, that most mysterious of creations which allows us to communicate not only concrete facts but the most subtle and ineffable of realities. Athene, a more pragmatic deity, teaches humans the arts of weaving and strategy in war; both weaving and strategy are dances in which opposites move together and apart in patterns which invoke the interplay of opposites in all life experience. Demeter teaches humans the secrets of decay and rebirth in both nature and the human soul. Prometheus, along with the stolen fire of consciousness, offers instruction in agriculture, astronomy and architecture and, as Aischylos puts it, makes human beings, through these educational offerings, "cease to contemplate their deaths". These great culture-bringing deities are symbolic portraits of the different facets of what we call education, and they convey in the language of the imagination the human need and capacity to apply knowledge and skills to enhance, improve and deepen the experience of mortal life.

The name that a group deliberately chooses, and the deeper spirit which animates that group unconsciously, may not always accord. These deeper energies arise, in part, from the chemical mix of the collective psyche of the group members. They are also reflected in the birth chart of the organisation as a living entity, and that birth chart is, in turn, a picture of the patterns of the heavens at that moment, describing what is emerging into life and manifestation according to the qualities of the time. The deeper spirit of the academy is different from the deeper spirit of a faculty, a school, an association, a centre, an institute or a lodge. In our present society, we associate the term "academic", at best, with intellectual excellence and major contributions to human progress; and at worst, with ineffectuality and intellectual arrogance – the mind divorced from both heart and body, abiding in its ivory tower and contemplating its metaphorical navel while the "real" world passes by unnoticed. Academia as it exists in the present day is thus respected in some quarters and denigrated in others, because it can present us with both the best and the worst in the realm of ideas. But academia is not always an academy in the deeper sense, and the spirit of the academy may often be found outside academia.

The academic ideal which took shape in the ancient world has, in many modern educational establishments, been replaced by narrow specialisation, intellectual dogmatism and a platform for covert or overt political agendas. In contrast, the academy is an archetypal dynamic, with its roots firmly in the mythic world. It reflects aspirations which arise when any group of people seeks a framework of learning which can unite the imagination, the intellect, and the quest for meaning. The term "polymath", which is no longer deemed attractive within many academic institutions, is appropriate for the nature of education in the academy. The academic ideal involved education as a bringing together of all the concerns of humankind into a harmonious whole, and a contemplation of what Plato called the "eternal realities." From this perspective, the goal of education is the expansion of awareness and the realisation of the individual's innate potential. In practically every traditional allegory, the path of education is portrayed as an ascent, usually to the celestial domain of the Muses. The most famous of these allegories is Plato's prisoner in the cave, who ascends from the shackles of opinion to ultimately gaze on the Sun, the source of being, beauty and goodness. Martianus Capella's fifth century work on the seven liberal arts, *The Marriage of Philology and Mercury*, presents us with an allegory of Learning's heavenly ascent. A similar allegory is offered in Alan of Lille's medieval work, *Anticlaudianus*, which portrays the celestial journey of Wisdom and the ensuing perfection of the human being. In all of these works, the goal of education is the quest for authentic understanding, which cannot be achieved through rigid specialisation or reliance on the conventional offerings of collective opinion. It can only be achieved through a multi-disciplined approach to knowledge, even when the main focus is in one particular field of endeavour.

This ideal was expressed by Pythagoras' school and then by Plato's academy and its offshoots, and continued through the Platonic Academy of Renaissance Florence, the Humanist academies of Rome and the French academies of the late sixteenth century. Although the academy was regularly destroyed or deformed through politics and religious intolerance, it surfaced again in the proliferation of academies in the seventeenth century. Like all fundamental human dreams, the ideal proved indestructible, even when forcibly repressed. But the ideal of the academy was never entirely achievable, and compromises often resulted in an entirely different kind of entity, even though the entity might still call itself an academy. In the fifteenth and sixteenth centuries, for example, the Roman academies, like that at Florence, were loyal to the traditions of Plato's academy: they were centres for the cultivation of philosophy in that larger sense so dear to the Greco-Roman world. But during the seventeenth century, the academy began to alter its nature, becoming a public body rather than a small circle of like-minded friends and fellow thinkers. This new type of academy set itself a fixed and limited scope, often of a polemic or apologetic character, in the fields of science, letters and the arts. Many academies from this time onward, such as the French Academy founded by Cardinal Richelieu, became the practical and effective instruments of existing, government-approved cultural norms rather than the creators of cultural innovation; in effect, they became the judges and custodians of socially defined excellence, rather than inspiring, instructing and nurturing excellence in the individual. Yet, despite these distortions, the ideal of the academy is still with us and is perhaps more urgent for expression now, when knowledge has become divorced from meaning, than it has been for many centuries.

The ancient ideal of the academy unites the arts and the sciences, fostering intellectual liberation, imaginative expression and religious tolerance. All knowledge, even when focused in a particular sphere, is perceived as interrelated and open-ended, rather than confined within narrow limits; rather than experts, there are instead simply people who are further along the road of endless discovery. This kind of academy is political in the broadest sense, not in the narrow "party politics" sense as we find it in education now. Plato intended his academy, devoted to research and instruction in philosophy and the sciences, to train young men who would eventually become statesmen and improve the political leadership of the cities of Greece. It is difficult to imagine what the world would be like if our present political leaders were required to undergo such a training. The academy as a psychological group dynamic thus reflects some element deep within the human being which aspires not only toward excellence, but also toward a synthesis of knowledge which allows a perception of a larger and interconnected cosmos. Facts are doorways, not immovable objects; systems are languages rather than definitions of reality; and truths remain truthful within a bewildering array of forms. This ideal of education is deeply Apollonian in nature, sacred to the Sun-god and his Muses. Kleio presides over history; Euterpe over lyric poetry; Thaleia over comedy; Melpomene over tragedy; Terpsichore over dance; Erato over erotic poetry; Polymnia over storytelling; Ourania over astrology and astronomy; and Kalliope over eloquence and the heroic epic. The Muses as sources of inspiration in the arts and sciences tell us that the goal of education in the ancient academy was to become "musical" in the broadest sense.

Plato founded his academy in 387 BCE on land which had once belonged to the Spartan hero Academos, who, according to Pausanias, left the land to the citizens of Athens for gymnastics. The land was surrounded by a high wall and was adorned with statues, temples and the sepulchres of the illustrious; it was planted with olive trees reared from cuttings of the sacred olive in the Erechtheum. It was, in effect, a *temenos*, a sacred place symbolically separate from the dense plane of everyday earthbound life and imbued with a serenity which fostered the contemplation of deeper realities. The landscape is mythic, and the setting was an integral part of the meaning of the school; the image of scholars strolling through the sacred groves and discussing the nature of reality has come down to us in innumerable paintings and poems. Roman frescoes of what are known as "sacro-idyllic landscapes" present us with a dream-world of gently rolling hills studded with little temples like jewels, majestic cypresses and magical streams, in which the philosophers – sometimes two and sometimes seven (embodying the seven then known planets) engaged in passionate but serene debate. Yet despite the romantic and rather precious image thus conveyed, Plato's academy and its branches managed to thrive for nine hundred years, undergoing various transformations and internal conflicts but retaining essentially the same ideals, until the Emperor Justinian, angered by the "pagan" implications and believing the academies posed a threat to the power of the Church, closed the last Platonic academy in the sixth century of the Christian era.

The academy embodies an ideal of education which is embedded in an underlying cosmological framework. This framework, while not necessarily Platonic, is nevertheless rooted in the fundamental perception that life is a unity, that all knowledge is interrelated, and that within each human being lies the capacity to recognise this larger unity. Through such recognition the individual personality can be brought to flower through the process of education as a form of inner "recollection" of the primary realities of universal and human nature. This approach to education has, as we all know, been virtually lost in modern times. It has even been lost in some astrological schools, for sometimes these have, like many collectively recognised educational institutions, forgotten that astrology is a language rather than a concrete thing, a bridge rather than an end in itself, and a piece in a much greater puzzle rather than a system of truth standing alone. The invocation of the Muses, the recognition of different forms of knowledge as languages and bridges rather than objects or closed systems, and the tolerance and openness to inspiration resulting from this recognition, have been all but lost in many modern universities. It may be that what we are attempting to do here at Bath Spa University College is revive the ancient ideal of the academy in modern form.

My dictionary defines "academy" as a higher, would-be higher or specialised school or university, or a society for the promotion of science or art. The operative word here is "specialised", which is the direct opposite of the ancient spirit of the academy. To the modern mind, the term "academy" conveys excellence and the highest possible standards in a specific field, and bodies which call themselves academies see themselves in this light. Not only the academy itself, but also the world around it, assigns the modern academy a status which implies that no better qualified judge or arbiter exists. This is a joint process, engaged on tacitly by both academicians and the general public. Once established in this way, the academy is deemed unassailable, although this approach is also directly contradictory to the ancient spirit of the academy. The term "academy" has, in some quarters, lost any claim even to academic achievement in the usual sense. The United States Naval Academy, Air Force Academy, and Military Academy at Westpoint ostensibly replace intellectual achievement with excellence of another kind, although the nature and value of that "excellence" are open to debate. America is rife with academies devoted to specialist sciences: the American Academy of Pediatrics, for example, or the National Academies (a body referring to itself as "advisers to the nation on science, engineering and medicine"), and, of course, the Academy of Motion Picture Arts and Sciences, purveyors of the coveted Oscar awards – a modern academy which generally answers to political correctness and internal favouritism rather than to Apollo and the Muses. The term "academy" has in some quarters deteriorated into breathtaking silliness, such as the Online Trading Academy, whose members specialise in day trading on the NASDAQ stock exchange. But oddly, none of these latter-day academies invoke collective opposition as Plato's academy once did, and there is no modern emperor Justinian who is likely to close them down.

In Britain, the idea of academic or artistic excellence still clings, although often cut off from its roots. For example, there is the Royal Academy of Art, which once upon a time nurtured innovation as well as excellence; now, like the Roman academies of the late seventeenth and eighteenth centuries, it rules as the mouthpiece of collective artistic taste. There is the Royal Academy of Music, and the British Academy of Film and Theatre Arts, and the British Academy for the Humanities and Social Sciences, which refers to itself as "an independent, self-governing fellowship of 750 scholars elected for distinction and achievement." These academies, and their international counterparts – such as the Académie Française, founded in 1635 – assume the position of judging bodies, claiming the high ground of standard-setting in their spheres, and making entry both exceedingly difficult and a most desirable thing for the aspirant. The Académie Française, for example, stubbornly refused to admit women to its ranks until it capitulated in the face of the intellectual brilliance and creative talent of Marguerite Yourcenar, the author of *The Memoirs of Hadrian* and the first woman to become an academy member. Anyone here who has read this novel will recognise that Mme Yourcenar tapped the deepest ideals of the ancient academy in her literary creation, for it fuses history, imagination and individual and social psychology into a magical whole which does indeed lead the reader to contemplation of the "eternal realities". But Marguerite Yourcenar is rare among academicians.

If the academy is rooted in an archetypal pattern and reflects a particular perception of the nature and value of knowledge, other kinds of schools and bodies of education are also linked to archetypal patterns, and these may sometimes violently oppose the ideal of the academy. In fact, the academy tends to invoke its opposite, as all archetypal patterns do, and thus in the ancient world and in the Renaissance, the academy came into conflict with certain presiding collective authorities. It continues to do so now, if the spirit is true to its roots, although the authorities in question today may be educational rather than religious. The collision between the Platonic academies and the early Church was inevitable, for wherever there is a devotion to power, the ideal of the academy is lost. Those who seek power demand the suspension of inquiry from their followers: knowledge, we are told, is the enemy of faith, and the burning of books, whether promulgated by a medieval Inquisition, a twentieth century Nazi party or a twenty-first century Taliban, is the most potent of symbols reflecting the dangerous independence fostered by knowledge of a broad-based kind. Of course knowledge is not the enemy of faith; it is the enemy of the idea that there is only one faith. The great edifice of the Church arose from humble beginnings: it began as a mystery cult, akin to the mystery cults of Mithras, Attis and Orpheus. This kind of group dynamic, as ancient and archetypal as the ideal of the academy, rests on the basis of belief rather than debate; subjective experience rather than objective reasoning and experimentation;

emotional identification rather than detached perception; established authoritative texts rather than new interpretations and methodologies; the longing for redemption rather than the pursuit of excellence; and the utilisation of secrecy and mystification rather than open discussion and dialogue as a means of disseminating knowledge. Doctrine replaces questioning, and the intellectual elitism of the academy is replaced by the spiritual elitism of the divinely chosen. While entrance into Plato's academy required a knowledge of geometry, no initiation rites were required, and no teachings were "secret." If any knowledge remained secret, it was only because an individual was unable or unwilling to understand.

Taking my cue from Cicero, I will refrain from commenting that certain areas of the modern scientific establishment function more like mystery cults than like academies, and that certain academic purveyors of scientific truths sound more like the Grand Inquisitor condemning heretics than like scientists. Perhaps our model of science from the perspective of the academy is the scientist of the seventeenth century Rosicrucian Enlightenment, whose commitment to research and respect for objective truths were rooted in a perception of the natural world as the visible manifestation of the intricate workings of a vast, unified and living cosmos. Despite these destructive examples, however, the value and importance of the mystery school tradition as an archetypal group dynamic is unquestionable; in its most creative form it complements and balances the academic ideal, although it springs from different roots and answers to different gods. Hybrids between the two can exist, although it is difficult to stand in the middle and hold the balance. Human beings have always needed a vision of redemption and a belief in the possibility of transformation and renewal through the rituals and symbolic language of religious experience, the essence of the mystery tradition. Doctrine as the expression of religious experience is as important to human culture as knowledge, although often the two seem deeply threatening to each other. The symbolic realm can be approached through both mind and heart, and while some disciplines – such as music, theatre and astrology – can appeal to both, in the main these different group dynamics are like two portals which, although leading to the same realm beyond, resonate with different temperaments according to the nature of the individual. More often than not, they fall into opposition. This is particularly the case when any educational edifice makes claim to absolute truth. Whether this is the medieval Catholic Church, the militant elements in Islam, the modern science purveyed by many of our universities, the sort of psychology which entrenches itself in a form of dogma which excludes other languages and dimensions of experience, or the sort of astrology which relies on an inflexible "system" to purvey its unassailable truth, such an edifice is always threatened by the academic ideal.

It is worth looking more deeply at why, over the centuries, the academy has flowered only to be opposed with great virulence. The flowering which we all hope has begun here will inevitably constellate its opposite, not only within the university structure, but within society in general and, more importantly, within the individuals involved with it. The enemy of the ideal of the academy is not really "the scientist" or "the sceptic" or "the academic;" it is that element within each of us which finds it easier to believe than to understand, and which seeks safety in the comfort of closed conceptual structures rather than risking the anxiety which comes from never being certain of the truth. We may find examples of this fear of open-ended thought in every academic discipline. In archaeology, for example, the mainstream view – which, fortunately, is currently being challenged – is that one should not ask too many questions of an artefact, and one must certainly not ask questions concerning its symbolism. The reality of symbolism is usually denied in this more "scientific" approach to archaeology; symbols, we are told, do not exist, and therefore there is no point in trying to explore them in the context of the buildings and artefacts left by ancient cultures. Attempting to enter into the world-view of an ancient culture through the symbolic dimension of archaeological finds is thus considered the "wrong" way to study archaeology; it is deemed impossible to understand world-views so different from our own, and therefore it is better not to try, and the archaeologist must restrict himself or herself to an assessment of the material evidence without imaginative speculation. We may read interpretations such as, "The purpose of this building is unknown, although it may have been used for religious purposes." Such an approach results in an arid and impoverished language and a complete inability to comprehend the roots of our past, because the necessary crossing of disciplines and the required comprehension of the various languages of ancient religion, astrology, myth, ancient literature, anthropology and psychology is perceived as chaotic, threatening and unscientific. Two of the greatest archaeologists – Heinrich Schliemann and Sir Arthur Evans – have for some time been out of fashion in academic archaeology because they interpreted their finds imaginatively and, most threatening of all, they pursued their discoveries with a passion fired by their love of ancient myth. Schliemann believed deeply in the reality of ancient Troy because Homer spoke so powerfully to his soul, and Evans believed equally deeply in the reality of the Cretan labyrinth because the story of Theseus and the Minotaur spoke so powerfully to *his* soul. Yet without their unscientific dreams and intuitions, Troy and the great labyrinthine palace at Knossos would still be buried beneath the earth and dismissed as "mere" myth.

The same problem exists in the study of history. It could be argued that one learns more living history by reading the novels of Mary Renault than by reading erudite scholarly texts on the political history of ancient Greece, yet historical fiction, even if it is impeccably researched and based on documentary sources, is deemed to be mere fiction. Plato's dialogues are also works of fiction (or more precisely, works of theatre); they are not philosophical texts in the usual sense; yet they speak to our imagination as well as our intellect, and communicate in a way no didactic philosophical treatise ever could. And what is history, anyway? Do we not perpetually recreate it through our subjective reinterpretations of the past? And what is its value, if we do not feel connected with the living people whose history we are studying? What is the ultimate purpose of such a study, if it is not to understand more deeply the real nature of the human being? Crossing disciplines, when practiced within spheres such as history and archaeology – and, sadly, within some astrological circles as well – seems to provoke deep unease, because once the imagination and the intuition are allied with lateral thinking and unleashed in education, deeper questions are asked which require not only the student but also the teacher to be transformed by what has been learned. All this is part of the ideal of the academy.

The ideal of the academy is threatening because it requires hard work, and I do not mean hard work of the usual academic kind. It challenges those collective elements within all of us that find it easier to accept the intellectual authority of others, whether that authority is academic or religious; and even more importantly, it challenges those elements within all of us that prefer the authority of a fixed system of thought. We want to be given answers rather than experimenting and reasoning them out for ourselves; we want absolute truths to be offered which ease our fear and anxiety about being human and mortal, rather than living with the uncertainty which comes from an endlessly expanding and changing body of knowledge that opens doors to the unknown rather than allowing us to settle comfortably by the fire. We also want our once-fresh inspirations to prove reliable enough to become dogma, rather than having to let go of our creative children in order to create more. The academic ideal challenges intellectual laziness, apathy and lack of imagination, and activates that fundamental anxiety which propels so many people into belief systems – however scientific or rational they sound – which give them assurances rather than raising more questions. A so-called academy which judges rather than educates is far more acceptable in collective eyes, for it can rest in its excellence without effort or self-questioning. The ideal of the academy is not only Apollonian but also Promethean, for its members aspire to be more than they are and are prepared to sacrifice the comfortable security of mediocrity. In myth, Prometheus is punished by the gods for his sin, and so too does the collective punish those who pursue knowledge in an individual rather than a collectively sanctioned way.

The innate elitism of the academy also constellates opposition, within its members, in similar groups, and in society. Plato's political vision is deeply politically incorrect, and highly offensive to those identified with a more democratic vision of society and a more egalitarian view of human nature. Although Athens was a nominal democracy, there is nothing democratic in the myth of the philosopher-king. The elitism of the academy lies not in any superiority of blood or wealth or family background, but in the qualities of mind. While we may believe that anyone can and should strive toward excellence, the reality is that any standard of excellence set by an educational body means there will be losers. The danger to those who espouse the ideal of the academy lies in too great an identification with the role of the philosopher-king, to the point where one believes too much in one's own superiority and becomes a judge rather than an educator. The shadow-side of Apollonian aspiration can begin to look just like its opposite, as all shadows do, and such an assumption of innate superiority rapidly becomes indistinguishable from the dogma of the divinely chosen, the shadow-side of the mystery cult tradition. It is only when teachers are still learning and still able to abandon cherished truths in the face of newly discovered ignorance that this shadow-side of the academic ideal can be contained. It is unlikely that it will ever go away.

It is possible that the academic ideal can be kept alive through a love of knowledge so great that it burns through the personal issues of power and self-aggrandisement, and the personal anxieties and uncertainties which are inevitably constellated when one recognises that no truth is absolute and no body of knowledge is ever complete. Such a love may not protect the academy from conflict with the outer world, but it may help to protect it from the more destructive elements in its members. The more we cling to rigid definitions in any sphere of knowledge in order to assuage our terror of the unknown, or to fill up the void created by our personal hurts, grievances and insecurities, the less we love what we are learning, for we are using it for our own purposes rather than giving ourselves to it as an act of love. The academic ideal is not democratic in the Neptune-in-Aquarius sense; not every individual is able to pursue studies in this way, nor able to afford it even if the ability is present. While Plato's school was free, modern universities are not. We are compromised even before we have begun. Yet we must be able to acknowledge and accept some truth in the accusations of elitism which inevitably arise when the collective is confronted by the academic ideal. The present trend to lower university standards so that everyone can have a degree reduces the value of all education; when learning becomes politicised in this way, excellence is lost. It is appropriate that we should have to study, memorise, take examinations and present papers and theses. It should be difficult, not easy. It is inevitable that some people will fail simply because they lack the ability to succeed, or because they are too lazy to try. Apollo was never a politically correct god, and he had little patience for those who did not strive for excellence. One key to the ideal of the academy seems to be, not specialisation for its own sake, but inclusiveness which coexists with the recognition that individuals have special talents that need to be applied in different ways. Another key seems to be a willingness to apply reason rather than belief to complex subjects such as astrology, which requires many levels of understanding and a respect for many different approaches. Perhaps the most important key of all is that we love astrology not merely for its own sake, or for the comfort it brings, but for what its language points to, what its doors open onto, and what its symbols awaken in us as a recollection of where we have come from and where we are going.

Verity and the Question of Primary and Secondary Scholarship in Astrology

From the paper originally titled 'Perils of the Occult Mentality'

Geoffrey Cornelius, University of Kent at Canterbury

The type of thinking employed in astrology is at root non-positivistic and metaphorical, a combination which, as a study in-itself, is academically acceptable only as a literary, poetic or imaginative exercise. Treated as a mode of knowledge this thinking is usually denigrated as a leftover remnant of naive idealism or worse still, occultism. There therefore exists an abyss between the prevailing epistemology and astrologers who understand that their practice concerns real knowledge of the world. Can – and should – the academy bridge the gap, or will the astrologers tumble into it?

In order to introduce the problematic relationship between astrology and the academy I will offer something that may seem untoward, but is in fact fully relevant to our discussion – a horoscope. The proposition that astrological symbolism, in and of itself, could yield insight into our academic proceedings constellates the very issue we are considering. It also raises the question, for which the astrologers must begin to account, of what order of knowing this is, and what place such knowledge might have in a university. But let me put these considerations aside for a moment and take up the astrological question of an appropriate horoscope for our debate. The horoscope for the inception of the conference, for 10:00am 13th June, is remarkable for the strong placing of Uranus, exactly on the western horizon. We might even suspect the guiding hand of election in this matter. Whether or not elected, this is a lively signature for our subject. However, bearing in mind the old dictum that 'the lights bring to light', I suggest that the major zodiacal event maturing over the weekend, the Full Moon, fully reveals the exact nature and the consequences of the challenge of Uranus, which is at the same time the challenge of this conference. It is to the Full Moon of 14th June that I will therefore turn.

There are two levels to the symbolism. The first is given in the

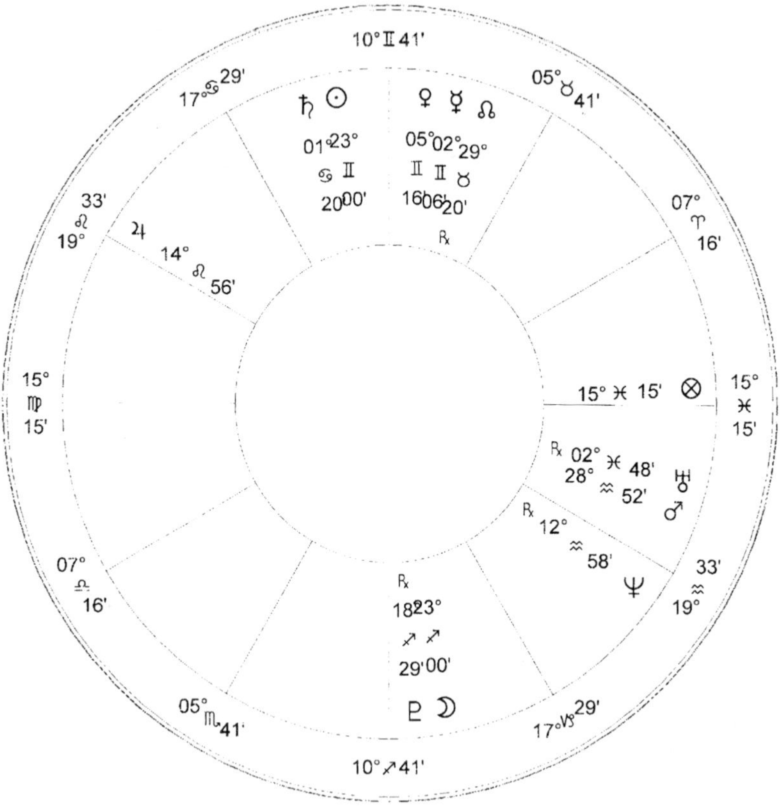

Horoscope for the Full Moon
14 June 2003, 12:16:27 pm GMD, Bath, England.

universal symbolism of the Full Moon, with the Sun in Gemini and the Moon in Sagittarius, The Gemini-Sagittarius polarity is an image of education and enlightenment, the journey of body, soul and intellect, the field of discourse and wisdom. The Full Moon brings to light and displays in the heavens the theme of our conference, *Astrology and the Academy*. So the timing of this event is a fortuitous election, bringing us together under this Full Moon, here, now. Observe also the Moon's separation from Pluto, in the depths of the fourth house: here is Plato's allegory of the cave, the metaphor for the academy. The Moon shows the shadow-play of figures at the back of the cave, the light of the Moon reflecting the Sun.

The second level of this symbolism is horoscopic, and is revealed through traditional horary analysis. The moment of Full Moon at 12:16 this afternoon falls in the planetary hour of Mercury. Mercury rules the Ascendant, swift in motion, in its own sign and term, free of beams, almuten. Mercury is a classical significator for the occult arts and astrology; placed in the ninth, the house of higher learning and the university, and applying to the lady of the ninth, Venus – here we find repeated the metaphor for the theme, astrology and the academy.

What is the union that astrology seeks in the perfection of the Mercury-Venus conjunction? This pair is a favourite motif in renaissance philosophy and art, and is the marriage of intellect and Eros, intellect consumed in love, desire exalted in intelligence. We see this symbolism in Botticelli's *Primavera*, it is a guiding thread for Ficino, and it is the heart of the work of the Platonic Academy in Florence.

With such radicality of symbolism and with Mercury in great dignity, ruling both Ascendant and Midheaven, lord of the syzygy and receiving the Sun, then we know it will tell the truth about its subject: the use of astrology reveals the use of astrology. We realise that this horoscope not only invites us to contemplate what we already know, but that by being led out or educated by the symbolism, we infer and discriminate things that as yet we do not quite understand. So, just as we form a symbolic picture of the goal of our endeavours, the joining of astrology and the academy, our understanding is brought up with a jolt by the square of Uranus.

Uranus, the first of the new planets, was discovered by Herschel in Bath in 1781. It is appropriate to our theme, for this planet has been adopted by the majority of modern practitioners as a universal symbol for their art, and it is not surprising to find it configured in some shape or form. But it is all awry in this horoscope, because Uranus interposes between Mercury and Venus by a powerful square, prohibiting the primary significators from perfecting their beautiful conjunction.

The traditionalist may be tempted to ignore Uranus and imagine that we could simply revert to an astrology of earlier times, but we have not been shown a symbol of this order just to wish it away. In an earlier age there was no impediment to astrology in the academy, but modern Uranus shows the condition we are in now, and that is what we are called to work with. The house placing of Uranus is significant, for the sixth shows the problem of *method* – what is the method of analysis and discrimination through which the question of astrology shall be raised? What actually does the 'academic' study of astrology mean, and what is the scope of this study? The importance of this concern is underscored by the conjunction of Mars with Uranus, with the Moon applying sextile as she begins her waning phase. In the struggle out of the cave, work must be done in search of an answer.

A creative move may be attempted, in the style of modern horary, applying the mutual reception by degree to Uranus and Neptune. This makes Uranus a friend rather than a foe, and this suggests a distinctive mode of theorising the question of astrology. Here is not the place to develop this line of interpretation, however, because nothing can come to fruit until we take up the message of Uranus in Pisces, and why it plays a pivotal and prohibiting role.

I suggest that we will approach an understanding only by taking on the signification of Uranus for the change in European and American culture and consciousness that we call the Enlightenment. From the philosophical watershed that is marked in time most exactly by Kant[1], we can demarcate an age when astrology was still possible from our age when, like every evocation of a poetic and enchanted universe, astrology has become absurd. A characteristic function of Uranus, as every astrologer knows, is splitting and dividing, a reflection of the primordial divide of Heaven and Earth, showing in tyrannical mastery over Nature, and in the exaltation of abstracted human reason. Uranus is a signifier of the subject-object split that has led to the objectification of scientific and literal reality as the ground of truth, with a whole mode of human-being cast into 'subjectivity' and secondary status. This symbolism is especially resonant with Uranus currently in the dual and slippery sign of Pisces. This placing reflects the epochal precessional movement ushering in the second fish of Pisces with the discovery of Uranus.

It is my interpretation of this horoscope that for astrology to have a genuine relationship with the academy, it is to be spoken *in* the academy.

We can hardly imagine Mercury in Gemini keeping quiet, can we? It is only Uranus in Pisces that might be tempted to throttle it. On the other hand, if Mercury is spoken, there is a demand that we take on the paradoxical task of laying out, understanding, and critically discoursing on the actual theory and method of astrology. I do not underestimate the intellectual problem involved. Not only is Uranus a symbol of division, but Mercury in Gemini delights in splits and polarities, and it can hardly help engineering them.

The paradox of the subject-object split is exposed the moment we use allegory. Allegory as a mode of analysis is usually denigrated as depending on an arbitrary and essentially mistaken mix of subjective and properly objective observations, and was entirely discounted by the scientific enlightenment. It is the supposed subjectivity of its operation that renders it opaque or occult to transparent and democratic rationalism. It is a commonplace for the historian of science to suggest that shaking off this earlier form of reasoning is a condition of entry to modern rational thought.[2] Hence any attempt to reintroduce consideration of this form, and to advance its truth-claim, can only be seen as regressive. It is allowable for allegory to be encompassed in the study of Shakespeare or Dante, and it is not a problem for the academy to take on the 'as if' of this mode of interpretation with respect to literary and artistic production. But do not forget that the Cartesian split has cast the *geisteswissenschaften*, the 'human sciences' wholly into the status of secondary knowledge, with the final arbitration of truth and method reserved for, and imitated from, the methods of logic, mathematics, and the natural sciences.[3]

So where do we locate astrology in this divide? Like all the inferential arts of divination, and despite its long-continued attempts to disguise itself as natural science, astrology is a *divinatory allegoric.* A liberal-minded attitude might allow it to belong to the humanities, where it can be humanely dealt with and not taken too seriously. However, astrology will not be put back in its box so easily, precisely because we cannot avoid the fact that its practitioners understand it to make a primary truth-claim.

When we probe closely the nature of the truth-claim made for astrology, then I suggest that a still more fundamental epistemological issue is uncovered. This has already been raised in this conference by Angela Voss; it is in the nature of the Full Moon in Gemini-Sagittarius and it concerns the distinction between knowledge and what we may call 'wisdom'. This term is almost a banal platitude when we use it today, so far has it fallen. Yet we can hardly avoid the fact that prior to our modern period the academy's quest for knowledge subserved the quest for wisdom. Plato's allegory is not about information theory – the people who are tied down in the cave and can only see the shadow-play at the back do not lack data. They have plenty enough information, they have all their horizontal and linear logic on one level, but they lack the wisdom to *see*.

This is problematic because the seeing is not, on the face of things, given to all; we reach issues of illumination, initiation, and elite knowledge. Here is the perilous question of the occult mentality, which can be located right the way back to that original allegory of western philosophy, Plato's cave. We astrologers are heirs to this way of understanding whether we like it or not. This is so out of keeping with our time that it is wise for us to be modest on entering the portals of the academy and not imagine that we are going to storm the barricades. There are too many barricades for us to take them all at once, and in any case they lie deep within our own imagination just as much as they exist in some sceptical world outside.

The question of a primary truth claim is pivotal and so far as the astrologer is concerned cannot be avoided. The attempt to avoid it would leave us with the academy studying astrology as some sort of belief-system, to be sympathetically annotated, dissected, and put up for comparison with various other belief-systems. That places it on a par with the way in which the sociologist or anthropologist chooses to study the belief-system of the ancient Celts, of west-coast New-Agers, or of the Ndembu, or any of countless other tribes and cultural groupings. Nothing wrong in that, one may say, and indeed such studies have their own particular lights of illumination. However, the various social sciences do all share a common avoidance strategy, which is to avoid allowing the material to touch the observer as *truth for the observer*. The actual meaning of things for the Ndembu is not supposed to become the meaning of things for the anthropologist, because that would undermine the fundamental category-logic implicit in the endeavour of what we call science. If this undermining were to occur then he or she has committed the cardinal error of 'going native'.

I have mentioned several times that astrology makes a primary truth claim. In order to bring out what is meant by primary truth with respect to astrology, I will adopt as a synonym the somewhat archaic term 'verity'. I take my cue from the weight given by William Lilly to this concept in the context of his lengthy judgment 'If Presbytery shall stand?', which is the most important single demonstration of astrology in his *Christian Astrology*.[4] This is a prophecy which falls within a wider pattern of mundane astrology predictions. However, taken in its own right it is an exquisite exercise in craft and a spell-binding interpretation where Lilly, writing in the spring of 1647, correctly predicts the execution of Charles I in 1649 and the rise to power of Oliver Cromwell. Beyond the circumstances of the prophecy Lilly has a further purpose:

> From these configurations we shall naturally frame our judgment, not positive or affirmative, but conjecturall, onely out of a desire that posterity may see there's some verity in Astrology, and the Clergies just cause to carp at the Art, if I lye [...]

The success of this prediction is therefore intended to demonstrate the 'verity' of astrology on the canvas of the greatest possible concerns of Church and State.

However, before Lilly could demonstrate astrology to others he first had to prove it for himself. Here is how he describes his passage into the art in 1633:

> I apply'd myself to study those Books I had obtain'd, many times twelve, or fifteen, or eighteen Hours Day and Night; I was curious to discover, whether there was any Verity in the Art or not.[5]

So what are we to understand by the word 'verity'? The Concise Oxford English Dictionary offers the following definition:

> *verity* n. truth (of statement etc); true statement, esp one of fundamental import; really existent thing [...]

Nearly all astrologers will affirm that their practice is rooted in something of fundamental import, and that knowledge of astrology is knowledge of a 'really existent thing'. Verity is for our purposes a preferable term to the more obvious word 'truth', because truth is usually also thought of as *the* Truth, and becomes abstracted as an absolute quality. All that is sought is the relative truthfulness of astrology in and of itself. Lilly seeks to demonstrate that there is *some* verity in astrology. This is the ground on which it stands or falls, its own raison d'être; and this is worthy of the most searching investigation.

The nettle to be grasped is that it is wholly insufficient to treat astrology as a belief-system that people have had in the past and sometimes have today, to be studied as an item of cultural history, or as a subject of sociological or anthropological analysis. The astrologer claims and knows that astrology has verity as a way in which reality shows itself. That is what is meant by a primary truth claim. Accepting this leads us to distinguish the study of the belief-system and the claim of astrologers from the issue of the verity that may lie behind their claim. Laying out the conditions of astrology's putative truth – and not simply analysing the cultural circumstances of its claim – is properly the work of the academy.

There is an ethical demand upon the academy with respect to verity in astrology, as in all other things, and it bears upon the individual choice we each make in studying anything or in undertaking the practice of anything. Verity goes to the heart of the matter. If I am going to spend a lifetime on astrology, then like Lilly I require to see whether there is any verity in it. I am not going to waste my time on something that does not in itself have verity, when some other discourse or practice, such as cognitive psychology and neurophysiology, or psychoanalysis and counselling technique, or solar flares and electromagnetic fields, will get to the heart of the results claimed by astrology, and when understood will be capable of achieving more reliable and truthful results. Where else is there a greater requirement to see and educe verity than in the academy? What else is a university for?

This brings us to consider the relative status of the intellectual pursuits that cluster under the umbrella of astrology in the academy, in the necessary distinction between *primary* and *secondary* scholarship. This is easily understood, at least in an approximate sense, and I can best exemplify the distinction in an anecdote from my experience. Many years ago, along with several other astrologers, I had the good fortune to meet a notable scholar concerned with our field who can be taken as standing for the whole genus of such scholars. He was an eminent authority on an astrologer of antiquity who is a major figure in intellectual history, and our scholar was concerned to advance the argument for the importance and influence of this historical figure. It was a delight and also a puzzlement for our scholar to meet studious modern individuals who were in some measure in the direct lineage of astrological practice of said intellectual hero: 'astrologists', he called us, using the archaic term. He was charming with us and we asked him interesting questions. It is a wonderful thing to ask questions of a scholar, and there was even a possibility that things we might say could illuminate some tiny corner of his own studies.

In the conversation, one of our party asked whether our scholar had looked at the methods of the hero from the past and seen what light they might throw on his own natal horoscope. We rather took it for granted that our scholar would have made some little experiment, if only out of passing curiosity. But this was a question too far. A momentary look of blank incomprehension passed across his brow. Why should he do *that*? Why should he for one moment take seriously the core of the life work and attempt at meaning – the verity – of the very figure he is studying?

Now I have to say that admirable though this scholar's scholarship is in his chosen area, it is entirely secondary to the question of astrology. This mode of scholarship does indeed bring many materials of significance before the astrologer, and it may incidentally assist the astrologer, but its whole project is secondary with respect to its subject matter. Scholarship that is primary with respect to the subject matter bears upon or offers a critique of, challenges, educes or brings forward, the verity of the thing, and if it does not aim to do that then it is secondary to the field.

The distinction between primary and secondary scholarship involves qualifications and considerations that go beyond the scope of this current paper, but for present purposes it is sufficient to establish a simple criterion, which is that primary scholarship treats of the verity of that discipline. This means that for astrology, primary academic scholarship treats of the verity of astrology as a discipline *in its own right*. An important qualification is that the distinction is not between different nominal discourses and disciplines, as if we were to say that 'history' can never be primary with respect to any other discipline outside of itself. The distinction is created by the intention of scholarship, not by its nominal form, and therefore it is possible to treat the history of astrology in the light of its bearing on the verity of astrology, in which case it becomes primary to the field.

Having said this, such an equation between disciplines is all too rarely achieved. We could name various of the current generation of intellects at work in historical studies in astrology who do not see the wood for the trees. It seems to be generally the case that the more a scholar can see of texts and transmissions and translations and mis-translations, the less they will see of astrology. If such scholars have not started off with the basic symbolic perception that makes an astrologer then there is no chance at all of them properly understanding their subject-matter. Such scholarship, however valuable elements of its discovery may be, is effectively dead with respect to astrology's verity.

It follows that in commencing the difficult task of laying out the material of astrology for the academy, we need to be especially clear in the distinction of primary and secondary. A discourse that has its own primary method and is treating of its own verity cannot be brought on as a substitute for primary method in another discipline. Sociology is not a substitute for jurisprudence in the field of legal studies. History is not a substitute for differential diagnosis in medicine. Likewise, porting in 'theories and methods' from social sciences is wholly inadequate as a means of providing theory and method for the academic study of astrology.

At the point that the academy engages in primary scholarship then it is fully engaged in the discourse, development and transmission of its subject matter. This means, however, that we astrologers should not for a moment imagine that what transpires will be a comfortable endorsement or rubber stamp for everything we do. The reverse is likely to be the case. As an illustration of the issues we might face, take the case of the interface that has occurred in recent times between orthodox astrology and modern science. Surprising as this statement might at first seem to most astrologers, the scientific and statistical researches into astrology that have occurred mainly in the last fifty years represent a genuine – if wholly misguided – attempt at primary scholarship in our field, precisely because they have taken fully seriously and then tested within their own methods the possibility of verity in the claims of astrologers. We all know what has happened to those claims, put to those particular tests – a dismal failure for astrology. Do not therefore for a moment imagine that the status quo will be endorsed by the critical gaze of the academy. The end result may well be that astrologers have to rethink much that they do, if not everything that they do. But if that is the truth of the matter, then the academy will have served its purpose for us all. This means that far from holding to a model of the objective observer, the academy will begin to shape and lead thinking within the subject area of astrology itself. Anything short of this is an abnegation of the responsibility of the academy. That, I suggest, is what is indicated in our conference's Full Moon in Sagittarius.

Endnotes

1. See Kant's condemnation of astrology in his description of 'the starry heavens above and the moral law within': see the Foreword to the *Critique of Practical Reason* transl. Lewis White Beck (Bobbs Merrill, New York, 1956).
2. Brian Vickers 'Analogy versus Identity: the rejection of occult symbolism 1580-1680' in Brian Vickers ed. *Occult and Scientific Mentalities in the Renaissance* (Cambridge University Press, 1984).
3. Hans Georg Gadamer *Truth and Method,* transl. revised by J.Weinsheimer & D.G.Marshall (Sheed and Ward, London, 1989).
4. William Lilly *Christian Astrology* (London 1647; reprinted Regulus, London 1985) pp. 439-42.
5. Katharine Briggs ed. *The Last of the Astrologers* (English Folklore Society, 1974) p. 23.

Psychological Aspects of Astrology's Return to the Academy

From a paper originally titled "Light from Dark Matter: The Burden and the Gift of Astrology's Shadow Position in Academe"

Jean Hinson Lall, MA

The reasons for astrology's long exile from the academy have been as much psychological as intellectual and political, for it represents the shadow of the scientific, professional and technical value-system of the contemporary academic culture. The reintroduction of astrology as a serious topic of university studies produces an inevitable collision between the norms of intellectual objectivity (the stance of the modern scholar who stands apart from the material being studied) and the reality of what C.G. Jung called the objective psyche, or collective unconscious, from which we can never fully separate our conscious standpoint. For astrology systematically reveals the unconscious, archetypal factors underlying conscious experience and collapses the subject-object dichotomy fundamental to the modern psyche and the modern intellect, thus undermining the assumptions and identity of the modern scholar. To reintegrate astrology into academic life requires bringing more objectivity into astrology but also bringing the implications of the objective psyche fully into the academy. This requires a historical perspective on astrology's psychological position since the Enlightenment and a capacity to do personal and intellectual 'shadow work' in academe – a slow and costly alchemical process, but a necessary one if astrology's full contribution is to be realized.

As we gather to celebrate astrology's return to the academy, it may be worthwhile to reflect on the psychological aspects of this rapprochement. I would like to consider the psychological position of the astrologer in academe, the reactions we may evoke in other scholars, and what our historic relationship to the collective psyche equips us to contribute to the world of scholarship.

Because the debates over astrology in modern times (to the extent that they take place at all) tend to be framed in intellectual and ethical terms, we can easily overlook the psychological barriers to the acceptance of our discipline. The assumption of most academics is that astrology has long since been proven invalid on scientific grounds; that it has no leg to stand on theoretically; and that the effects of astrological practice must therefore be either null or actually harmful, hence its practitioners must be charlatans or fools. Modern astrological practice is of interest only sociologically, to the extent that one might want to research what sorts of people persist in superstitious beliefs and why. The historical study of astrological texts suffers from the same prejudice: we find for example the biography of Elias Ashmole[1] published without due attention to his horoscopy, while the astrological writings of no less a figure than Johannes Kepler have generally not been considered important enough to translate into English. Those of you who are historians of astrology could no doubt multiply these examples endlessly.

The bias which we encounter so frequently among educated people does not arise solely out of faulty reasoning or incorrect or insufficient information. It is also an expression of the biased person's psychological and emotional makeup, a function of the imaginal structure of his or her personality. Each of us lives mythically, and academic and professional disciplines have their own guiding myths which give meaning to the work of individual practitioners. The agnostic physicist or rationalist philosopher is as deeply embedded in irrational images as any theologian, astrologer, or Jungian psychologist. All have the same problem, of which they may be more or less aware: that of becoming conscious of the myths they are living and learning to reflect on the profound images that inform their theory and practice. While most scholars do not seem to consider this an issue, it is in fact a responsibility, when one judges the work of others or attempts to place one's own work in relation to other disciplines or ways of thought, to engage in this kind of reflection. Otherwise one is simply operating from prejudice and dogma and obstructing the search for truth.

We begin, then, with the obvious challenges of finding acceptance for our theory, methods and subject matter; of unearthing and interpreting material that has long been neglected or censored; and of reckoning with the difference in underlying metaphors between ourselves and other scholars. Less obvious is the challenge of realizing the split *within* ourselves as people of the twenty-first century who in many ways base our existence on modern and post-modern assumptions, yet who are practicing an ancient form of divination. A closely related problem is to come to terms with the gap between ourselves and our counterparts who lived in earlier times when our discipline was taking form. There are biases at work in our relationship to our own material, for we do not dwell any longer in an ensouled cosmos, we do not see with the same eyes as did Babylonian astronomers, we do not reason or inhabit our bodies in the same way as did the ancient Greeks, and both the concept and the experience of human personality have undergone a metamorphosis since the time of our medieval ancestors.

My reflections on this topic come out of thirty years' experience as an astrologer who happened also to be married to an academic scientist, so that I was continually brought into contact with people who could not find any point of contact with my work. I also had to reckon with the changes astrology brought about in my own mentality and inner makeup. In the early years of my studies I had a dream which was a simple mental realization: "I have been robbed of my objectivity". Just that. On reflection, I felt that it was so: As a young mother who had left her career to care for a child, who was also studying astrology and depth psychology and undergoing analysis, I was no longer the proper educated Western adult who could stand above and outside of reality and analyze, discuss and control it. I was now in the soup, not only immersed in female existence (the official address of subjectivity) but engaged in traffic with the *mundus imaginalis*. It took many years for me to become fully comfortable with that position and to feel thoroughly grounded in the objectivity of astrology, which is that of the oracle.

In earlier times, of course, the way to gain an objective view was through divination. The ancient Greeks journeyed to Apollo's temple at Delphi to find an objective reference point in their turbulent world.[2] Right up through the Renaissance, astrology was looked to as a source of objective insight into matters great and small. Enlightenment thinking, however, consigned astrology to the scrapheap of subjectivity and superstition.

Depth psychology has opened a new avenue of approach to the old divination methods. C.G. Jung revived for psychology the classical understanding of psyche as an infinite cosmos of which we are an inseparable part. He recognized not only the personal unconscious but also the collective unconscious, which he also called the *objective psyche*, pointing to the experience of the archetypal world as something far larger than our personalities, not under our control, which stands over against our ego, often frustrating our wishes but pressing us towards our fullest possible humanity. It is through our participation in this greater cosmos that divination is possible. Jung argued that modern education, which omits this half of reality, is

> morbidly one-sided. No doubt we are right to open the eyes and ears of our young people to the wide world, but it is the maddest of delusions to think that this really equips them for the task of living. It is the kind of training that enables a young person to adapt himself outwardly to the world and reality, but no one gives a thought to the necessity of adapting to the self, to the powers of the psyche, which are far mightier than all the Great Powers of the earth.[3]

As astrology is a method of working directly with the unknowns of the psyche, perhaps the return of our discipline to the academy will contribute in some measure to correcting this one-sidedness in the education of our young people. It might also help to address some limitations in the prevailing academic world-view. For example, in conventional scholarship today it is assumed that a paper is independent of the time of its presentation. Astrologers notice, however, that topics sometimes choose their moments, and that what stands forth, what is available to be grasped about a particular subject, varies according to the day and the hour. We know that time is qualitative as well as quantitative. This awareness allows us to avoid the superstition of believing in reproducibility as the sole standard for truth (for in a certain sense, no situation and no experiment can really be replicated). It also permits us to make a divinatory move in our studies, turning to the objective psyche for insight into the material and guidance regarding our approach to it. So let us take a few minutes to examine the cosmic picture of our conference and of this particular hour.

Horoscopic reflections

What does astrology itself have to say about the return to the academy? The chart for the opening of the conference (Figure 1) gives us a view of the event as a whole and its subject-matter. Aries is the sign on the cusp of the ninth house, which has to do with higher education, philosophy and scholarship; hence Mars, ruler of Aries, should have much to say concerning the question of astrology in the academy. Mars is in Aquarius, the sign associated with astrology as well as with science and other objective studies, in the seventh house of partnerships, social adaptation

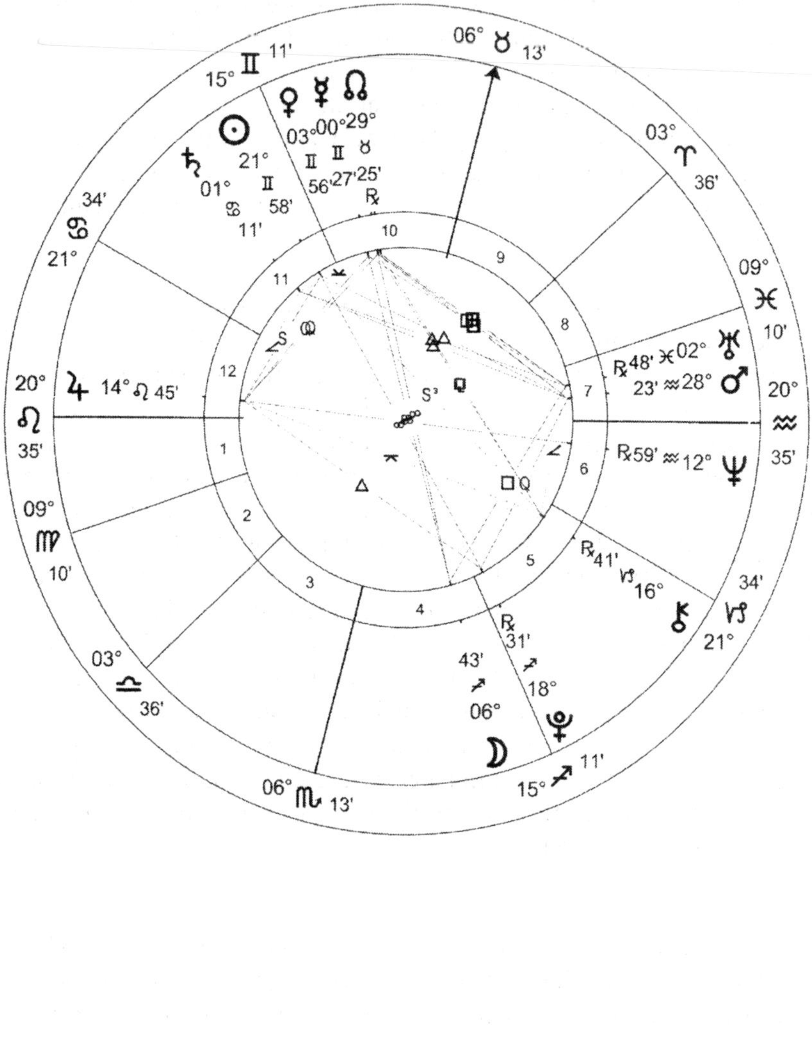

Figure 1: Horoscope for the opening of the conference on *Astrology and the Academy*
Bath Spa University College, 13 June 2003 at 10:00 BST.

and 'open enemies'. It applies (though still out of sign) to the conjunction with its co-ruler Uranus in the seventh house and to the trine with its other co-ruler Saturn in the eleventh. Mars the pioneer and warrior forges a new trail and rides straight up to the gates of the academy, laying down a challenge and demanding a real encounter, among ourselves and between astrologers and other scholars. The Sun, ruler of the Ascendant, applies to the trine with Mars, indicating good prospects for the success of the endeavour.

Turning now to the chart (Figure 2) for the present hour, when our focus is on the psychological situation, we find that Mars has moved to within two and a half degrees of the Descendant, bringing the issue of astrology's self-assertion into even sharper focus. While the Sun is nicely positioned in Gemini on the eleventh cusp and sextile the Leo Ascendant, promising the joys of collaboration and the flourishing of friendships and networks of communication, Mars angular conjoined with Uranus accentuates the disruptive effect of our arrival on the scene, the potential for open opposition and conflict, and the changes that may be stimulated by the confrontation. There may be battles over turf and testing of boundaries. We'll be called upon to think and act with courage, facing the conflicts in our own thinking and the tensions within our field as well as defending ourselves against outside attack. There should be abundant energy available for the forging of creative relationships that help to bind our work into the fabric of intellectual culture.

Exciting days lie ahead as we enter into debate and competition, testing our ideas in the arena of established scholarship, but also renegotiating the rules to allow the true nature of astrology to express itself. Mars in Aquarius is, to say the least, intellectually assertive, ready to fight through to the truth, and (certainly in the seventh house) eager to engage. If not spoiling for a fight, he is dying for a good debate. Perhaps he is best able to uncover and clarify his views through energetic encounters with other keen minds. This bodes well, I think, for the long-overdue emergence of robust criticism within astrology.

Mars on the Descendant can indicate projected aggression or the displacement of an inner conflict onto an external situation. Here, through the conjunction with Uranus in Pisces, Mars is carrying the highly charged burden of astrology and magic, the shadow of the scientific culture that dominates the academy. We can see in this constellation both our own assertion of the right to enter the scholarly conversation, and also the resistance and hostility we may encounter on the part of scientists and rationalists or 'skeptics' who do not realize the mythic, magical and even

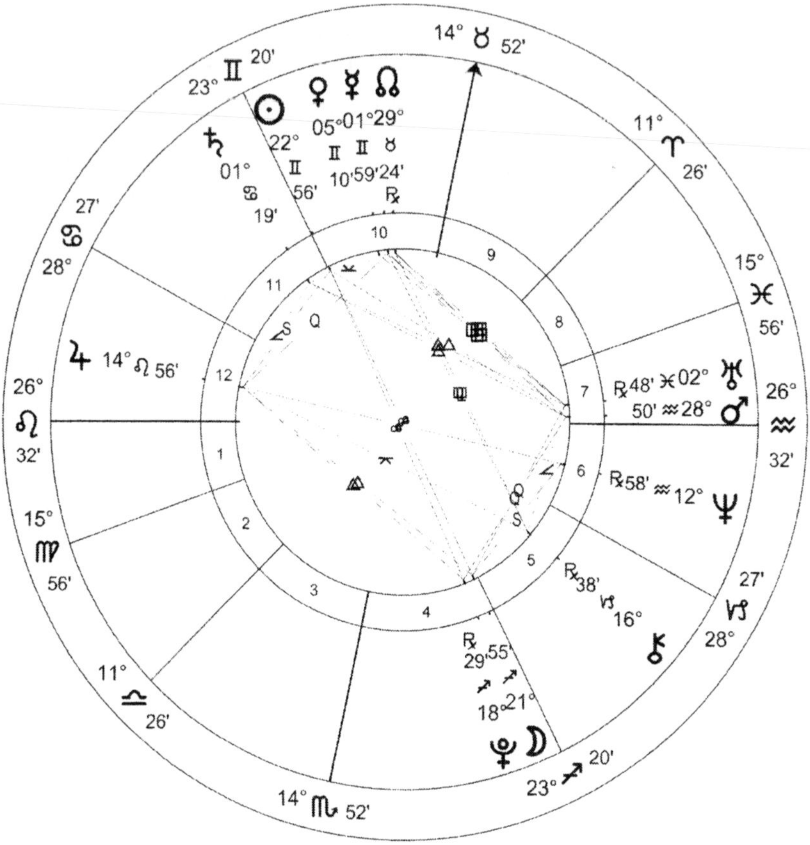

Figure 2: Paper addressing "Psychological Aspects of Astrology's Return to the Academy", Bath Spa University College, 14 June 2003, 10:30 BST.

superstitious underpinnings of their own standpoint. The fact that Uranus and Aquarius rule *both* astrology and science underlines the point that this struggle involves projection and thus calls for a psychological attitude.

Mars in the seventh can also be a psychologist, however, probing fearlessly into relationship issues including the shadow projections, and uncovering the images and metaphors (Pisces) within the intellectual attitude or theory (Uranus/Aquarius). Finally, Mars approaching the conjunction with Uranus in Pisces might bring to awareness the psychological and intellectual costs of the schisms in our past – the bloody religious wars; the split between scientific and magical world views; the amputation of the soul from psychology and philosophy; the relegation of the *mundus imaginalis* to the heretical, the superstitious, or the merely imaginary – and give voice to the soul's prophetic anger at her condition in the contemporary world.

The Moon in this morning's chart, ruling the twelfth house of seclusion and exile, has completed the conjunction with Pluto in Sagittarius on the way to her opposition to the Sun, perhaps showing that our discipline has learned something from her long sojourn in the wilderness, and also from her extensive twentieth-century involvement with depth psychology. At the Full Moon she can reflect back to the Sun the fruits of these underworld (Pluto) journeys (Sagittarius).

The goal of the work is indicated by the Taurus Midheaven and the North Node in the tenth house, both ruled by Venus, who is moving toward the alchemical conjunction with final dispositor Mercury in Gemini, suggesting hopes for a revival of the deep principles of classical and Renaissance humanism in astrology and in the academy. The square of Mars and Uranus to the North Node, Venus and Mercury shows the drive toward this *coniunctio* and the hazards and difficulties along the way (including, as Geoffrey Cornelius has pointed out, the interposition of Uranus between Mercury and Venus). Neptune and Jupiter, the planets of inspiration, oppose each other and square the Midheaven, showing an intense engagement of spirit and imagination in this new direction for astrology, and the possibility of inflation.

The instability of the Mars-Uranus pairing, along with the stress on the 'mutable' planets generally, is ameliorated by the 'fixed' angles and by the trine to Saturn in Cancer. Mars will in fact reach the exact trine to Saturn just before it conjoins Uranus in the third degree of Pisces later this month. Saturn here alerts us that the work will be constrained by emotional limitations – our own and those of other people. We may feel the impact of other scholars' emotional biases and find our own maturity being tested. Scholarship requires emotional restraint and self-discipline, the capacity to give criticism objectively and to receive criticism without taking it personally. Saturn in Cancer might help astrologers rein in some of the lunar excesses of our field, the tendency to accept uncritically any and all astrological opinions, techniques, theories, levels and styles of practice. At the same time, we might call upon the fathering capacities of Saturn to shelter, in the potentially inhospitable academic climate, the lunar gifts of astrology, its ability to receive, mediate and give body to symbolic truth and to reveal by its reflected light the unity of all things. Saturn can guide us to the appropriate professional forms for the expression of astrological values and demonstrate their philosophical foundations in ancient tradition, the ancestral 'homes' (Cancer) from which they proceed.

Much more could be said about this chart, but I hope that these brief reflections have served to orient our thinking about the psychological position of the astrologer returning to academe. I would like now to examine more closely the nature of the shadow that falls upon astrology and some of the 'psychological history' behind our displacement from the world of scholarship, drawing upon some insights of C.G. Jung and on the work of historians of science and culture.

Astrology's exile

Human personality and culture unfold together. Thus in the transition from one historical period to another, along with significant changes in political theory and governance, theology and folk beliefs, economic structures and trade relations, language and literary forms, building technologies and architectural ideals, we can also observe shifts in the way the human being is imagined and placed in relation to society and cosmos, and in the actual reported experience of being a person. In fact, the emphasis on the human individual has been a distinguishing feature of Western civilization, and its history is of particular relevance for our concern with the recovery of astrology.

The last great flowering of astrology, during the Renaissance, coincided with the emergence of a greatly enhanced sense of human creativity and the powers of the individual. From this newly sovereign, self-aware personality, nourished on classical learning and Hermetic magic, would come a powerful new science, a new humanism and individualism in art, religious and political reform and revolution, immense economic changes, and a drastic restructuring of social institutions.

To the humanists of the Renaissance, science was not separate from 'natural magic' any more than it was unrelated to Christian theology. The serious researchers of the day, whose work fed directly into modern sciences, were practitioners of astrology, alchemy, and other Hermetic disciplines. Yet as the Renaissance gave way to the Reformation and the Enlightenment, the magical and mystical elements in science and philosophy were gradually stripped away, while the Western psyche underwent a corresponding surgery.

The history of this transformation is complex and fascinating, and far from being fully understood. It is often viewed simply as 'progress', the inevitable leaving behind of outmoded views, and indeed most people today assume that the decline of alchemy and astrology came about because they simply lost out in fair and open competition with the new 'mechanical philosophy' of natural science. In fact, however, the Hermetic sciences were argued against, and defeated, largely on theological and political grounds rather than on the basis of experimental results or an objective comparison of the validity of their theories and methods with those of the new scientists. As Evelyn Fox Keller notes, at the time when these debates were at their height, "the very notion of scientific success in the modern sense was as yet unformulated".[4] Nor was there an established forum in which agreed-upon criteria for the validity of scientific work could be applied to the testing of one approach versus another.

To understand the decline of astrology we have to consider the forces threatening the stability of political and religious institutions during this period. Many parts of Europe were undergoing severe political strains at the same time as the Catholic Church faced the challenge of Protestant reform, and often (since Church and state were so intimately related) the religious and the political issues were closely intertwined or even identical. To take one example, in seventeenth century England, which in the course of a few decades endured civil wars, plots against the government, the overthrow and execution of the monarch, the Puritan interregnum, continuing religious unrest and strife, a major epidemic of plague, and the Great Fire of London, civil and religious order were obviously at a premium. The involvement of many astrologers in both radical politics and nonconforming religion therefore attracted the opprobrium of those in power and helped to seal astrology's eventual doom as a respectable academic and professional field.[5]

The crisis of the Church meanwhile was not simply a matter of resisting or implementing institutional reform, but of preserving, restoring and extending the very means of salvation. Following the shock of schism, Europe became more thoroughly Christianized than ever before, as both Catholic and Protestant reformers sought to root out lingering pagan practices and folk beliefs and to inculcate in all believers a high level of personal piety, moral rigor, awareness of sin, and sense of responsibility for their own salvation. Belief in the Devil as an active force in the world against whom the faithful must continually struggle was heightened by Protestant preaching.[6] "In both Catholic and Protestant quarters there arose a zealous commitment, sometimes strengthened by millenarian beliefs, to purify the world by declaring war against Satan. The war was to be waged both internally, by resisting temptation, and externally, by prosecuting witches and heretics".[7]

Renaissance magic and astrology were targeted in this campaign because their methods relied upon the power of imagination, which unfortunately was precisely the realm in which the Devil was thought to be able to make contact with human beings. As a consequence, all forms of divination and the entire Hermetic world-view became suspect. The Reformers set out to eradicate the Renaissance and classical imagination, with which Catholicism had made an accommodation, and to reinstitute the iconoclastic purity of primitive Christianity. As the Reformation progressed, the Catholic Church responded by joining in the repression of imagination, so that ultimately the two branches of the Western Church collaborated in the creation of modern, anti-imaginal consciousness and culture.[8]

We see, then, that the institutions that held Western civilization together were stretched to and beyond the breaking point by the changes in consciousness that were unfolding. The often draconian actions taken against those accused of nonconformity, heresy, witchcraft and occultism are heartbreaking to read about, yet hardly surprising. Churches and governments simply found it impossible to contain the full range of human strivings and possibilities that had emerged during the Renaissance.

What was the psychological condition that accompanied this crisis of institutions? Jung addressed this question in the Epilogue to *Psychology and Alchemy*[9], observing that with any expansion in consciousness there is a danger of inflation. The ego (or the group) is gripped by the energy of a newly emerging archetype, identifies with it, and loses its sense of limits and proportion. From this point of view, the widening of consciousness in the European psyche during the Renaissance brought about a crisis. Until that time, the spiritual problem of Western man had been more or less effectively contained by the Church and by esoteric practices such as alchemy.

So long as the psyche was understood to dwell not only in the human being but everywhere in nature, alchemy provided a systematic and highly meaningful method of psychological and spiritual work. The alchemists projected the psyche's transformative processes into chemical substances and worked upon their own inner nature through their laboratory experiments. The wisdom of this approach lay partly in its implicit insight that although the ego assists and nurses the psyche's process of realization, much of that process takes place outside the ego and does not belong to it. For the 'psyche' being worked upon is not only the soul of the individual person, but the world soul, the *anima mundi.* This awareness would have been reinforced via the close links between alchemy and its sister discipline of astrology, which tracks so intimately the links between microcosm and macrocosm, person and world.

With the decline of astrology and alchemy and the rise of Enlightenment science and modern consciousness, the projection of the psychic process was gradually withdrawn from the external world and the human individual lost all sense of connection with the world-soul. Moreover, since the new consciousness identified itself entirely with the ego, all the impersonal and collective contents of the process which had formerly been contained in the alchemist's retort or observed in the constellations of the sky were now taken upon the ego as part of personal identity, producing the crisis of inflation.

For Jung, this crisis found its literary embodiment in Goethe's *Faust*, a work written in the late eighteenth and early nineteenth centuries, i.e., after the decline of alchemy and the emergence of the modern individual for whom the ego is the centre of the work of transformation. Faust, the power-magician, stands as a prototype of the new man who took upon his own personality many psychic contents that had formerly belonged to the world of nature. Faust, allied with Mephistopheles, uses his magical-scientific powers to summon the divinely beautiful Helen of Greek myth into manifestation in order to unite with her. The *coniunctio* or divine marriage, a holy mystery which in classical alchemy would have occurred between the 'King and Queen,' the symbolic substances in the retort, here becomes a personal conquest. Faust claims the treasures produced by the alchemical *opus* as possessions to be enjoyed and used to augment his own powers. "Faust's sin," Jung writes, "was that he identified with the thing to be transformed and that had been transformed".[10]

So the new consciousness that began to emerge during the Renaissance overloaded the ego, just as it overtaxed institutions. Both for the individual and for political and religious authorities, the forces unleashed by the Faustian inflation created a crisis. The newly emerging powers of the individual carried great potential for creation but also for destruction. In order to take full possession of the good, creative, 'light' powers and to employ them with a clear conscience, it was necessary to project and banish the dark side. This was accomplished through the scapegoating of suspected witches and heretics and the discrediting of occultists, and concomitantly through the intensification of Christian moral identity and the establishment of a new model of the professional scientist and scholar as part of a rational, morally sober, anti-imaginal society.

When the witch-hunts were at their height in England, the scientists who adhered to the new mechanical philosophy tended to be strong believers in witchcraft, and many actively advocated the prosecution of witches for their exercise of dangerous supernatural powers. Their witch-phobia included an obsession with the demonic sexual powers and lustful nature of woman, together with a depreciation of nature and a deliberate repression of the inner femininity of the scientist himself. The image of the new scientist was that of a virile ascetic, immune to the allure of emotion, sensation, and subjective fantasy. This identity and attitude stood in sharp contrast to that of the alchemists, who had sought to bring about the transformation of matter through a 'marriage' between masculine and feminine principles in nature. They acknowledged the equality of the feminine principle (the male adept often working alongside a female partner, the *soror mystica*) and described their *opus* in terms of loving combinations, not only between aspects of matter but between mind and nature. The new natural science also imagined itself as involved in a 'marriage', in this case between the male scientist and female Nature who was to be subdued and enslaved for human purposes. This union was to be anti-erotic, characterized by the absolute mastery of the scientist over his own emotions and inner 'female' tendencies. Its imagery and ideology were vividly expressed in the influential writings of Francis Bacon, whose "central metaphor – science as power, a force virile enough to penetrate and subdue nature – has provided an image that permeates the rhetoric of modern science".[11]

One means by which occultism was discredited was through literary propaganda. Frances Yates[12] shows how the Faust story in particular was used to attack well-known natural magicians or hermetic philosophers who in reality were not Faustian either in their philosophy or their way of life. Couliano[13] similarly analyzes the use of the Faust theme by the Spanish playwright Calderón, showing how effectively the Reformation spirit demonized the world of nature, woman, eros and natural magic. This modern spirit, in which we are all steeped, makes an irrevocable split between the real and the imaginal, and thus declares the occult or imaginal arts to be *without effect* in the real world. This was not a scientific but a religious, doctrinal move, yet out of it would arise, with increasing vigor, a new science and a new way of life.

The figure of Faust in this polemical literature would seem to be less an authentic portrayal of the Renaissance occultist than a personification of the demonic power shadow of the new science, which was soon to consolidate its political and spiritual hegemony. By projecting this shadow onto the alchemist and the witch and driving occultism and natural magic from the field, science was freed to pursue its goal of total enslavement of the material world. The historical result is a society dominated by Faustian magic in the form of 'values-free,' technocratic science, unleashing and manipulating natural forces which are beyond our capacity to manage, either practically or ethically. The sacredness of nature, the reality of the soul, the unity of the cosmos, the subtle identity between subject and object, the balance between masculine and feminine, along with the symbolic imagination through which these realities could be understood, have been sacrificed in favor of the myth of masculine science and the cult of the heroic secular personality.

As astrologers re-enter academic life, then, we must realize that this is the baggage we carry. The scholars we meet do not merely have different opinions than we have about the nature of reality and how best to study it; they also have *built into their personality structure* a denial of all that our discipline represents and therefore an incapacity to perceive it accurately. Because astrology embodies a different kind of objectivity than that of post-Enlightenment thought, it is experienced as merely subjective. Because its model of the cosmos, its imagery and its way of thinking balance masculine and feminine, it stirs up old fears of the feminine and androgyny which persist despite decades of feminist analysis and activism. Because it works by means of imagination, it is mistaken for mere fantasy or entertainment or shadowed by the spectre of occult manipulation and the pact with the Devil. And although the dread of religious heresy has receded, it has been replaced by the fear and loathing of scientific heresy.

And we ourselves, to the extent that we belong to our own time, have the same limitations in dealing with our material. We are defended against the imagination and insensible of the soul, easily caught by fantasies of finding a scientific basis for our theories, and readily seduced into reinventing astrology as yet another modern technology for empowering the personality and conquering nature through expertise. The Faust problem is never far away.

Restoration of astrology's gifts to the academy

This brings me back to the chart for the hour, to revisit its Jupiter-Neptune-Midheaven T-square. Perhaps this can keep us mindful both of our highest ideals for astrology in the academy and of the potential for inflation, both as a nightmare in our distant past and as a contemporary problem. The Faustian inflation was not cured by the projection of the shadow, but only managed, as we can see by the titanic character not only of modern science but of modern life generally. The return of astrology to the academic and professional worlds raises the issue of additional 'powers' being taken on by an already overloaded twenty-first century ego. Jupiter and Neptune both tend to inflate, especially in hard aspect, and here they are in hard aspect to each other *and* to the MC. Jupiter rising in Leo (applying to a trine to Pluto) suggests a new birth of classical learning and Renaissance humanism, full of potential, but still in the twelfth house where it lacks clear boundaries. Neptune in Aquarius in the sixth suggests the imaginal-scientific practices of the Renaissance magus. Their square to the MC in 'fixed' signs shows an intense drive to achieve a visionary ideal – the recovery of astrology and the cosmos to which it belongs – in a visible and tangible (Taurus) way.

How can this dream be realized in a way that does not simply add to the inflationary load of our present civilization? We must first of all cultivate an intimacy with our own shadow, the inner Faust that we can see so easily in our scientific counterparts but seldom notice in ourselves. There might, for example, be more than a touch of hidden egotism and self-importance in the outsider discipline of astrology, a desire to have special knowledge or special powers to compensate for our lack of professional status and respectability. We must also face honestly the actual inferiorities of astrology which result from its long exclusion from academe: the paucity of sound theoretical work, critical reflection and appropriate standards for establishing quality and verity. Finally, we must ground our scholarship and our practice in a cosmological perspective which places humanity appropriately in relation to Heaven and Earth; cultivate the alchemical attitude that returns the mysteries of transformation to the world soul; and revive the art of true imagination through which we may serve her processes.

Both the greatest challenge and the greatest gift presented by astrology to the world of scholarship derive from its cosmic-psychological character. Astrology systematically reveals the archetypal factors underlying conscious experience and informing all theories about the world. It collapses the subject-object dichotomy fundamental to the modern psyche and the modern intellect, thus undermining the assumptions and identity of the modern scholar, but pointing the way toward new kinds of thinking and a different sense of self. By showing the correlations and resonances between the planets and many different levels and kinds of phenomena, inner and outer, it releases psyche from her imprisonment in personal subjectivity, as a mere epiphenomenon of the brain. It reawakens our active participation in the *anima mundi* and engenders philosophical reflection on the unity of being.

All of this we must bring with us, without apology or compromise, as we return to the academy.

Endnotes

1. C.H. Josten, ed. *Elias Ashmole (1617-1692), His Autobiographical and Historical Notes, his Correspondence, and Other Contemporary Sources Relating to his Life and Work.* (4 vols., Oxford: The Clarendon Press, 1966).
2. E.R. Dodds, *The Greeks and the Irrational* (Berkeley and Los Angeles: University of California Press, 1951), p. 75.
3. C.G. Jung, "The Meaning of Psychology for Modern Man", *Collected Works*, Exec. ed. William McGuire (Princeton: Princeton University Press) [hereafter Jung, *CW*], Vol.10, para. 326
4. Evelyn Fox Keller, *Reflections on Gender and Science* (New Haven: Yale University Press, 1985) [hereafter *Reflections*], p. 55.
5. Patrick Curry, *Prophecy and Power: Astrology in Early Modern England* (Polity Press, 1989).
6. Brian P. Levack, *The Witch-Hunt in Early Modern Europe* (2nd ed., New York and London: Longman, 1995), pp. 103-106.
7. *Ibid.*, p. 106.
8. Ioan P. Couliano, *Eros and Magic in the Renaissance* (Chicago: University of Chicago Press, 1987) [hereafter *Eros*].
9. Jung, *CW* Vol. 12, paras. 555-565.
10. *Ibid.*, para.560.

11. *Reflections*, p. 48. Cha. 3 of this volume outlines the contrasting sexual metaphors and attitudes toward nature, woman and witchcraft of the hermetic and mechanical philosophers.
12. Francis Yates, *The Occult Philosophy in the Elizabethan Age* (London/New York: Routledge, 1979), pp. 136-42.
13. *Eros*, ch. 10.

Astrology, the Academy and the Early Modern English Newspaper

Prof. Anna Marie Roos, University of Minnesota Duluth

Between 1691 and 1711, London "coffeehouse" newspapers devoted to a "question-and-answer" format, such as the Athenian Mercury *(1691-1697) and the* British Apollo *(1708-1711), employed anonymous experts to answer readers' questions and impart simplified knowledge about natural philosophy and phenomena. At the same time, they marketed a "culture of civility" to non-elite individuals, which included encouraging gentlemanly curiosity about the natural world. Not only did the* Mercury *and* Apollo*'s editors spend a good deal of effort convincing their audiences they were credible sources of knowledge, an authoritative virtual "academy" of experts, but audience responses can be assessed in the running "conversations" of questions and answers. These papers therefore may be utilized as gauges of public attitudes towards particular topics in natural philosophy, such as astrology, and to what extent astrology was considered a legitimate subfield within "scientific" studies in the early modern period. Both the* Mercury *and* Apollo *also served an expressly didactic function, wittily illustrating to their less-informed readers which scientific theories were currently fashionable, and which ideas were the provinces of only "vulgar beliefs"; a comparison of the two papers is a measure of the progressive vulgarization of belief in astrology between 1690 and 1711. Although previous scholars were correct in their claim that many elite natural philosophers largely disavowed astrology (both natural and judicial) by the first decade of the eighteenth century, among the literate cits of London who were largely the audience of the* Mercury *and* Apollo*, the legitimacy of astrology was still a matter of active debate.*

Introduction

Between 1691-1711, London "coffeehouse" newspapers devoted to a "question-and-answer" format emerged, such as the *Athenian Mercury* (1691–1697) and *The British Apollo* (1708-11.) These newspapers employed anonymous experts to answer readers' questions and impart simplified knowledge about natural philosophy and phenomena.[1] At the same time, they marketed a "culture of civility" to non-elite individuals, which included encouraging gentlemanly curiosity about the natural world. Not only did the *Mercury* and *Apollo's* editors spend a good deal of effort convincing their audiences they were credible sources of knowledge, an authoritative virtual "academy" of experts, but audience responses can be assessed in the running "conversations" of questions and answers.[2] These papers therefore may be utilized as gauges of public attitudes towards particular topics in natural philosophy, such as astrology, and to what extent astrology was considered a legitimate subfield within "scientific" studies in the early modern period.

Although several works have examined the importance of books, journals, almanacs, and public lectures in disseminating knowledge of the natural world, little analysis has been done to elucidate the role and influence of the first subscription newspapers in this diffusion of natural philosophy.[3] Johns and Bond have made a preliminary analysis of the skill of the *Mercury's* editors in fabricating a virtual Athenian Society or Academy to rival the authority of the Royal Society and the *Philosophical Transactions of the Royal Society*.[4] However, I will analyze the *Mercury* as well as its imitator *Apollo* in their own right, elucidating to what extent these newspapers were able to become trustworthy purveyors of knowledge for their wider coffeehouse audiences. I will focus upon the techniques by which they established a didactic relationship with their readers, and the nature of their audiences' response to their efforts, utilizing editor and audience attitudes towards astrology as a case study.

The success of both the *Mercury* and *Apollo* in establishing their authority had to do with sage marketing, and most importantly with their editors' manoeuvring around the growing tenuousness of social norms and boundaries of class and professionalization that existed in natural philosophy and society in the late seventeenth and early eighteenth century. The editors of the *Mercury* and the *Apollo* both traversed the semi-permeable boundaries between aristocrats of landed property and lineage and those merely aspiring to polite behaviour, between amateur curiosos and experimental scientists, between Scribelarian satire of natural philosophy and its actual practice. Specifically, the anonymity of the editors was key in the establishment of their credibility. Although the editors were not aristocratic, both publications were masterly in their appropriation of the language of the virtuosi, as well as the language of politeness and the reformation of manners to appeal to the fashionable taste for natural philosophy their audiences cultivated. The anonymity of the editors also was reminiscent of the "gentlemanly" reluctance to publish, their modesty of not wishing to draw attention themselves in public an aristocratic pretence (see Figure One).

Since the boundaries between professional and amateur science were hardly firmly drawn at the turn of the eighteenth century, the *Mercury* and *Apollo* took advantage of this state of affairs to make connections with their audiences. Both papers became virtual salons for the discussion of natural philosophy, allowing their readers to participate vicariously in a Royal-Society like meeting that they could never attend, reporting on their own experiments just as professional virtuosi did in the *Transactions* and virtually witnessing those of others.

Both the *Mercury* and the *Apollo* also served an expressly didactic function, wittily illustrating to their less-informed readers which scientific theories were currently fashionable, and which ideas were the provinces of only "vulgar beliefs"; a comparison of the two papers is a gauge of the progressive vulgarization of belief in astrology between 1690 and 1711. Although scholars such as Patrick Curry were correct in their claim that many elite natural philosophers largely disavowed astrology (both natural and judicial) by the first decade of the eighteenth century, among the literate cits of London who were largely the audience of the *Mercury* and *Apollo*, the legitimacy of astrology was still a matter of active debate.[5]

The paper academy: editors, audiences, and marketing

The *Mercury* and the *Apollo* answered a large volume of readers' questions about a variety of subjects, including love, divinity, and history, but querists in both the *Mercury* and *Apollo* were also extremely curious about the natural world.[6] Both publications subsequently employed anonymous experts to answer a significant proportion of readers' queries about the astronomical discoveries of Copernicus and Galileo; in the case of the *Mercury*, Cambridge mathematician Richard Sault, bookseller John Dunton, divine Samuel Wesley, and Dr. John Norris perused the *Philosophical Transactions* to answer questions for their readers, with a particular fondness displayed for the work of Robert Boyle and Rene Descartes.[7] In the case of the *Apollo,* the identity of the writers of the newspapers is a bit more controversial; there were probably as many as twelve men in this 'society of gentlemen' who answered questions, and of these only six can be identified with certainty.[8]

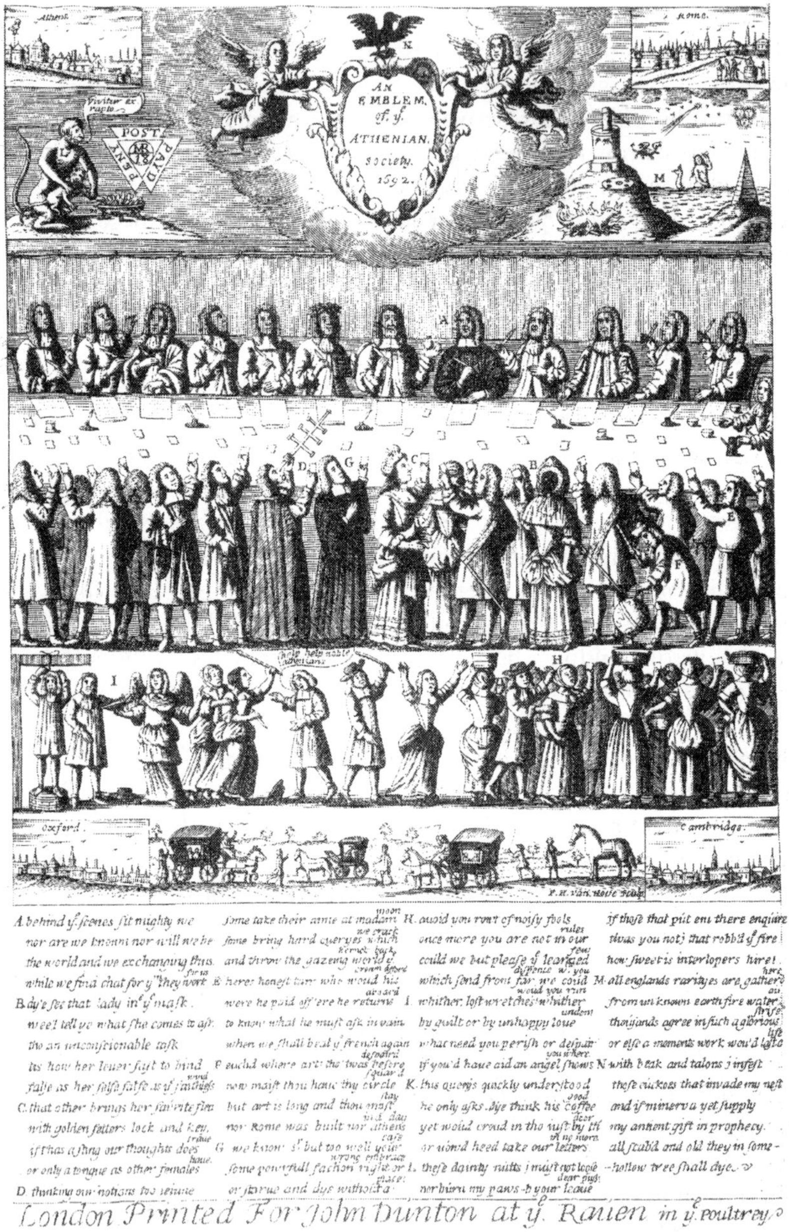

Figure One: Frederick Henrick von Hove, "An Emblem of the Athenian Society." (London, 1692). Note how the editors are veiled to emphasize their anonymity. Reproduced by permission of the Huntington Library, San Marino, California.

Of these six, two were professionals in the sciences. Dr. William Coward (1657?-1725) was an oculist and an intimate of Dr. Hans Sloane, president of the Royal Society (1727-1741). Sloane corrected proofs for Coward's *Ophthalmoiatria* (1706), a work that ridiculed the Cartesian placement of an immaterial soul in the pineal gland.[9] Dr. James Mauclerc was a physical scientist and theologian, who answered some seventy questions in each of the first two volumes of the *Apollo*.

An average of 39 questions in natural philosophy was addressed per volume of the *Mercury*, the total of 760 amounting to 20 percent of all questions in the twenty volumes of the newspapers; the *Apollo* had a similar percentage of queries about natural philosophy, and in fact, there were more printed inquiries about "science" in the *Apollo* than in any other subject.[10] The inquiries sometimes went beyond letters; the *Mercury* mislaid a partial skeleton that it was sent by a reader.[11] This miscellaneous inclusion of subjects of natural philosophy with those of literature and politics likely had more influence in introducing "scientific" subjects to the audience of these coffeehouse newspapers than journals purely devoted to natural philosophy. Although the *Mercury's* weekly print run for subscribers was only in the hundreds, because copies of newspapers were also sold in bookstores, passed around in coffeehouses, read aloud there, and sold in the street by hawkers, the total audience was likely in the thousands; the *Apollo* had similar audience numbers.[12]

The readers of these papers were those who frequented coffeehouses, which ranged from aristocrats and the "politer sort of mankind" that Dunton claimed was his audience, to washing women, milkmaids, and the London mob who had semi-respectable dress and could afford a penny for a dish of coffee. However, the range of advertisements, and analysis by other authors such as Berry and Roos suggests a good proportion of middling sorts read the paper, many who wished to ape the polite and aristocratic interests of the virtuosi in natural philosophy--in Larry Klein's terms, these papers marketed "politeness for plebes" much as did the profligate *vade mecums* being published.[13] Though some gentlemen did read the *Mercury*, such as Sir William Temple, most readers did not have the resources to collect expensive tomes, but could well afford a penny paper, and these periodicals marketed to their audiences accordingly. So well did the *Mercury* target its audience, that it was the most commercially successful periodical in its day.[14] And, the "society of gentlemen" who edited the *Apollo* wished to emulate the *Mercury's* economic success, so much so that a print war resulted between Dunton and his imitators soon after the *Mercury* was first published in 1691.[15] Even after the *Mercury* folded in 1697, Dunton attempted to revive it with other publications including the *Athenian Oracle* and *Athenianism;* he was thus protective of his proprietary rights. Hence, when the *Apollo* began publishing its paper in 1708, Dunton wrote a number of letters to its editors, accusing them of "interloping" with his "Question-project," and he promised that the moment he was financially able would "buy out their WHOLE SOCIETY of British Apollo's (which [...] consists of [...] Simpletons only) at least forty times."[16] The *Apollo* responded in kind, announcing a satirical issue on the subject of John Dunton which was distributed free of charge to subscribers upon request.[17]

Although the *Mercury* and *Apollo* were very much competitive penny sheets to appeal to their coffeehouse audiences, their editors intimated to their readers that they were not Grub Street Hacks writing the papers for mere commercial gain. The editors styled themselves as an anonymous "society of gentlemen" who did not need to write a paper to earn income, but rather who published to serve their country by creating a virtual academy, and who would never accept gifts in exchange for publication of a poser's inquiry. Over the time of the *Mercury's* production, Dunton increasingly announced his desire to move away from the large amounts of questions of the heart published in his paper to more incorporation of natural philosophy and mathematical questions for the betterment of greater society.[18] His supporters and boosters, like Charles Gildon, also made overstated claims in other publications about the nature of the altruistic work of the *Mercury*; Gildon wrote the *History of the Mercury*, a work done in imitation of Thomas Sprat's *History of the Royal Society* that also traced the ancestry of the *Mercury's* noble work back to antiquity and claimed the *Mercury* was even more eminent than the Royal Society.[19] Gildon's claims were most likely bordering on the satiric, as he also poked fun at a number of publications that popularized natural philosophy such as the Pierre Motteux's *Gentleman's Journal* (1692-1694). But some readers were convinced by the tone and stated purpose of the editors of the *Mercury* and *Apollo*. One reader of the *Apollo* was "credibly inform'd, that none of you make a Dependance on this Paper, being all in plentiful Circumstances; nor is it possible for so many to subsist on it, and to make that Appearance as I have seen some of you do."[20] Other readers of the papers, however, were still skeptical. In the preface to the first volume of the Mercury, Dunton answered objections from one querist who claimed the *Mercury* was merely "a Mercenary

Design to get a Peny" that used techniques much like a flying Stationer or ballad-monger.[21] Dunton sarcastically responded, "A wondrous Estate in the mean time he is likely to raise by a Peny-Paper" and assured his audience that:

> as for those concerned in the Composition (they are not very ambitious of the name of Authors,) most, if not all of 'em can safely protest they never had, not ever expect one Sixpence for their Pains, nay scorn any such thing, and would even go near to desist from their share therein were it once offered.[22]

There were a number of questions published that revealed reader skepticism of the paper's true intentions, and perhaps a good more pointed questions that were never brought to light. The *Mercury* was also the subject of a satirical play-- "The New Athenian Comedy"-- by Tory Elkanah Settle, subsequently advertised by John Houghton, whose *Collection for Improvement of Husbandry and Trade* competed with the *Mercury* for subscribers.[23] In Settle's play, Jack Stuff, a character representing John Dunton, asserts that "Truth and Honesty, Religion or Conscience are no Athenian Arguments, we write for the penny, and there's an Answer for all."[24] And, in fact, the editors of the *Mercury* and *Apollo* did use "mercenary designs" to get readers to buy more papers. They referred readers in their answers to questions to other volumes or editions, published tantalizing extracts from foreign journals in quarterly supplements which carried an extra charge, and claimed that they had not room to publish the answer to a particularly intriguing question until the next issue.[25]

Trustworthy interpreters and the judgment of astrology

Despite outside criticism and questionable marketing practice, the *Mercury* and the *Apollo* did succeed in convincing many of their readers they were gentlemanly and trustworthy interpreters of natural philosophy. One key to this was the editors' conscious appropriation of the format and content of the *Royal Society Transactions*; some of the reason for this was because the *Transactions* were irregularly published by the 1690s.[26] One reader of the *Mercury* in fact asked what the Royal Society was doing "for these several Years last past? And the Reason that we hear so little or nothing from 'em?"[27] The editors explained that the "death of several of their Worthy members," their patron Charles II, as well as William I's wars meant he was "too busie to have yet leisure for the cultivation of the softer Arts of Peace in his Kingdom" were the reason.[28] But, this meant the *Mercury* and *Apollo* could fill in the vacuum, likewise providing miscellanies of information about natural philosophy, including information from the foreign journals.

Both papers also not only received questions about the natural world, but also accepted and confirmed reports of natural phenomena and experiment from subscribers.[29] Like the Royal Society's ventures to create Histories of the Trades in which mechanic's arts were analyzed to find scientific truths, Dunton proclaimed, "every *Smith, Carpenter, Mason &c* that makes an Improvement in his Craft or Mystery deserves the title of Virtuoso."[30] Therefore, in May, 1691, the *Mercury* advertised:

> If any Person whatever will send in any New Experiment, or curious Instance, which they know to be truth, and matter of fact, circumstantiated with Time and Place, we will insert it in our Mercury; (but we shan't use the Authors Name without his License) and if it wants a Demonstration to the Senders, we will endeavour to find one, for the satisfaction of them as well as of all other Ingenious Enquirers into Natural Speculations.[31]

The editors not only portrayed themselves as reviewers of experiments in natural philosophy, but they styled themselves as arbiters of "scientific taste," clearly delineating which ideas of natural philosophy were fashionable and which were "vulgar" to espouse. When readers of the *Mercury* wrote questions asking if particular old-wives tales were true, such as if the "chameleon lived only by air," Dunton borrowed extensively from Sir Thomas Browne's *Pseudoxia Epidemica* to illustrate which popular beliefs were "vulgar errors."[32] Comparison of the *Mercury* and *Apollo* also illustrates to what extent other ideas in natural philosophy like judicial and natural astrology were "vulgarized" from 1691 to 1711.[33]

Judicial astrology in particular was increasingly circumscribed in these didactic newspapers. Whereas astrology and astronomy had been part and parcel of the same discipline in the late Middle Ages, they were increasingly separated into two types of study. In the *Mercury* and the *Apollo*, the pursuit of judicial or Ptolemaic "genethialogical" astrology [based on the geniture or time of birth], which posited that human fate could be predicted or controlled by occult effects of the planets, was carefully separated from that of astronomy, which was the study of planetary systems. In these works, the discipline of astronomy also came to include the study of previously astrological effects of the planets, particularly the Sun and Moon, on weather and health.

The editors of the *Mercury* further limited astrological effects on the human body to planetary heat and light, denying that there was any basis to judiciary astrology. In answer to a question about whether the stars and planets influenced "humane bodies and consequently humane affairs?", the *Mercury's* editors responded that the stars and planets have

> some real influence on human Bodies, we are sure from experience, because they have all Light and some of 'em heat [...]. But that they have any occult influence such as Astrologers fancy, on the Bodies and very Minds of Men, much less any such as forces 'em to good or bad Actions, we cann't beleve, having never seen any solid Reason for't.[34]

This distinction between judicial astrology and medical astrology would later be reflected in Ephraim Chambers's popular *Encyclopedia* (1724) which noted that judicial astrology, "is that which pretends to foretell moral events; i.e., such as have a dependance on the free will and agency of man; as if that were directed by the stars [...]. The same superstition has prevailed in more modern ages."[35] However, it was evident that a consideration of the planetary effects of heat and light "properly belongs to physiology, or natural philosophy, and is only to be deduced *a posteriori* from phenomena and observations, that the properties of moisture, heat, cold &c. employed by nature to produce the two great effects of rarefaction and condensation almost wholly depend on the course, motion, position, &c. of the heavenly bodies."[36] In fact, when asked why the "generality of Male or Female die in the Night," the *Mercury's* editors stated that: "We question the truth of the Observation, unless when the Moon happens to change then," a reflection of the belief still prevalent among learned physicians that the lunar cycles regulated the crisis days of a disease, or the turning point towards death or recovery.[37]

The *Apollo's* editors also challenged the idea that any occult planetary "blasts" outside of their heat and light caused illness. One of the tenets of Paracelsian medicine was that the Sun could strike a person ill when the astral concordance between it and the body were disrupted; a victim could thus die of being "blasted" by the offending planet. In fact, being "planet struck" was listed as the cause of death in 5% of the mortality bills in seventeenth-century London.[38] The *Apollo* felt that such a diagnosis of death was ridiculous, stating that the searchers, women hired to assess the cause of death by the government, were "ignorant" if they said "it is so, when they fancy the Cause of Death ariseth from a Blast."[39] It was far more likely that disease was "not from any Planet, but a Malignant Air."[40] This opinion probably had its precedent in the work of Robert Boyle, who in a 1685 treatise stated that "the Vulgar have entertain'd such strange Conceits and Stories about these Blastings, on which account some of them say that Men are Planet-struck, that the fabulous things mingled with those that are possible, have made intelligent Persons reject them all."[41]

As well as denying that any solar and lunar effects except heat and light could affect the body, the *Apollo* and the *Mercury* refuted the idea that any occult power of the planets could be trapped and used for magical purposes. One reader of the *Mercury* was not certain "Whether the force and virtues of the old Egyptian Talismans and their other Magical Operations were true and real, or only Imaginary and Illusion?"[42] Specifically, the reader was referring to the procedure when at the propitious time, when the desired planet was at its strongest influence (for instance usually at noon on the vernal equinox for the Sun, and midnight for the Moon the same day), sigils made of the appropriate metal (gold was associated alchemically with the Sun, silver with the Moon) were stamped with an image of the celestial body, usually along with a magic square with characters and symbols from the Kabbalah. Each of the planets had its own magic square or KAME'A, in which sixty-four figures in a square grid would add to the same number in four directions.[43] The *Mercury*'s editors denied that talismans or planetary sigils which the maker or user "believed wou'd receive and keep the Critical Influences of the their [the planet's] design'd aspects" had effects upon medicine or anything else.[44] The editors reasoned that the engraving of the sigil "wou'd be too long an Action, and wou'd not be finish't before its proper [planetary] aspect was over, and another begun."[45]

The *Apollo* also denied that Moon beams, claimed to be intrinsically cold and moist by astrologers, could be trapped. One reader with the initials "T. A." remarked that if one takes a mirror, one could "contract the sun-beams into such a Point as will be real Fire, that you may kindle a Pipe with it."[46] By the same logic, "T. A." wrote that he had read if one took the same mirror "when the Moon is at full, you may with it contract the Beams of the Moon into a waterish dew upon your Handkercheif; so that if you please you may wash your Face with the Moon-shine."[47] But "T. A." apparently did some reasoning on his own, for he then asked, if the Moon "being said to give Light only by reflecting from the Sun, how can his Beams, being Fire be when darted back conversed into Water?"[48] The *Apollo* basically told this reader that he was correct that moon beams had no occult principles and were "intirely owing to the reflected Beams of the Sun."[49] Thus, "we must not take the Dew gathered upon the Handkercheif to be the Beams of the Moon contracted and turned into Water."[50] Rather, the handkerchief was moist because it received and imbibed the "Moisture of the Ambient Air."[51] So much for washing your face with lunar beams!

These examples illustrate that the editors of the *Mercury* and *Apollo* were attempting to instruct their readers that belief in occult forces was a vulgar belief, but I would like to offer a gentle correction to Curry's assertion that by the eighteenth century, astrology was no longer a topic for polite conversation.[52] The middling sorts who were reading these coffeehouse newspapers certainly fashioned themselves as members of "polite society," and they were actively reading and discussing natural and judicial astrology; their repeated queries about astrology revealed that they were also not apparently convinced that it was a false discipline. The vehemence of the stance that the editors took in disavowing astrology of both types also suggests that they were combating a rather strong set of beliefs among their reading public.

Although readers of the newspapers were not sure whether to discount occult effects of the planets, by the early eighteenth century, editors of the *Mercury* and *Apollo* certainly were. They would accept only that the heat and light could have effects on the human body, rejecting other astrological emanations. Moreover, the editors of the newspapers participated in the common practice of making judicial astrology an exemplar of vulgar belief, guiding their readers in what and what was not polite discourse. Jonathan Swift, an early contributor to the *Mercury*, wrote in a mock almanac about astrology that "all pretenses of foretelling by astrology are deceits, for the manifest reason that all the wise and learned, who alone can judge whether there be any truth in this science, do unanimously agree to laugh at and despise it, and that none but the ignorant vulgar give it any credit."[53] The subscription newspapers were broadcasting much the same message to their subscribers in their rejection of the occult emanations of the luminaries. Whether they convinced their readers, the members of their paper academy, of this lesson remains an open question.

Acknowledgements
I would like to acknowledge Edward Ruestow, recently retired from the University of Colorado at Boulder, as well as Natasha Glaisyer of the University of York and Sara Pennell, independent scholar, for their insights and advice. I would also like to thank the University of Minnesota for providing a Grant-in-Aid and McKnight Summer Research Fellowship that allowed me to do research in London, as well as the librarians in the Rare Books and Music Reading Room at the British Library, and William Hodges of the Duke Humfrey Library at the University of Oxford. Lastly, I would like to thank Michael York, Nick Campion and Patrick Curry for giving me the opportunity to present my work at the Sophia Centre's Inaugural Conference.

Endnotes
1. *The Athenian Gazette or Casuistical Mercury Resolving all the most Nice and Curious Questions. Proposed by the Ingenious of Either Sex* (London, 1691-7); *The British Apollo Or, Curious Amusements for the Ingenious. To which are Added the most Material Occurrences Foreign and Domestick. Perform'd By a Society of Gentlemen* (London, 1708-11). Previous studies of natural philosophy in the *Mercury* and *Apollo* are almost entirely empirical, counting the numbers of questions in the newspapers that are scientific in nature. See Gilbert D. McEwen, *Oracle of the Coffee House: John Dunton's Athenian Mercury* (San Marino, 1972), p. 114. Subjects covered in McEwen's survey of the *Mercury* included astronomy, chemistry, geography, geology, mathematics, medicine, meteorology, mineralogy, natural history, navigation, physiology, physics, and psychology. For a survey of the amounts and types of questions asked of the *Apollo*, see William Francis Belcher, 'A Study of the British Apollo, 1708-1711', Ph.D. Dissertation (University of North Carolina, Chapel Hill, 1950), pp. 175-306. For a recent working concerning the Mercury and gender, see Helen Berry, Gender, Society and Print Culture in Late-Stuart England: The Cultural World of the Athenian Mercury (Aldershot and Burlington, VT: Ashgate, 2003).
2. Formal literature of religious and political controversy commonly used the question-and-answer format in, as did L'Estrange's *Observator* of 1681. The difference with the *Mercury* and the *Apollo* was that the editor did not pose questions for the sake of the point he wished to make. The question of the authenticity of these sources is also one that must be addressed; because actual letters from John Dunton, the editor of the Mercury, to subscribers survive at the Bodleian Library in Oxford, most of the questions can reasonably be assumed to be authentic. See Helen Berry, 'Nice and Curious Questions': Coffee Houses and the Representation of Women in John Dunton's *Athenian Mercury*', *The Seventeenth Century*, 12 (1997): pp. 257-76, on p. 258; William Belcher's study of *The British Apollo* also indicated that the boys that delivered the newspaper also collected queries from subscribers, indicating that the paper had authentic

materials, although some of the humorous poetic questions may have been inserted by the editors. See William F. Belcher, 'The Sale and Distribution of the British Apollo', in *Studies in the Early English Periodical,* ed. R.P. Bond (Chapel Hill, 1957), pp. 75-101.

3. Bernard Capp, *English Almanacs 1500-1800: Astrology and the Popular Press* (Ithaca, 1979); William Eamon, *Science and the Secrets of Nature: Books of Secrets in Medieval and Early Modern Culture* (Princeton, 1994; Adrian Johns, *The Nature of the Book: Print and Knowledge in the Making* (Chicago, 1998; Larry Stewart,. *The Rise of Public Science: Rhetoric, Technology and Natural Philosophy in Newtonian Britain, 1660–1750* (Cambridge, 1992.)

4. Adrian Johns, " Miscellaneous methods: authors, societies, and journals in early modern England," *British Journal of the History of Science* 33 (2000): pp. 159-186; T. Christopher Bond, "Keeping up with the latest transactions: the literary critique of scientific writing in the Hans Sloane years," *Eighteenth-Century Life* 22, 2 (1998): pp. 1-17. One recent and key historiographic issue has been the means by which scientific journals such as the *Philosophical Transactions of the Royal Society* established their credibility and authority in the latter half of the seventeenth century when the norms of scientific practice and communication were just being established. In their articles, Johns and Bond both have considered how readers of the *Transactions* could believe that the matters of fact they were reading about were reliable and trustworthy.

5. Patrick Curry, "Astrology in Early Modern England," in *Science, Culture, and Popular Belief in Renaissance Europe*, ed. Stephen Pumfrey, Paolo Rossi, and Maurice Slawinski (Manchester: Manchester University Press, 1991) pp. 274-91.

6. General biographical information about the editors of the *Apollo* and *Mercury* is taken from my article: "Polite Society and Perceptions of the Sun and the Moon in The *Athenian Mercury* and *The British Apollo,* 1691-1711," *Expertise Constructed: Didactic Literature in the British Atlantic World, 1500-1800*, eds. Natasha Glaisyer and Sara Pennell (New York and Aldershot: Ashgate, 2003), pp. 78-118. Barbara Benedict also explores the role of curiosity as a fashionable attitude in the *British Apollo*. See Barbara M. Benedict, *A Cultural History of Early Modern Inquiry* (Chicago, 2001), pp. 98-101.

7. Dunton writes in the Preface to the first volume of the Mercury, "for Philosophy, we sometimes read (without being ashamed to own it) the Great Aristotle, the Ingenious Descartes, the Incomparable Mr. Boyle, and the *Transactions* of the Royal Society, with those of the Foreign Virtuosos [...]" (Dunton, Preface to the *Athenian Gazette: or Casuistical Mercury*, 1691, vol. 1, p. 1).

8. Belcher, "A Study of the *British Apollo* 1708-11," pp. 156-7.

9. *Dictionary of National Biography,* 1937-1939 ed., s.v. "Coward, William."

10. McEwen, *Oracle of the Coffee House,* p. 114.

11. *Athenian Mercury*, 24 November 1691, vol. 4, no. 17, p. 2.

12. Berry, "'Nice and Curious Questions,'" p. 258.

13. *Ibid.;* Anna Marie Roos, *Luminaries in the Natural World: Perceptions of the Sun and the Moon in England, 1400-1720* (New York, 2001), pp. 228-230; Lawrence E. Klein, "Politeness for plebes: Consumption and social identity in early eighteenth-century England," *The Consumption of Culture: Word, Image, and Object in the 17th and 18th Centuries,* ed. Ann Bermingham and John Brewer (London and New York, 1995), pp. 362-382.

14. Not only did it last seven years, but at the end of the first year, its editors claimed they had recieved near "four thousand Questions which no lie upon our Hands." ("Preface to the Second Volume," *The Athenian Gazette or Casuistical Mercury* (London, 1691, p. 1.)

15. Comparing a *Mercury* and an *Apollo* side-by-side shows the extent to which the *Apollo* went to imitate its predecessor; the size of the sheet, column width, numbering style, and even the fonts were nearly identical, along with the emphasis on "curious questions" and "curious amusements for the Ingenious." The *Apollo* however, also had its trouble with plagiarists; it scheme to publish a six penny book of all of the Poems commemorating the death of the Prince was short-circuited when "some Mercenary Persons are upon printing them in a small Character, to undersell it." (*British Apollo*, 19 November to November 24, 1708 vol. 1, no. 82, p. 1.)

16. John Dunton, *Athenianism, or, the New Projects of Mr. John Dunton* (London: Tho. Darrack, 1710), p. x.

17. *British Apollo*, 30 July to August 4, 1708, vol. 1, no. 50, p. 1.

18. Bond, "Keeping up with the latest transactions," p. 12. Dunton's dealt with his increasing reluctance to publish questions about love from women in the *Mercury* by creating another publication called the *Ladies Mercury*. The *Ladies Mercury* in its first edition carefully addressed the editors of the *Athenian Mercury,* and claimed their paper was "not at all intended to encroach upon your Athenian Province. We acquiesce to yield up to You that fair and larger Field; the Examination of Learning, Nature, Arts, Science, and indeed the whole World; being contented to bound our narrow Speculation to only that little Sublunary, Woman." (*The Ladies Mercury*, 27 February 1693, vol.1, no. 1, p. 1); The *Ladies Mercury* also specifically requested of its readers that "All Questions relating to Love, &c., are still desired to be sent into the Latine-Coffee-House in Ave Mary-Lane, to the Ladies Society there, and we promise they shall be weekly answered with all the Zeal and Softeness becoming the Sex. We likewise desire we may not be troubled with other Questions relating to Learning, Religion, &c. We resolving (as we said before) not to infringe on the Athenians." (10 March 1693, vol. 1, no. 3, p. 2).

19. Charles Gildon, *A History of the Athenian Society* (London, 1692), reprinted in *The Athenian Oracle*, eds. John Dunton, Richard Sault, Samuel Wesley and Charles Gildon (4 vols, 3rd edn, London, 1728), iv, p. 6.

20. *The British Apollo. Being the Quarterly Paper, in which are Inserted those Questions and Answers, for which we had not room before*, vol. 1, no. 1, 1708, p. 12.
21. "Preface," in *The Athenian Gazette: Or Casuistical Mercury, Resolving all the most Nice and Curious Questions Proposed by the Ingenious: From Tuesday March 17th to Saturday, May 30th*, 1691, p. 2.
22. *Ibid.*
23. Elkanah Settle, *The New Athenian Comedy, Containing the Politicks, Oeconomicks, Tacticks, Crypticks, Apocalpyticks, Stypticks, Scepticks, Pneumaticks, Theologicks, Poeticks, Mathematicks, Sophisticks, Pragmaticks, Dogmaticks, &c.* (London, 1693); John Houghton, *A Collection for Improvement of Husbandry and Trade*, 29 September 1693, vol. 3, no. 61, p. 1.
24. Settle, *Athenian Comedy*, 16.
25. The *Apollo* even promised to provide new musical compositions for its readers, a promise that it largely could not keep. See Rosamond McGuiness, "Musical Provocation in Eighteenth-Century London: The 'British Apollo,'" *Music and Letters* 68, 1 (1987): pp. 333-342.
26. Johns, "Miscellaneous methods," p. 160.
27. *Athenian Mercury*, 24 November 1691, vol 4, no. 17, p.1.
28. *Ibid.*
29. Johns, "Miscellaneous methods," pp. 164-5.
30. "Advertisements," in *the Athenian Mercury*, 9 May 1691, vol. 1, no. 14, p. 2.
31. *Ibid.*
32. William C. Wright, "Sir Thomas Browne's *Pseudoxia Epidemica* and English Coffee House Journalism," *Journal of Popular Culture* 12, 1 (1978), pp. 36-41.
33. "Polite Society and Perceptions of the Sun and the Moon." (see footnote 6).
34. *The Athenian Mercury*, 13 April 1692, vol. 6, no. 22, 1.
35. Ephraim Chambers, *Cyclopedia, or a universal dictionary of arts and sciences.* (London: D. Midwinter, et.al., 1738), 162-63.
36. *Ibid.*
37. *The Athenian Mercury*, vol. 2., no 29, 1; Nancy Siraisi, *Medieval and Early Renaissance Medicine: An Introduction to Knowledge and Practice* (Chicago and London: University of Chicago Press, 1990). 135.
38. Webster has a fascinating account of the searchers, women hired to ascertain the cause of death in London and the bills of mortality in *Health, Medicine and Mortality in the Sixteenth Century* (Cambridge: Cambridge University Press, 1979).
39. *The British Apollo*, Wednesday 14 May to Monday 19 May 1708, vol. 1, no. 28, pp. 1-2.
40. *Ibid.* Robert Boyle discusses a "malignant air" as the cause of death in his consideration of different types of effluvia, planetary and terrestrial. Boyle thought terrestrial effluvia from malignant air could cause disease, their

corpuscles insinuating themselves into bodily skin pores, but he doubted celestial effluvia could have such an influence. See Barbara Beguin Kaplan, *"Divulging of Useful Truths in Physick" The Medical Agenda of Robert Boyle* (Baltimore and London: The John Hopkins Press, 1993), Chapter four, passim.

41. Robert Boyle, *An essay of the great effects of even languid and unheeded motion: whereunto is annexed An experimental discourse of some little observed causes of the Insalubrity and Salubrity of the Air and its effects* (London: M. Flesher, 1685), 69.

42. *The Athenian Mercury*, 22 December 1691, Vol. 5, no. 7, question 1.

43. See E.A Wallis Budge, *Amulets and superstitions: the original texts with translations and descriptions of a long series of Egyptian, Sumerian, Assyrian, Hebrew, Christian, Gnostic, and Muslim amulets and talismans and magical figures, with chapters on the evil eye, the origin of the amulet, the pentagon, the swastika, the cross (pagan and Christian), the properties of stones, rings, divination, numbers, the Kabbalah, ancient astrology, etc.* (London: Oxford University Press, 1930). See also Martha R. Baldwin, "Toads and Plague: Amulet Therapy in Seventeenth-Century Medicine," *Bulletin of the History of Medicine*, 1993, 67, 2: 227-247.

44. *Ibid.*

45. *Ibid.*

46. *The British Apollo*, Monday January 9 to Wednesday 11 January 1710, vol. 3, no. 86, pp. 1-2.

47. *Ibid.* The work that "T. A." was referring to was Thomas Robinson, *An essay towards a natural history of Westmorland and Cumberland [...] to which is annexed, A vindication of the philosophical and theological_paraphrase of the Mosaick system of the creation* (London: J. L., 1709). This book, via scriptural exegesis and Cabala, tells the story of the creation of the world.

48. *The British Apollo*, Monday January 9 to Wednesday 11 January 1710, vol. 3, no. 86, pp. 1-2.

49. *Ibid.*

50. *Ibid.*

51. *Ibid.*

52. Curry, "Astrology in Early Modern England," in *Science, Culture, and Popular Belief in Renaissance Europe*, pp. 274-91.

53. Jonathan Swift, *The Accomplishment of the First of Mr Bickerstaff's Predictions* (London, 1708), p. 3.

The Lure of Egypt or How to Sound Like a Reliable Source

Joanna Komorowska, Paedagogical Academy, Kraków

The paper will briefly outline the manner in which the authority of the ancient Egyptians is invoked in several surviving astrological works of antiquity, with the focus on the second century works of Vettius Valens and Claudius Ptolemy, representatives of two vastly differing approaches toward the astrological lore. Consequently, the argument shall involve the question of Valens' alleged Egyptian travels and the stance he assumes with respect to Nechepso and Petosiris, to end with the discussion of Ptolemy's way of dealing with the inherited tradition. It will be shown that while sharing in some general tendencies and, moreover, facing the same tension between the contrasting urges of tradition vs. innovativeness, the two astrologers choose separate ways to extricate themselves from the dilemma.

My interest with the topos of Egyptian travel starts with a French commentary and translation of Vettius Valens' *Anthologiae* Book One, completed by Joelle Frederique Bara in 1989: while outlining Valens life, or rather what can be reconstructed from the text of the nine volumes-long impressive work, the French scholar writes: "c'est au cours d'un sejour en Egypte sans doute que les prêtres l'initierent a la genethlialogie".[1] Thus, one is led to believe that Valens has actually been in Egypt, and that it is there that he was introduced to the mysteries of advanced astrology. The issue, however, may be considerably less straightforward: after all, in investigating such claims, one has to consider the character of the society that produced them.

Indeed, it may be symptomatic that the fateful travel to Egypt is mentioned only once in Valens' work, in chapter IV.11.4. Next, there is the mystagogic character of astrology, a notion steadfastly supported by the author throughout his work, to consider. As it has been persuasively argued by Tamsyn Barton, there is much to be said for the rhetoric component of such assertions (at this point we have to note that according to Aristotle, the art of rhetoric would entail portraying oneself as trustworthy and competent, and, by contrast, portraying the others as untrustworthy and incompetent).[2] To turn a science into mysteries is to give it a divine sanction, and therefore to protect it against both adversaries and irresponsible and incompetent practitioners. This setting of astrological cognition apart from logic and rational thought can be considered as rhetorical, but it also has far reaching consequences where an astrologer's self-image is concerned. Namely, if one agrees that astrology is initiatory lore, leading to the discovery of the mysteries of the universe (and henceforth to contemplation of the divine order), acquisition of wisdom becomes a divine endowment, a prize to be won by specific, though mostly unnamed, *ponoi* (labours). As a consequence the search for this wisdom must be all too frequently frustrated, even if only to test the practitioner's perseverance and his desire for the truth (*egkrateia* and *epithymia*).

Thus, what we need to consider is whether we can actually trust Valens when he speaks of his travel to Egypt: this will give us plentiful opportunity to look at Egyptian travel as a rhetorical *topos* of astrological and occult writings and, moreover, to consider a number of contemporary writings ranging from philosophy to satire. What we have to realize is that, by asserting the irrational element as present in astrological cognition, Valens implies that his position is in a way better than that of his adversaries (including those who have another view of astrological tenets). Hardly surprisingly, the sort of knowledge that results from revelation would be generally considered as more valuable than the ordinary one.

Travel to Egypt in literary tradition

Traveling to Egypt has a long tradition in Greek literature and even more importantly, in Greek science, with Herodotus and Plato constituting the standard examples of Greeks drawing from the Egyptian tradition (Herodotus in Books II-III, and Plato foremost in his *Timaeus*). Strabo states that Eudoxus and Plato were the very first Greeks who managed to persuade the priests to accept them as students:

> ... at Heliopolis the houses of priests and schools of Plato and Eudoxus were pointed out to us; for Eudoxus went up to that place with Plato, and they both passed thirteen years [meanwhile Diogienes Laertios gives 16 months only] with the priests, as is stated by some writers; for since these priests excelled in their knowledge of the heavenly bodies, albeit secretive and slow to impart it, Plato and Eudoxus prevailed upon them in time and by courting their favour to let them learn some of the principles of

> the doctrine; but the barbarians concealed most things... But at that time the true year was unknown among the Greeks, as also many other things, until the later astrologers learned them from the men who translated into Greek the records of the priests; and even to these days they learn their teachings and likewise those of the Chaldeans.[3]

On the other hand, the neoplatonic philosopher Proclus maintains that Thales' excellence in mathematics was due to the instruction he received from the Egyptian priests. Characteristically, Thales and Eudoxus belong to the most eminent astronomers of antiquity, and Plato was similarly praised for his cosmological theories. Indeed, in his commentary to Iamblichus, Gregory Shaw notes that by the fifth century the claim to Egyptian experience became a stock argument in any apology of revealed wisdom:[4]

> Why would Iamblichus adopt the pseudonym of an Egyptian priest in order to explain his Platonic mystagogy? According to latter Platonists, the answer was clear. Plato himself had acknowledged that his writings were merely a propaideia to deeper mysteries and in several dialogues he spoke of the influence of Oriental, particularly Egyptian, wisdom on his thought. Although he probably never participated in Egyptian or Chaldean mysteries, he was believed to have done so by Platonists and therefore the Oriental element in Iamblichus' Platonism should not be seen as alien but merely as an attempt to reveal more completely the wellspring of Platonic wisdom. Just as Plato turned to his lady of prophecy, Diotima Mantike, to reveal erotic mysteries, so Iamblichus deferred to his persona, the Egyptian priest Abammon, to explain theurgic mysteries, the *hieratike techne*. In the role of Egyptian mystagogue responding to the questions and criticisms of Porphyry the philosopher, Iamblichus played divine revealer to the wayward Hellene, guiding Porphyry back to the primitive initiations that Plato and Pythagoras received from the Egyptians.

The fame of Egypt as a source of wisdom, particularly Hermetic wisdom, is also attested even by sources quite distanced from the excessive enthusiasm for hermetism: One such testimony comes from the fourth century work of the great historian Ammianus Marcelinus, who when speaking of Alexandria confirms the fame it enjoyed as a centre of astrological studies (astronomicis studiis calet). Another interesting passage comes from Roman senator, Firmicus Maternus, who in his Mathesis notes the audacity of astrologers, Asclatio and Apollinarios who dared to forge the world horoscope and promptly attributed it to Hermes himself (III.1). In fact, even the short warning issued to Tat in Corpus Hermeticum XVI.2 where he is instructed to prevent the teachings of Hermes from any attempt at the translation into Greek, is proof of the deep respect for the wisdom of the Egyptians and of the disdain due to the maze of words and apparent rationality of Greek philosophy. It may also be important to note that Alexandria's position as the centre of astronomical studies would be consciously upheld by the local government, a fact recently discussed by Liba Taub.[5]

The story

Having investigated the contextual aspect, we may turn to the passage covering IV.11.4-10. It is here that mention of Egypt emerges. The sequence of events depicted is as follows: having traveled a lot, Valens arrives in Egypt and there meets a number of false and greedy teachers; what he does not find is the truth. As a consequence of this disappointment he refrains from an extravagant lifestyle and continues studying on his own; again, after some time, the old fascination with life-periods gets hold of him; seeking a solution to his doubts he convenes with the learned, and finally one of them guides him toward instruction by a divine spirit (*daimon*). This brief outline of the whole story still manages to capture its most important elements: travel, disillusionment, independent study, consultation with sages, and, finally, illumination. What point was there in confessing all these to the reader? Let us consider both the general pattern and every element on its own.

First, let us focus on the disillusionment brought about by the author's failure to reach true cognition through ordinary instruction. Obviously, fil£rguroi did£skaloi he mentions are astrologers like those mentioned in the *Anthologiae* V.8: vain, pretentious, given to theatricals and greedy. They also correspond to those mentioned in VIII.5.16 described as gÒhtai and pleÒnektai ¥nqrwpoi. All things considered, they are hardly equipped for the advanced study of the lore. We may conclude that at this precise point Valens is misled by the appearance of knowledge, and this causes major strain to his finances. We would do badly to disregard this element of his tale as merely descriptive: the claim that one giving false prognosis is simply incompetent and his incompetence should not be transferred to the whole lore remains relatively frequent throughout astrological literature.[6] Moreover, there is much difference between them and the learned appearing later in the story, the true experts in genethlialogy. These latter are significantly referred to as o*f* per˜ tÕ toiaàta ™spoudakÒtej (7) – thus, we may infer, they have given much time and effort to the study of the matter in question. The word choice and the use of perfectum seem hardly accidental in this context, for they underscore both the experience possessed and effort involved in acquiring it, hinting at the difference separating the learned from charlatans. Thus, there exists some correspondence between the former and persons endowed with all the qualities considered necessary for attaining the true cognition in IX.15.11. Moreover, the learned can be compared with the meticulous person juxtaposed with the false astrologers in V.8.112.

It is important to note, though, that contact with the learned alone is said not to be enough. To achieve true knowledge, claims Valens, a higher, divine, intervention is needed. Yet this contact is far from being irrelevant: our author is quite explicit on its importance, when he says: di£peiran ™lamb£nomen (*I kept acquiring experience*, 7). Two factors are decisive here: one has to study the matter by himself *and* to consult the learned. And it is owing to both diligence and contact with the right men that one may arrive at illumination. Concerning the pe‹ra aspect, however, we have to consider a particular of the *Anthologiae* hitherto laid aside.

If one had to number three features of Valens' work most frequently professed by the author himself, these would be respectively generosity, clearness and, finally, experience. This last is advocated with utmost zeal throughout the work, for it serves to establish double claim to *Anthologiae*'s originality: first, that Valens has enough practical experience to lecture others on astrological matters; and second, that he managed to prove the inherited material he describes through practical application. These are obviously two aspects of the same activity, still their implications remain somewhat different, the former being related to originality *sensu stricto* while the latter may be regarded as relating to more general contribution to the lore.

Now, let us consider other elements of IV.11. We learn that following the disillusionment resulting from his meeting with so-called astrologers, Valens embarked on a much calmer, moderate lifestyle (™gkratšsteron ka˜ aÙt£rkh ˜lÒ menoi b…on, 4).[7] This is a significant point, for it forms a straightforward allusion to the lifestyle advocated at other points of

Anthologiae. Even more importantly, with its choice of words it forms an explicit opposition with the ardour with which Valens claim to have pursued astrology earlier (di¦ t¾n perˆ tÕ œrgon ™piqum...an, 4). Even if this ™piqum...a reappears shortly afterwards, this time it seems to result from author's own studies: it is said in IV.11.5. tÕ prÒblhma tîn ple...stwn maqhm£twn kaˆ ¹ tîn kaqolikîn crÒnwn dia...resij ¢nqe ‹lkon ¹m©j kaˆ me...zw t¾n ™piqum...an kateskeÚazon ktl. And connected as this particular desire is with ™pimÒnh, *perseverance,* we may view it as a stable, coherent disposition toward study rather than a feverish thirst for immediate knowledge.

Moreover, there is another hint latent in the passage: Valens claims that disillusioned as he was he occupied his mind with other questions (perˆ ›tera °scol»meqa, 4). What were those ›tera? Obviously, we should not think that he refrained from astrological studies in general, for he would be unable to deepen his insight enough to make an ™pimÒnh over a particular problem. Thus, he would be occupied with other, still astrological, matters – and this leads straight to the problem of the right sequence of learning.[8]

Finally, we come to the divine revelation. Given the characteristics of second century literary milieu, with the widespread belief in daimonic powers and influence of mystery cults, a mention of such an occurrence is hardly surprising. The revelation of Isis in Book Eleven of Apuleius' *Metamorphoses*, a passage of quite haunting beauty and sophistication in what seems to be adventure novel is generally perceived as a reflection of the author's own devotion to the cult of the Egyptian goddess. Lucian, though in a much different vein, describes himself as being instructed with regard to his life choices by a prophetic dream (*Somnium* 5ff.), when the two goddesses Art and Philosophy stood before him – a picture patently alluding to that of Heracles at his crossroads, but rightly interpreted by C. P. Jones as reflecting something of the mentality of second century society.[9]

The pilgrimage motif

Now that we have noted frequency of other elements that are appear in our passage, let us turn to Valens' travels themselves. In IV.11 he says that he arrived in Egypt having crossed many lands (4). It is interesting that twice within the *Anthologiae*, when discussing Critodemus' *Horasis*, Valens quotes the opening statement of this lost work: *having traveled through sea and wilderness I was finally considered worthy of attaining a safe harbor and most secure shelter.*[10] Thus we have the same travel element being claimed to guarantee Critodemus' reliability and experience, its purpose remaining all the more obvious should the fragment truly represent the opening of the whole *Horasis.*[11] The emergence of this fragment in the proem to Book Nine of the *Anthologiae* is particularly interesting because of Valens' employing the very same image (and the very same words) to apply them to himself and his search for knowledge (IX.1.10). Certainly, the mimetic aim remains primary, yet it is striking that the author introduces considerable changes as he seeks to elaborate on the instructive character of the experiences involved: *and I have seen many lands and many people, gaining knowledge through long experience and pain* (kaˆ poll¾n gÁn diodeÚsaj, klim£twn te kaˆ ™qnîn katÒ pthj genÒmenoj, polucron…v pe…rv kaˆ pÒnoij sunemfure…j). The vicinity of Critodemus' text and obvious similitudes between the two discourage eventual biographic inferences – the passage seems too manifestly modeled after Critodemus' own and destined to put Valens in position.[12]

Travel in search of knowledge is a motif which appears in other works as well – in Artemidorus' *Onirocritica* we read of the author's vast travels that led him to collect the experiences of other interpreters. Though he never mentions a revelation (his principal aim being to establish oniromancy as what we would nowadays call exact science), he describes his having talked to many wise and experienced diviners. Obviously, this may be considered as corresponding to Valens' assertion that he sought the company of the wise. Certainly there are some notable differences as well, for Artemidorus is quick to indicate that the wise he addresses are ordinary, market-based diviners, mistrusted by the crowd, while Valens speaks of persons of somewhat priestly dignity. Yet the common elements are too evident to be missed.

The story yet again

To put IV.11 in an even wider perspective, we need to have a look at an interesting document surviving in cod. Montepessulanus and published in CCAG VIII.4, pp. 254-262. The text is a Latin translation of a letter allegedly sent by a famous medicine man and astrologer, Thessalus of Thralles, to Nero.[13] That such a letter actually existed is confirmed by two sources, Galen and Plinius. The point I intend to make here is not that the Montepessulanus text is an authentic letter of Thessalus – it is rather that the story used by him to support his claims bears a marked similarity to the one appearing in *Anthologiae*.

Before Thessalus begins an account of his travels, he makes some interesting introductory remarks, obviously intended to highlight his achievements. These bear a marked similarity to those made by Vettius in IV.11. Similarly, he refers to the earlier Hermetic tradition established by Nechepso, which bears comparison with Valens' opinion on both Critodemus (IX.1. 4) and Nechepso himself (in VI.1.9): *rex Notopso, vir sapientissimus et ornatus omni virtute, hac voce divina non attigit, sicut tu quaeris* (257.11-13).

Turning to Thessalus' account of his studies, we note immediately that he seeks to portray himself as a man obsessed with learning. He traveled because he thirsted after true cognition (in his case, iatromedicine). Searching for the right teachers, he came to Egypt: *transferendo me in Alexandriam cum pecunia multa perseveravi cum philosophis causa scientiae ac doctrinae* (255.9-11). That is, he retraces the route taken by numerous other students of the occult, aiming at the very center of mathematical and astronomical investigation. Alexandria, a city famous for its doctors and advancement of medicine, is certainly a right choice for an aspiring student.[14] And it is hardly surprising that Thessalus' companions are defined as philosophers, any aspiring Hermetist would consider himself one. Then, Thessalus states that he came to Alexandria equipped with a considerable amount of money – is this not reminiscent of Valens' statement: t¦j m n tîn crhm£twn dÒseij ™ poihs£meqa (IV, 11.4)? The similarity becomes even more evident with Thessalus' next statement; concerning himself he says: *desiderabam desiderio vehementi* (255, 12). Thus he seems to be agitated by the same urgent desire that is mentioned by Valens, the ™piqum…a (ibid.). During the course of his studies, Thessalus comes across a book written by the famous king Notopso (obviously identical with the famous Nechepso). Significantly, he is astounded at the ornate language employed in the work, for he notes: *et admirabar de promissionibus illius libri, qui videbatur pluribus verbis incredi-bilis et vanagloriosis uti* (255.19-20), which echoes the severe criticism Valens directs at Critodemus (III.9.1). One has to note that even if Thessalus' remark has no exact equivalent in *Anthologiae* IV.11, it stresses the aspect of misunderstanding and obscurity so frequently dealt with in Valens' own work. The point is that even this element, albeit seemingly absent from Valens' story itself, may be found explicit in other parts of his work. Now, due to lack of any advancement in his studies, and deeming deception worse than death itself (this seems to echo Valens' complaint on the charlatanry of Egyptian astrologers), Thessalus is deeply saddened and departs from

Alexandria to undertake excessive travels in Egypt: *antiqui Aegypti civitates et multa loca sacra perquisivi* (256.5). Now, however, he no longer converses with philosophers – those whom he meets are priests (*sacerdotes*), and it is from them he strives to obtain the truth.[15] Finally, mediating one of these sages, Thessalus receives a visionary instruction from Asclepius himself. Thus we see him claiming to have obtained his knowledge by supranatural means – exactly what Valens claims for himself in IV.11!

The marked similarities between the two accounts are of crucial import for our discussion. As we see Thessalus practically retracing Valens' footsteps in achieving the ultimate revelation, we are led to wonder whether we are not faced with an element traditional in hermetic literature. The tale, to stress it once more, is built of motifs quite frequently met in astrological literature: suffering, disappointment with the popular astrology, gaining experience, labour, and finally, a revelation by a supranatural being. All these are present in both Thessalus and Valens. Moreover, notions of revelation being achieved only after overcoming considerable difficulties, of wisdom being hard to find and of the moral perfection of those who are graced with instruction by the divine are hardly surprising – these are standard elements of most initiation stories (it would be enough to consider the ordeal of Lucius in the *Metamorphoses*). And this very repetition may lead a careful reader to doubt the biographical value of data contained in the tale.

Ptolemy

Having spent considerable time analyzing Valens (who owing to his Hermetic sympathies is very much the more interesting source) let us turn, albeit briefly, to his Alexandrian contemporary Ptolemy. The attitude he assumes with respect to his illustrious Egyptian predecessors is vastly different from that displayed in the *Anthologiae*. The *Apottelesmatica* rely on the data collected by the Egyptians and indeed Ptolemy invokes the authority of iatromathematicians in I.3 when discussing the utility of astrological foreknowledge. Then, some interesting remarks are found in his treatment of the *horia* terms. First he criticizes the Egyptian traditional division, which we also know from Dorotheus' work. Yet this critical attitude, exemplified by the objection of illogical and unsystematic character, does not stop his admission that the division is working in actual prognostic. Moreover, when introducing his own attribution system, which, as we know, is absent from other sources, its validity is corroborated with a tale of its being found in the sand of the Egyptian desert: as we know, one of the principal arguments in favour of astrology is its long tradition of practice, and in I.2 Ptolemy took particular care to stress the importance of the data pool. Obviously, for him it is a claim to antiquity rather than Egypt par excellence, it is Egypt as a homeland of Hermetism that counts.

Conclusions

Now, the easy way out of the dilemma is to assume that Thessalus, or whoever wrote the Montepessulanus passage, relied on the tradition derived from Valens and therefore cannot be considered decent comparison material – still, the popularity of references to Egypt in a number of earlier works attests to the fact that we are actually speaking of a tradition much older than the *Anthologiae*. Like numerous other elements of the auto-adverstising tendencies of the latter work, such as the ability to converse with the divine powers – which is also attested for the great Neopythagorean Apollonius (who, however, preferred to claim the Indian, rather than Egyptian, authority to give weight to his teachings) – the travel to Egypt or notion of Egyptian provenience of teachings remains commonplace among hermetists, mathematicians and astro-logers. To say that it is commonplace does not equal a rejection of any possibility of Valens actually paying a visit to the Nile valley, particularly given that *wanderlust* is a well-attested phenomenon in second century CE, its most famous exemplification being the emperor Hadrian (characteristically, his visit to Egypt is usually connected to advanced magical and divinatory consultations).[16] Certainly, inhabitants of the Empire were not alien to the concept of travel and pilgrimage and it is highly possible that one aspiring to astrological knowledge would endeavour to travel to Alexandria or Hermoupolis.[17] Moreover, to stress the conventional nature of the passage is not to reject the possibility of its author experiencing a divine revelation, it is only to signalize that drawing a definite, biographical conclusion from a passage similar to *Anthologiae* IV.11 is to be possibly misled by the rhetoric of his time – which of course is the very thing any aspiring rhetorician would have desired.

Endnotes

1. *Vettius Valens: Anthologies, Livre I*, etablissement, traduction et commentaire par Joelle-Frederique Bara, EPRO 111, Leiden, EJ Brill, 1989, p. 15.
2. T. Barton *Power and Knowledge: Astrology, Physiognomics and Medicine under the Roman Empire* , Ann Arbor, University of Michigan Press, 1994. Some remarks on the persuasive character of medical writings can be also found in M. M. Sassi *The Science of Man in Ancient Greece*, tr. P. Tucker, University of Chicago Press, 2001, pp. 143ff.
3. Strabo XVII, 1. 29 tr. H.L. Jones, vol. VIII, pp. 83-85.
4. *Theurgy and the Soul,* Pennsylvania State University Press, 1995, pp. 7-8.
5. L. Taub "Instruments of Alexandrian Astronomy: The Uses of Equinoctial Rings" , in C. J. Tuplin and T. E. Rihll (eds) *Science and Mathematics in Ancient Greek Culture*, Oxford University Press, 2002, pp. 133-149.
6. Thus, Ptolemy blames incapacity of the diviner in I.2.12, while Firmicus Maternus states in his *Mathesis* I.3.8: "si vero interroganti ei male magister respondit, non matheseos, sed hominis fallax notatur inscientia".
7. Both adjectives are given much import in the Stoic system, *egkrateia* and *autarkeia* forming the qualities of the Sage; considering the philosophical proclivities of Valens and his adherence to strict determinism their emergence in this context can hardly be considered accidental. Moreover, the two virtues would be generally regarded as prerequisite in initiatory rites. Then, perhaps some hint may be provided also by the ˜lÒmenoi: the word comes from a*f*reomai and entails a conscious decision, an act of will. Then, it may be relevant that according to Valens *egkrateia* forms a necessary prerequisite of astrological cognition in IX.9.11
8. Cfr. *Anth.* IX.9.7; according to Valens, astrological science demands very precise sequence of study and cannot be mastered quickly, just through reading number of handbooks; in fact, most passages of *Anthologiae* put much weight on the amount of time one uses to study astrology.
9. C.P. Jones *Culture and Society in Lucian* Harvard University Press 1986, p.10.
10. Respectively *Anth.* III.8.3; IX.1.5. There are two versions of this quotation: 1. pelagodrom»saj ka˜ poll¾n œrhmon ÐdeÚsaj °xièqhn ØpÕ qeîn limšnoj ¢kindÚnou tuce‹n ka˜ monÁj ¢ sfalest£thj; and 2. ½dh pote pelagodrom»saj ka˜ poll¾n œrhmon **diodeÚsaj** °xièqhn ØpÕ qeîn limšnoj ¢kindÚnou tuce‹n ka˜ monÁj ¢sfalest£thj.
11. Apologetic and polemical components of scientific prologues formed the main focus of C. Santini, N. Scivoletto & E. Zurli, *Prefazioni, prologhi, proemi di opere tecnico-scientifiche latine* vol. I-III, Roma 1990-1998.
12. Symptomatically, Book Nine is said to deal with problems that were left untouched until Valens' times (IX.1.2: nun˜ de taÚthn sunt£ssw [t¾n ¢rc¾n] leipomšnhn ™n oÙden…).

13. Concerning the letter see I. Moyer "The Initiation of the Magician: Transition and Power in Graeco-Egyptian Ritual", in D. B. Dodd & Ch. Faraone *Initiation in Ancient Greek Rituals and Narratives: New Critical Perspectives*, Routledge, London and New York, 2003, pp. 219-237.
14. Cfr J.-M. André, M.-F. Baslez *Voyager dans l'Antiquité*, Paris: Fayard, 1993 [hence: André- Baslez 1993], pp. 207-246.
15. The close connection between temple and astrology in Roman Egypt has been investigated by A. Jones, " The Place of Astronomy in Roman Egypt" , in *The Sciences in Greco-Roman Society,* ed. T.D. Barnes, Apeiron XXVII/4, 1994, pp. 25-51.
16. Cfr A. Birley *Hadrian: the Restless Emperor*, London: New York, Routledge, 1998, pp. 235-253.
17. Cfr André- Baslez 1993, pp. 247-282 (on pilgrimage), 317-372 (on tourism).

Marco Polo and the Chinese Zodiac

Derek Walters

Despite Chinese Astrology's long history, the celebrated 'Chinese Zodiac' did not appear in China until the sixth century. Whatever its origins, it was indeed a happy invention, for in replacing ancient Chinese seal-script signs, the twelve animal names helped the astrologer and client to understand the astrological significance of the hours of the day, the months of the year, and the harmonious relationships between them. This paper offers suggestions regarding the possible sources of the Twelve Animals, and shows briefly how they are used in interpreting Chinese horoscopes.

"Let me begin with Armenia"[1] are the opening words of what is perhaps the world's most fascinating travelogue. The tales of Marco Polo's journeys are familiar enough, but in recent years some scholars have expressed doubts concerning whether the traveler ever actually got as far as China. Firstly, they say, he makes no mention of the Great Wall; secondly, there is no reference to tea; and thirdly, it is remarkable that he does not describe Chinese script. Well, for a start, the Great Wall as we know it today was built during the Ming dynasty, a few centuries after Marco Polo. In his day, the remains of the First Emperor's fortification would have been little more than a ridge, which would not have merited a passing glance. Secondly, the fact that Marco Polo does not allude to tea (though he does describe the taste and brewing of spiced rice wine) is often cited as evidence that in earlier times tea drinking was not as commonplace as it is today. As for his failure to describe Chinese characters, since he was already familiar with the Greek and Arabic alphabets, he probably considered that the ideograms of Chinese were no more a novelty than the vertical script of the Mongolians.

But where Marco Polo's writings do convince me that he was in China was his chance, and wildly inaccurate, rendition of the animals of the Chinese zodiac and the curious form of words that he uses to describe a Chinese horoscope. After recounting that in Khan Balik (the Mongolian name for Beijing) there were no fewer than five thousand astrologers plying their trade, he refers to the signs of the Chinese zodiac: "The first bears the sign of the Lion [!], the second the Ox, the third the Dragon [!!] the fourth the Dog [!!!] and so on up to twelve".[2]

In comparing Marco Polo's remarks with the actual order of the Chinese zodiac signs (Rat, Ox, Tiger, Rabbit, Dragon, and so on) the fact that the only sign he gets completely right is the Ox is probably because this is the only sign common to both the Chinese and the familiar western zodiacs. There is no Lion in the Chinese zodiac, although there is a Tiger, conventionally the third sign. Confusion between Leo/Tiger and it being the first of the Chinese zodiac is understandable. Elsewhere in the *Travels* Marco Polo makes the point that the Chinese New Year begins in February, which is a Tiger month, followed, two signs later, by the Dragon. The Dog, however, is the eleventh sign. This garbled version of the Chinese zodiac must indicate that while Marco Polo may not have had a working knowledge of the Chinese zodiac, he certainly had a passing familiarity with it. In all fairness, his list of examples should be compared with those trotted out by Joseph Needham: "[…] the ox, sheep, dragon, pig and so on […]"[3] which seem to have jotted down from a book on Chinese astrology opened at a random page.

Yet it is a simple off-hand remark that provides an even more significant clue to the fact that Marco Polo not only visited China, but also during his meanderings actually witnessed a typical horoscope being drawn up. Any educated westerner of the time would certainly have been familiar with the basic principles of astrology and the construction of a horoscope. And it would have been commonplace knowledge that an astrologer would need to know the date and time of birth, and probably the place as well. So does the Chinese astrologer. But Marco Polo takes pains to spell out exactly what it is that the Chinese astrologer requires:

> If anyone proposes to embark on some important enterprise or […] some other project whose outcome he would like to know, he will consult the astrologers, telling them the year, month, hour and minute of his nativity. This he is able to do, because in accordance with custom everyone is taught from birth what he must say about his nativity, and parents are careful to note the particulars in a book.[4]

But note the way that Marco Polo refers to the essential data on this early form of birth certificate. Instead of writing "date and time" he refers specifically to the "year, month, hour and minute". Actually, this time he gets seventy-five percent of the possible full marks since although he mentions precisely four factors of the date and time, he ought to have said "year, month, day and hour". These four specifics form the foundation of all Chinese horoscopes, and on account of their being written vertically, are known as the *Four Columns* of Chinese astrology.

When Dr Needham made his passing reference to the animal signs, he had probably glanced at a page dealing with the seasons or elements pertaining to the twelve animals, for it seems to be rather more than a coincidence that all four animals are collectively known as the Four Earths, or Coaching Posts. It is a great pity that in his remarkable account of the history of Chinese astronomy he should be so dismissive of the contribution made by the diviners and sages on whose studies and observations Chinese astronomy was founded. "Whoever invented the animal cycle is welcome to it", he sniffs. So who did?[5]

Early Conjectures

The twelve animals as a repeating cycle are found in the calendars of Mongolia and Tibet, but not, remarkably, in 'official' Chinese calendars, where the animal names, if present at all, are usually relegated to the bottom of the page in small print. The animal names are known from one side of Asia to the other. Stone figures of the animals line the route to the tombs of Kings in Silla, Korea; they appear carved on a mediaeval ceremonial gate in Sivas, Turkey; shepherds in Turkey and Iran use the animal names to reckon the years just as the nomads of Mongolia do. In China, they were represented in some exquisite tenth-century drawings in the Dun Huang manuscripts, and on bronze astronomical plates of the sixth century. Exactly when the animal names first appeared is impossible to say; they may have belonged to an oral tradition, but there is no material evidence to suggest that they are earlier than the fifth century. Attempts to suggest that they are earlier than this (such as P. Pelliot's *Le Plus Ancien exemple du cycle des douze animaux chez les Turcs*) confuse the twelve animal names with the Twelve Branches, which, in popular usage, they supplanted.

The Twelve Branches

The ancient Chinese reckoned their days in tens and twelves, the former being known as the Ten Heavenly Stems, and the latter as the Twelve Earthly Branches. The signs for the Branches had nothing to do with animals, and everything to do with the course of the hours through the day, and the months through the year. The first branch, which stood for the midnight hour, (dawn of a new day) and the month which included the winter solstice, was represented by the graph for a baby; the seventh branch, mid-day or mid-summer, by a sign represented mid-way. Other recognisable signs were a plough for late summer, and a wine bottle for sunset or autumn. The fourth, fifth and sixth signs, which would correspond to the months of March, April, and May, represented constellations (the Pleiades, Dragon and Snake) which became visible at those times of the year. The eleventh sign showed a man holding a spear (on night-watch) and the final sign, two people asleep in bed.

The Twelve Animals replace the Branches

At some point in the fifth or sixth centuries, the Animal Zodiac replaced the twelve branches. Did it originate in China and spread outwards across the whole of the Asian continent? Or conversely, did it make its way from Central Asia into China? Whichever was the case, the dissemination of the animal cycle throughout Asia seems to have happened suddenly, and this fact may prove to be a significant factor in determining the origin of the animal cycle.

A consideration of the twelve animals alongside the branches which they superseded reveals some remarkable coincidences. The rat (or mouse in some translations) is busy at night; the midnight hour. Rabbits favour the dawn hour, and in many cultures are associated with spring. The Dragon and the Snake stand in the place of the very branches which represented the similarly named constellations. The Horse, invariably associated with masculine interests, stands at the position – noon and midsummer – when the Sun, still known as the Great Yang force in modern Chinese, is at it highest point. The Chicken comes home to roost at the sunset hour; the Dog takes the place of the watchman; the snorting Pig resonates like the snoring of the sleeping couple.

The Chinese year begins with the month of the Tiger, which bears on its head the Chinese character for King, showing that he is the leader of the animals. It is difficult to dismiss the notion that the animal names were very carefully chosen to represent the original symbolism of the twelve branches. The few remaining names could only have been chosen for their astrological symbolism. For example, the seventh sign, the Horse, represented the yang, or masculine force; it follows therefore that its partner, the next sign, should represent femininity, and what better animal to indicate this than the sheep, since flocks of sheep are all female?

The Four Harmonies

But there is another intriguing side to the symbolic nature of the animal names. In Chinese astrology, signs that are four places apart are regarded as extremely harmonious. Thus, for example, the Horse (Branch VII) harmonises with the Tiger (Branch III) or the Dog (Branch XI). Remarkably, not only are these three animals associated with hunting, predominantly a masculine pastime, but form a triangle, the apex of which is the Horse, sign of the Great Yang. The Sheep, Pig and Rabbit form another triangle. Astrologically, each of these signs is connected with family life: the Pig with home comfort (remember the couple in bed); the Sheep with married life, and the Rabbit with children and procreation – an accomplishment in which rabbits are said to excel.

The case for the astrological origin of the animal cycle seems irrefutable. It only remains to say who invented it, and why. The era of the first recorded evidence of the cycle, about the sixth century, coincides with the growing interest of Buddhism in China. I would suggest that Buddhist monks, during their journeys to bring the Buddhist scriptures to China, maintained themselves through the sale of horoscopes.

Unfortunately, the desiccated algebra of the standard system of stems and branches for reckoning the years, months, days and hours, may have been acceptable to the learned classes, but for the unlettered it was an obstacle to the understanding and interpretation of the horoscopes. The decision to replace the Branches by memorable names was a stroke of genius, and the simplicity of the system meant that within a century or two at the most, the calendar of twelve animals was established throughout Asia. There was only one sign which presented a challenge - what animal could possibly represent the second of the signs? What springs to mind when you think of late January, or two o'clock in the morning? It seems that the creator of the animal cycle was equally stumped – and therefore borrowed the second sign – Taurus – from the western zodiac and so gave the Chinese the Spring Ox, which to this day graces the first page of every Chinese almanac.

Endnotes

1. Latham, Ronald, *The Travels of Marco Polo*, Harmondsworth, Middlesex: Penguin, 1958, p. 33.
2. *Ibid.* p. 133.
3. Needham, Joseph, *Science and Civilisation in China,* Cambridge: Cambridge University Press 1959, Vol. III, p. 405.
4. Latham, *Marco Polo*, p. 132.
5. Needham, *Science and Civilisation*, p. 406.

Astrology and Brazilian Culture: A Personal Perspective

Ruth Cunha Cintra, TRIOM (Centro de Estudos Marina e Martin Harvey Editorial e Comercial Ltda), Brazil

Astrology and Astronomy have been present in the history of Brazil since its 'discovery' – the Brazilian flag was designed according to astronomical (and astrological) standards. This paper will look at the astrology of our native people. There has been significant progress in studies on Brazilian ethno-astronomy, especially on the astronomical lore of the Guarani nation. Lastly, the paper will provide an overview of Astrology in Brazil today as an accepted academic subject, as a profession and as a professional help for businesses.

What I will try to do here today is give you a small idea of what is going on in Brazil regarding astrology. Michael York said in the opening session that astrology has been accepted on-and-off for the last 400 years. Brazil has only 500 years of history, so our culture is quite recent and we don't have a history or culture in astrology.

Brazil is a huge country; it is the fifth largest in the world, or the fourth if we consider the United States without its discontinuous territories. I live in São Paulo, Brazil's business centre. It has a population of eleven million. Brazil is called a continent country because it covers seventy-five percent of South America. The Tropic of Capricorn passes through São Paulo, and you cross it when you arrive at the international airport and go into the city.

Together with my sister Renata and our friend Vitoria we have established TRIOM, a study centre that opened in 1991 and was named after our uncle, James Martin Harvey. Mr. Harvey was an Englishman who went to Rio de Janeiro in 1923 to work as an employee for the Western Telegraph Company. He soon fell in love with the country and with my aunt Marina. They got married and, from 1935, on they lived permanently in São Paulo. My uncle graduated in Economics, but he was also a historian and a writer. He came back frequently to England for his studies and research and also to nurture a childhood dream: to learn more and more about the stars. He also had a passion for old antique books, so on his travels back to England he would buy enormous amounts of them and he managed to compile a very precious library. In his presentation,

Dr. Halbronn showed us some pictures of *Monarchy or No Monarchy*, and that is one of the books in the precious library that Mr Harvey had collected.

With his studies he became not an astronomer but a highly respected astrologer, very well-known in Europe, especially in Germany, France, England and the United States, but hardly known at all in Brazil until a few years ago when we started our centre and published his research on historical natal charts.

Why was this so? I think it is because our culture is so recent. When the *Zacuto Almanac* (one of the most ancient books of my uncle's collection) was printed in 1525, Brazil had just been discovered. It was thanks to books such as the *Almanac* that the fifteenth century explorers managed to sail around the world and discover new lands. When William Lilly's *Monarchy or no Monarchy in England* was published in 1651, showing, among other things, his vision of the fire of London, Brazil as a colonised country was only a hundred-and-fifty years old. So we were way behind and had to start from scratch, with the inheritance of a European education but in a completely new environment. The study of astrology in Brazil as an acceptable subject is something that has emerged only in the last thirty to fifty years.

Nevertheless, astrology/astronomy was always present in our culture, helping the explorers to "discover" us for instance. At that time the pilots of the "caravelas", the Portuguese men-of-war that reached Brazil and other far away lands were usually doctors and Jews, and they knew how to make use of the astrological instruments that had been brought to Spanish Europe by the Arabs. Arriving in Brazil in one of these caravels, Mestre João, or Master John, was able to calculate the position of the stars of our most beautiful constellation, the Southern Cross, and send it to the King of Portugal, Dom Manuel the Fortunate. In the first volume of Mr. Harvey's nativities is the natal chart of Dom Manuel, which shows Jupiter at the Midheaven, indicating that he would bring expansion, glory and fame to Portugal.

Brazil's independence from Portugal was proclaimed on 7 September 1822, 16h08, in São Paulo, articulated by a group of European educated men – all of them freemasons, including the future first Emperor of Brazil, Dom Pedro I – so I believe that the knowledge of astrology would be natural for them. This date is the one considered to be the horoscope of Brazil by a consensus of Brazilian astrologers.

When the Republic was established in 1889, a new flag was created. One of the collaborators for the project was the astronomer and university

Professor Manuel Pereira Reis. Among other details, it was decided that the blue circle in the middle of the flag would reflect the image of the celestial chart at an angle that corresponds to the latitude of the city of Rio de Janeiro at 12 Sidereal H, 8h30 on 15 November 1889, the day of the proclamation of the Republic.

The words "Order and Progress" displayed on the white stripe were inspired by the French positivist philosopher Auguste Comte, who had many followers in Brazil. The word "Order" may be seen to relate to Brazil's astrological Sun sign, Virgo, and "Progress" relates to the sign at the Ascendant, Aquarius.

The star above the words is Spica, from the constellation of Virgo, again Brazil's astrological sign. Each of the other stars signify one state, and if another state should be created and incorporated, a specific star from that specific celestial chart should be chosen to represent it. The stars on the flag cannot be put there at random. All the stars have five points, and it is nice to remember that the five-pointed star is the esoteric symbol of man.

Now, going back to the year 1500 when Brazil was discovered. As with many other native peoples, the rhythm of the stars determined the cycles of life of the native Brazilians, and nature was the master, not simply a collaborator. The Brazilian astronomer Prof. Germano Bruno Afonso, classifies the native knowledge in two kinds: (1) the everyday knowledge, where the sunny and rainy periods define the seasons and the constellations mark the rituals and (2) the religious knowledge where the acts of gods and spirits explain the most important celestial events, like the eclipse.[1]

Although not as sophisticated as the Aztecs, Mayas or Incas, the different tribes of the Tupi-Guarani group all looked at the stars to determine the time to plant, the time to harvest, and so on. Many inscriptions on rocks show that they knew every corner of the sky, and they believed that everything that happened on earth was a reflection of the sky. Through the sky the natives determined their calendar and oriented themselves.

Many references are made to two of the more important constellations that are seen only from the Southern Hemisphere; the Southern Cross and the Three Maries. The group of blue stars in the Taurus constellation was important to them. These stars, the Pleiades or "seven sisters", would in many tribes determine the beginning of the year and the time to start planting. For some tribes, like the "taulipangs" who lived in Roraima, the disappearance of these stars on the western horizon signified the rainy season was about to begin, and with it the season of the "piracema", when the fish swim upriver, making it easy for the natives to catch them. So it was time of abundant food, with all the harvesting and fishing.

When the stars reappeared on the east, completing a year of the native calendar, they coincided with the beginning of the drought season and the ensuing scarcity of food. For the Guarani and the Tupi groups, two main constellations determined their year: the Ema and the Tinguaçu. These constellations are opposite each other in the sky and were used to determine the opposite seasons of the year. When the Ema is seen in the sky it indicates winter, cold weather and scarce food. When the Tinguaçu is seen, it is a sign of warm weather, abundant food and socialising. This is the time to celebrate life. The Tinguaçu configuration occupies the sky in the area of the constellations of Taurus, Aries and Perseus. The Tupinambá group relates the appearance of the Tinguaçu with that of the Pleiades: the bird's beak appears two weeks before the "seven sisters".

The great pre-Columbian civilisations and the Tupi-Guarani all used the stars to count time. The complexity of the calendars varied according to the respective degree of cultural development. What all had in common was the notion of respecting nature's cycles as an important way to live more harmoniously.

The Guarani nation lived mainly in the Southeast of Brazil, below parallel 20 where São Paulo is located. They were gradually absorbed by the new settlers. Many traditional families like my own can go back to some Portuguese ancestor who married a Guarani native. It is interesting to note that in the city of São Paulo, an important business and academic centre with many industries, signs of the native culture have been retained through the naming of streets and places by the "Caboclos".

So let us now return to the present and astrology in Brazil today. Since 1977, astrology has been placed in the CBO, Brazil's list of registered occupations. At present there is a law pending in the Congress and the Senate that declares astrology to be a legal profession. In São Paulo, we now have the first astrology course in Latin America with the establishment of a regular two-year course at the Bras Cubas University, with a total of 1600 hours of classes, 1000 of which are dedicated to astrology and 600 to supporting subjects such as psychology and philosophy.

In addition, there is some academic work that has been dedicated to relating astrology with other subjects such as medicine, psychology and teaching, but to date we still lack published material in these areas.

In her talk, Angela Voss mentioned the need for "the desire to learn". I feel this desire strongly in Brazilian students. I think it is easy for Brazilians to accept spirituality and mysticism, since we are used to the syncretism that exists in our culture. Nick Campion has said that "popular culture easily accepts astrology", and I think this also applies in Brazil. An informal study suggests there are at least eleven thousand professional astrologers in Brazil. They study in at least ten schools of astrology, mainly in São Paulo and Rio de Janeiro. These schools have university accreditation to produce professional astrologers. Some of these schools have already existed for more than twenty-five years, such as the Instituto Paulista de Astrologia and Escola Regulus in São Paulo, led by Prof. Waldir Bonadei Fücher, a well respected astrologer and teacher.

In Brazil we have a National Association of Astrology and seven state syndicates. Many local as well as national astrological events are organised each year. I have brought a book called *Brasil Corpo e Alma (Brazil Body and Soul),* compiled by my sister Renata, that includes the papers presented by our Brazilian astrologers in a national conference that took place in São Paulo two years ago. I have translated some of the articles into English.

Moreover, Brazil has developed astrology software that is being exported to Europe, like such programs as Pegasus, Vega and Canopus. Business Astrology has been developing these last few years, with able professionals like Maurício Bernis. Maurício has given assistance to more than six hundred businesses, including multinationals, using his skills in strategic planning and organisational restructuring together with his great astrological knowledge. He has recently been invited to participate in the International Society of Business Astrologers Congress in London.

Acknowledgment

I would like to thank the Sophia Centre for inviting me to present this paper. It was a great challenge and I could not have done it without the help and loving support of my partners and my team at Triom, my friends and my family. I am deeply grateful to Maurício Bernis, business astrologer and author of many books, a friend who patiently helped me through all the phases of the process of putting this presentation together. Many thanks to Amancio Friaça, astronomer and astrologer, who introduced me to Prof. Germano Bruno Afonso's Archaeoastronomy.

Endnote

1. Afonso, Prof. Germano Bruno, *Arqueoastronomia Brasileira*,

http://fisica.ufpr.br/tupi

References

Harvey, James Martin, Ed. (1992) *Nativitas – Astrological Studies*, vol. I, São Paulo: Triom.
Ramos, Renata C. L., Ed. (2001) *Brasil Corpo e Alma – Re-conhecendo o Brasil pela Astrologia*, São Paulo: Triom.
Bernis, Maurício, Ed. (2001) *O Brasil Astrológico,* São Paulo: AstroBrasil.
Bernis, Maurício, Ed. (2001) *Astrologia Vocacional – Escolha da Profissão para Obter Realização Pessoal*, São Paulo: Roca.
Afonso, Prof. Germano Bruno, *Arqueoastronomia Brasileira*, http://fisica.ufpr.br/tupi

Astrology as a Language Game

Mike Harding, Regents College

Astrology is often referred to as a symbolic language. Does this make it different from an 'ordinary' language, and what are the implications of describing it as such? In short, what makes one form of language more 'real' than another? The talk will introduce Wittgenstein's concept of 'language games' to explore how language can be used in various ways to describe our experience of the world. This will address many confusions regarding concepts of 'causes', 'principles', and 'underlying laws' which are often used to bolster the scientific, as well as the astrological paradigm, which is itself an increasing victim of psychologism. Also drawing on other ideas from the philosophy of language we shall place the language of astrology within a wider frame. This will raise the question as to the extent that astrology itself can usefully contribute to the debate that dominates much current philosophical thinking on the nature and experience of language.

Many astrologers have referred to astrology as some form of language, often as a language of symbols. In this paper I would like to explore some of the implications of treating astrology as a language, and in doing so will draw mainly on the work of Ludwig Wittgenstein. This is not done to 'explain' astrology in terms of an alternative system of thought, but in an attempt to clarify how we use its unique language.

Wittgenstein's approach was to examine the manner in which language is used to describe the world, and his examples consistently demonstrate that we all fall victim to language itself. In his words, we are often 'bewitched by language'. What did he mean by this?

Rather than our words having clear and specific meanings – as if they stand in place of objects or ideas, much as a picture might illustrate a certain scene – Wittgenstein came to believe that language has a multiplicity of meanings which emerge from their *use*. However, the logic of their use in each case cannot be separated out from the statements themselves, for their meaning becomes clear only within a particular context. There is no hope that the scientific approach – that is, to seek underlying principles or causes to explain how words are used – can ever be successfully employed, as such concepts as 'principles' and 'causes' are themselves examples of language use, and do not refer to something *underlying* what we perceive, but are variant observations of it. I will return to this point later.

At first glance it may seem absurd to suggest that words do not have specific meanings. Surely a table is clearly a table. Well, laden with food it can become 'a groaning board'. Examples of poetry and metaphor show us at once that everyday words can be used in novel ways. Thus, if we catch ourselves saying 'this word only means this' we are ignoring our actual experience of living in language. Much like the psychotherapist, Wittgenstein always asks us to stay with what we actually say and do, and explore the implications of it.

Wittgenstein speaks of our 'following a rule' when we use language in a particular way; this rule is not an underlying principle, but a way of understanding. If I declare that my heart is full of love, I am using the concept of the heart as a container in a *poetic* way. This is quite different from the manner in which a doctor might speak of the heart as being full of diseased material, and if anyone really believed that the heart was literally full of a substance called 'love', then they will have failed to grasp the complexity of language. Young children typically have that problem when they are learning to find their way with words. They will often have confusions when metaphors are used, having the tendency, as Freud pointed out, to see words as things. One client told me that when she was little her uncle had died on holiday, and she had heard her parents say that his body was being brought home. She was alarmed, as she wondered what would be done with his head and arms. Later, of course, she would learn that 'body' can also mean a group of people, that the body can be politic, that there can be a body of water or a body of opinion. In each case a different rule of usage is being employed, which we can see at once, although, and this is most important, we cannot formulate a rule that will explain which is the correct meaning. Wittgenstein named these different ways of using words 'language games'.

Wittgenstein used the word *game* because all games have rules of some kind, and it is these rules that make the game possible. We can see that chess is a game, and so is football. Both involve strategy and movement, both have 'players' with different functions, both have legal and illegal moves. However, both games are also totally different, and do not have interchangeable rules. So it is with language. What Wittgenstein demonstrates, however, is that this point is generally not recognised. We tend to act as if a word means the same thing in all circumstances, and thus transfer its meaning from one area of life into another, creating confusions for ourselves. For example, it makes sense to speak of 'night' as being opposite to 'day'. Yet we also speak of thoughts as being opposite to feelings. Clearly we cannot be using the word 'opposite' in the same way, because my thoughts and my feelings may be in exact agreement on many occasions. But the absence and presence of light cannot ever be regarded as being similar. Yet how many systems of psychology are based on such a fundamental confusion, where thoughts and feelings are given a geometric relationship, which is then claimed to be an inherent dynamic. In such ways language bewitches us, and leads us down impossible paths.

The various ways of using the same word, and the fact that it will have a different meaning in each context, is the core idea of the 'language game'. To tell someone to 'keep their shirt on' is not an instruction to remain clothed, but to stay calm. In this context the word *shirt* does not mean a shirt. A dictionary may tell us what a word *signifies*, but its meaning ultimately exists in the ebb and flow of life. It Wittgenstein's hands, this is a very powerful idea. It means that words like 'cause', 'reality', 'scientific law' and so on, do not, and cannot have finite meanings. Each different language game is a way of *being* which embodies language in a direct and immediate manner. Each game refers to a way of engaging with life, which only makes sense when we understand how it is used. In this respect Wittgenstein also referred to language games as 'forms of life'.

Unless we understand the context in which something is said, we will not know what the word means. But no theory about the meaning of a word is required for us to understand it. Indeed, no such theory would be possible. For this would demand that we know, in advance, every conceivable usage that the future could bring. Who would have guessed that words like 'bad' and 'wicked' could come to mean their exact opposite?

The language game of chemistry accurately describes the organic structure of a piece of wood, and can be used to predict its performance under stress, but is hopeless for the carpenter. There the demand is for a more visually-orientated language of texture, colour and feel. This embodied language game provided the old craftsmen with an ability to select the correct timbers for the task without any knowledge of its organic structure.

Though both carpenter and chemist might be speaking of the identical object – a plank of wood – they are describing it quite differently. They are, in effect, living in different worlds. In both cases, their worlds and their different concerns emerge out of the language games they use. We could think of the astrologer and the scientist at this point, and note that such questions as *how can the position of Mars cause wars to happen?* emerge primarily from confusions of using language.

It's less a matter of just 'seeing things differently', and more a case of recognising that how we use the words that describe the world are coincident with how we see the world. As Wittgenstein commented, only in a pathological condition can someone say: 'I can see that it's raining, but I believe that it isn't'. For a language game to 'work', to be seen by people to be relevant to their lives, it must relate to the nature of the world. It's no good inventing a language game of colours if there were no colours to perceive in the first place.

The scientist may choose to say that red, for example, is the numerical expression of a particular wave-length of light. But it would be wrong to suggest that this form of expression is more correct, or in some way underpins what is meant by 'red'. After all, if I ask the scientist what is referred to by the number, I would have to be shown the colour. It is the nature of the world that ultimately dictates whether a language game is valid, not some personal feeling or theory about it. And it is this point that moves our discussion more directly towards astrology.

There can be little doubt that astrology is a language game. It has its own rules, and ways of talking about life and the world that are relatively consistent and coherent. Indeed, it is quite a remarkable example of a language game, in the fact that its rules allow for a word to have a multiplicity of meanings, where one is not favoured over another. For example, Lee Lehman's *Book of Rulerships* lists nearly six hundred objects, situations or concepts that can be signified by the Moon.

But the point that is invariably raised against astrology is this: does its language refer to anything *real*. That is, do astrological statements carry the same validity as claims such as 'humans are mortal', 'ice is cold', 'the earth goes around the sun'? Or is it merely a poetic way of talking about our experience of such phenomena? Let's start with the chart itself.

The temptation here is to treat the chart as if it were a picture or a map, and stood in some kind of *relationship* to what it is saying. This image is compelling – I know this only too well – and it is very easy to be drawn down this particular road. But let's consider where it takes us. If we say that a *relationship* exists, then there must be a primary separation, and we're back to Descartes, splitting mind from world. Or, as

Wittgenstein would say, attempting the impossible trick of splitting language from the world.

Perhaps our problem here might stem from thinking that the astrological glyphs are somehow different from *words*. Is this really the case? Suppose we look at a chart and write down everything we can say about it. In other words, everything that the glyphs *mean*. If we were competent astrologers, then the report would be saying exactly what the chart says. There would be no difference. Would we then regard our finished report as being some kind of map or symbolic representation? Would the report be 'explaining' the chart, or the chart 'explaining' the report?

To be sure, the formal language of the chart is visually different from our typed report but, in terms of its meaning, why is one symbolic and the other not if they contain the same information? If I wrote my report in Japanese, would we claim that it was of a fundamentally different order? If someone asks me where the door is, I may say "over there", or I may simply point. Pointing is not symbolic of speaking, for in order to understand what pointing means one has already to be familiar with the meaning of signs and gestures, which are part and parcel of knowing a language. I stress this point because it is so easy to see glyphs, signs, numbers and symbols as if they are somehow apart from language, when they are inextricably bound up with it. The view that they are fundamentally different can lead us down false paths, and stop us seeing the chart *as* language.

Let's now take a closer look at how similar astrology is to our ordinary speech. We know that some people are more assertive than others. The astrologer might say that such people 'have a strong Mars.' At this level the two statements are identical. To say of someone 'he is assertive' or 'he has a strong Mars' can mean the same thing, and our choice of description merely a matter of convention. Astrologers often make the mistake of pointing to Mars in such a chart and saying that its placement 'explains' the personality of the native. It does not. It offers a description. To speak of explanations here is to fall into the language game of science, and take on some of science's inherent confusions. For example, astronomers claim that Mars circles the Sun because it follows Kepler's laws of motion, and that these laws explain the planet's movement. They do not. The concept of 'following a law' is a linguistic convention, a way of talking about things that the astronomer employs to make sense of what is perceived. The claim that a planet is following a form of Latin words is pure anthropomorphism, and a good example of what Wittgenstein described as the capacity of language to bewitch our intelligence.

At its basic level astrology offers us a way of describing and talking about the world, just as science does, and, like scientists, we can get carried away by language into reification, where a description is magically turned into a casual principle, and a way of talking about something becomes an operating system to explain what has just been observed. If we stay with *description* we can recognise that astrologers use the word 'Mars' to denote anger, 'Saturn' to signify guilt, 'Aquarius' to stand for innovation, and so on. Again, at this level, there are no problems for either the scientist or the philosopher. There is no logical reason why the word Mars cannot be used to signify anger, any more than there is a logical reason why we should quibble over calling someone 'sad' or describing them as 'unhappy'. The real problems start with the astrologer's claim that their language game uses the names of the planets and signs, not for reasons of poetic whimsy, but *because the positions of the planets dictate how the language is to be used.* The meaning of the Moon in Virgo is not the same as for the Moon in Libra. Ultimately, the Moon's mathematical position dictates how the concept of 'Moon' is to be employed.

Thus, at its core, lies the claim that astrological language is above and beyond us all, and that this language is inextricably bound up in the nature of the cosmos, and is signified by the motions of the planets and the rotation of the earth. Surprisingly, much of this is in accord with current thinking. The idea that language is above and beyond us all and that we are to some extent its creation is taken by many philosophers as a fact. Thinkers such a Martin Heidegger, with his claim that 'man does not speak language, he is spoken by it', that we do not have thoughts, they have us, that language is the 'home of being', the 'great stream that moves all things along', that language itself can give or withhold a word, all point to a radically different view of thought and speech. In this view language itself has the possibility to reveal or conceal. As he put it:

> […] man does not have control over unconcealment itself, in which at any time the real shows itself or withdraws […]. The thinker only responded to what addressed itself to him […]. But unconcealment itself, […] is never a human handiwork.[1]

Such views, which give us the image of language as alive and powerful, with a drift and movement of its own, have been extended by psychoanalysts such as Jacques Lacan to portray a picture of the human being created and structured by the nature of language itself. For Lacan, language is far from being 'natural' and 'within us'. Language is seen as akin to an alien life form into which we are born, and into which we have to fit ourselves. We are limited by the possibilities of language to the extent that even the physical body is named and determined by the conjectured power of words. Wittgenstein, too, draws our attention to language as the final limit of our world. And it is worth noting here that one of the foremost post-Lacanian feminist philosophers of language, Luce Irigary, claims that women have "an irreducible relationship to the universe".[2] While astrologers may wish to grant men similar possibilities, it is intriguing to find such a comment lurking within established thought.

However, it is when astrologers insist that *the positions of the planets are the moving signifiers of life* that they go beyond even this example of current philosophical thought. Here we have to consider whether the views of astrologers have to fall because their key claim finds no general support in language theory, or if astrology *itself* can extend the boundaries of our concepts of language, and thus contribute to, and not fall victim to, philosophical claims. As Wittgenstein has observed, when we make a claim that something 'must' be a certain way, we have merely indicated the point at which we have stopped thinking.

Let us now think further. We can start with one of the most common objections to astrology: that no causal mechanism exists which explains how the position of a planet can correlate with a specific event or character trait. Such a question is fatally flawed.

If, for the astrologer, the position of Mars in the sky signifies a possibility on Earth, what part could causality possibly play? If the position of Mars means such-and-such, and this indeed does occur, to suggest that such a description *causes* the phenomenon it actually describes demonstrates only confused thinking. The meaning of something cannot act *causally* to bring about the very phenomenon which arises from the description itself. Nor does meaning have a location. It does not arise from an object, anymore than the meaning of a news story lies in the nature of newsprint and ink, or the meaning of a television report lies in flickering electrons. Neither is there a need to resort to a conjectured 'a-causal connecting principle'. To suggest that an event may be explained by an underlying *a-causal* principle is essentially no different from positing a *causal* one. Except, as Heidegger has point out, an a-causal event could never be predicted, and thus this may not be the best analogy for the nature of astrology.

Jung was on far safer ground when he stayed with his original, astute observation, that synchronistic events are *meaningful* to the individual. But finding meaning and seeing connections between disparate phenomena is a human act which is ultimately inexplicable. Consider a sheet of music, the grooves on a gramophone record, the distribution of magnetic particles on a tape, the sequence of digital codes on a CD, the way the pianist moves her fingers, the vibrations in the loudspeaker cones and the way the conductor's arms wave. All these, if they refer to the same moment of the same music, must express some common form, but we cannot say what it is. What links all these disparate examples of human activity and production is *our perception* of them as being connected. It is our thought that links them together, but there is no 'formula' for describing the nature of that linkage, any more than there exists a formula for describing how a particular word or phrase can be used. Thus to seek a causal relationship between a planet and an event it describes is to be substantially misguided about the nature of language.

If we ask, instead: *how does astrological language connect to the world* we ask a question that cannot be answered of any language, because we are seeking a place *outside* of language, some point that sees the world, sees how language 'works' and observes the relationship between it and the world. All our attempts here would fail, as they would be conducted *within* language, and not from the point we are seeking, a place which is impossible to conjecture. The same problem exists with concepts such as 'laws' and 'principles', where an attempt is made to suggest that we can explain what is 'underlying' that which we describe as taking place before our eyes, by recourse to something that we *cannot* see. Our attempts to describe this invisible 'something' are invariably just different ways of talking about what we have seen, but they do not underlie our observation.

As with all language, and the music example given earlier, we can *see* the connection, but we can never actually name what it is. With all attempts to describe the 'underlying', we easily get bewitched by the nature of that word into thinking we have achieved this, when all we have done is to give another *meaning* to what we see. Many examples in science and psychoanalysis are riddled with such confusions, indeed, some psychologies appear to be built on them, and astrology is not immune.

We can see that it is a mistake to think that astrological language *causes* something, and that, similarly, it is a mistake to extend the concept of causality via the concept of laws and principles, and ask *how* this language relates to the world. But we are still left with the astrology's central, and problematic, claim: that a planet's position, by sign, house and aspect will dictate the usage of a language that can describe events before they come about, and indicate the probable date of their occurrence.

In this claim astrology gives us a picture of language which operates with specific reference to space and time. But Wittgenstein has this to say of *all* language:

> What we understand by the word 'language' unwinds in physical time.[3]

and:

> The stream of life, or the stream of the world, flows on and our propositions are, so to speak, verified only at instants. Our propositions are only verified by the present.[4]

It is only in the *present* that we can see or know something. It is only in the present that meaning can exist. In trying to work this through, which unfortunately for us occupies only a small fragment of his writing, Wittgenstein used the analogy of a cinema projector[5]. The moving picture we see on the screen we generally call the 'now' (Although 'now' no more names time than 'here' names a place). Yet the picture emerges from a strip of celluloid which has life both before and after the 'now' moment, and is accessible to physical measurement. Our engagement with what the film reveals on the screen – the now – is of a totally different order from our examination of the celluloid frames, and we are playing different language games with the concept of time.

If we extend this film analogy, the planets, the rotation of the earth and so forth similarly follow the same inevitable, frame-by-frame sequence of the film. But in 'real time', in the moment of the flickering image, when time and language are coincident, the correctness of our propositions face verification.

Here astrology extends the unique relationship between time and language that Wittgenstein and Heidegger strove to describe. It is when we are in *accord* with what is being said, when language speaks through us and the world, that language ceases to be a system of infinite and abstract possibilities and becomes coincident with the moment. What is said is what is taking place. Then it is language, as Heidegger put it, that speaks.

As with the frames on a waiting film, our ephemeris writes not a fixed and immutable fate, but a shifting lexicon of possibilities – a picture made up of pictures – which, like all forms of language, we cannot step outside, and in which, as in all forms of language, we find, or fail to find, meaning. The scientist may claim that the future is hidden, but, as Wittgenstein commented, "does the astronomer really think like this when he calculates an eclipse of the sun?"[6] Heidegger suggests that so many of our confusions about time stem from posing scientific questions. We ask 'what is time', as if wanting an object to be pointed out to us. For him, time is not a 'what', but a 'how'.[7] In seeking to make time a 'thing' that is 'out there' we are trying to avoid our own expression of it, often unwilling to face that *how* we are is how time *is*. Time shows the 'how' of things. And for him, the 'how' of things comes to us through language. From the astrologer's point of view, when the future aspect comes into exactitude in time, we can then speak of *how* things are.

In their different ways, both Wittgenstein and Heidegger insisted that our use and understanding of language emerges primarily from our embodied sense of the world, that we are part and parcel of a world that pre-dates us at every turn. If we abandon the false security of the Cartesian vision which attempted to separate consciousness from physicality, we find ourselves in an enormous realm. A realm in which such a question as 'where do I stop and the world begins' is both confused and meaningless. While much of science still adheres to Descartes, much philosophy, and some psychologies, increasingly involve the world in their understanding of the human being. What we have in astrology is a clear recognition that even attempts to extend the boundaries of the person to a particular culture, or to a specific language, is insufficient. The boundary may be moved, but Descartes still lurks on its horizon.

In astrology we have a unique form of speaking about the world, in which mathematics and poetry coexist. Its richness and complexity open up the possibilities of language in ways that no other form of thinking – no other language game – appears to match. But, like all language games, there is a deep mystery in how we come to understand it. As Wittgenstein put it: "But how can a language game become clear [...]

God only knows. – One day it starts doing something”.[8] Let us hope that this conference is a productive step on astrology’s long road, and the “something” that we are doing today makes astrology a little clearer to the world – and ourselves.

Endnotes

1. Martin Heidegger *The Question Concerning Technology*, New York: Harper Torchbooks, 1977, p. 18.
2. Luce Irigary *Thinking the Difference,* London: Athlone Press, 1994, p. 25.
3. Ludwig Wittgenstein *Philosophical Remarks*, Oxford: Blackwell, 1980, p. 89.
4. Ibid., p. 81.
5. Ibid., p. 81f.
6. Ludwig Wittgenstein, *Philosophical Investigations*, part 2, Oxford: Blackwell, 1980, p. 223.
7. Martin Heidegger, *The Concept of Time*, Oxford: Blackwell, 1992, p. 13.
8. Ludwig Wittgenstein *Last Writings on the Philosophy of Psychology*: Volume 1, Oxford: Blackwell, 1988, p. 112.

References

Lehman Lee, *Book of Rulerships*, West Chester, PA: Whitford Press 1992.

The Importance of Comets for the Cause of Astrology: the Case of Pierre Bayle in the Years 1680-1705

Dr Jacques Halbronn, Bibliotheca Astrologica, Paris

I would like to suggest a re-reading of the work of Pierre Bayle, concerning his assertions of the scientific status of History, and emphasizing in particular his critique of astrology in the writings dealing with comets which were translated into English in 1708. Those who have written about Bayle's thinking have not understood that when Bayle deals with comets he is actually looking at the way they had been previously viewed by historian, and by religion. I therefore take the opposite standpoint to those who consider that Bayle's proposals on comets are no more than a pretext through which to approach other subjects. Indeed it is better, I feel, to re-position Reflections on Comets in the line which we would call astro-history, and to place it closer to the critical work of Claude Duret, published in 1595, a century earlier. Speaking of pretexts, it must be understood that the debate on astrology and its effects on events is an integral part of a larger debate on History which is, at its heart, similar. Moreover, it is no accident that Bayle, from the opening pages of his Reflections, fiercely criticizes historians before even beginning to develop his critique of astrology. This critique is not as superficial as we might be led to believe; it involves a methodology which Bayle shows to us in great detail, and which aims less at traditional astrological knowledge, in which comets have a somewhat secondary role, than at those works which will not accept such a traditional view about astrology at all, except with certain reservations. In many cases, the word 'comet' can be replaced with any astral configuration without Bayle's argument losing its pertinence.

At first sight, comets seem to be a minor issue for the contemporary history of astrology and especially for those who practice astrology (see our study, which the present work prolongs: "Les variations d'impact des 'cométes' en France, Etude bibliographique"). It can be regarded as an archaic expression of the interest of men in the heavens, and a much less sophisticated matter than planetary conjunctions, eclipses, natal charts and so on. Until the eighteenth century comets were not predictable and, when they became predictable, they were still considered as a marginal factor, much the same as the fixed stars, astrology tending to rely heavily on planets.

However, comets offered a unique opportunity to gather people around an astronomical phenomenon, a cosmic show as it were, perhaps evoking collective memories of more ancient times. It is doubtful that comets were considered significant at the origins of astrology since they were not convenient for establishing a regular calendar, but they are still a reminiscence, a souvenir, of a sort of early collective astrology.

As late as the end of the seventeenth century, a major French Protestant thinker, Pierre Bayle, wrote about a comet that appeared at the end of the year 1680 – pretending at first to be a catholic author, and adding new considerations at the beginning of the next century, in 1705, with his lesser known work,[1] that is the *Continuation des Pensées Diverses écrites à un Docteur de Sorbonne à l'occasion de la cométe qui parut au mois de décembre 1680 ou Réponse à plisieurs difficultez que Monsieur ***(Basnage) a proposées à l'auteur*).[2] But, in the meantime, Bayle had also in the 1690s written on astrology in some articles of his famous *Dictionnaire Historique et Critique.*[3]

This is rather a unique case of one author who writes repeatedly about astrology within a period of twenty-five years, and who in both cases is concerned by the circumstances, since he pretends to answer objections in connection with publications of his time.[4] In several ways, intellectual as well as political, our study concerns the relationship between England and Holland where the French language was quite well known.

At first the work was published at the beginning of 1682, anonymously under the title *Lettre à M.L.A.D.C. docteur en Sorbonne où il est prouvé par plusieurs raisons tirées de la philosophie et de la théologie que les comètes ne sont point le présage d'aucun malheur. Avec plusieurs réflexions morales et politiques et plusieurs observations historiques et la réfutation de quelques erreurs populaires,* under a fake address (Cologne, Pierre Marteau). Someone finally discovered that the writing of Bayle was also the writing of the manuscript, and Bayle had to both use his name and suppress any reference to the pretended Catholicism of the author in the subsequent editions. The title, with the second edition, changed in *Pensées diverses sur la Cométe etc,* (Rotterdam; R. Leers) and was republished, augmented and translated many times. One passed from the plural to the singular, from the *Lettre* sur *les* Cométes to *Pensées Diverses* sur la Cométe but in fact, Bayle does treat of the case of many comets of the seventeenth Century, since 1618, and not just of the 1680 Comet so that the final title is rather inadequate, specially since he barely comments upon the effects of such an already old cosmic event..

The work belongs to the genre of anti-astrological literature and is not only concerned with the comets – far from it. However, Bayle's 1682 work, translated into English in 1708, is built as a dialogue with someone more-or-less imaginary, who is inclined towards astrology, and is actually, rather significantly, a Doctor of the Sorbonne (which was at the time a Faculty of Theology), which means that one can also read in it arguments constituting an apology of astrology based on some astrological literature of the time.

In 1689, the abbot Laurent Bordelon (1653-1730) also was to publish a Dialogue, his *De l'Astrologie Judiciaire. Entretien curieux où l'on répond d'une manière aisée et agréable à tout ce que l'on peut dire en sa faveur et où l'on fait voir en même temps la superstitieuse vanité de sa pratique et la dangereuse fausseté de ses predictions,*[5] with a new edition in 1710 under a new title, *De l'Astrologie Judiciaire. Entretien curieux 2ème édition augmentée des sentimens Modernes de plusieurs fameux auteurs du jardinage où ils jugent et condamnent comme erreurs populaires les anciennes observations des quadratures de la Lune et les influences des astres en matière d'agriculture et de jardins. Le Tombeau de l'Astrologie judiciaire.*[6]

Influence of England upon French astrology

English history was, in the seventeenth century, a major element in Nostradamus' prophecies. William Lilly quoted the *Centuries* concerning the execution of the king in 1649 (*Century* IX, quatrain 49, verse 2) upon his execution.[7] Afterwards, in 1666, the fire of London was also said to have been prophesied in one quatrain, and many editions of Nostradamus' *Prophecies* in the 1660s include images of both events as a frontispiece to the book, with an introduction underlining the most striking correlations. Dutch editions in French were published in Amsterdam in 1667-1668, one century after the death of Michel de Nostredame, with a specific "Advertissement au Lecteur: Tu y remarqueras la fin honteuse & cruelle du Roy d'Angleterre par la main d'un Bourreau dans la centurie IX, quatrain 49, page 106 [...] l'embrasement de la ville capitale de ces Isles dans la centurie II, quatr. 51, page 20". That is: "you will notice the horrid and cruel death of the King of England at the hands of the executioner, in Century IX, quatrain 49 [...] the fire of the capital city of those islands in Century II, quatrain 51 [...]".

Actually those two quatrains mention the name of Londres (London) twice: in "Senat de Londres mettront à mort leur Roy", that is "The Senate of London shall put their King to death", and "Le sang du juste à Londres sera faulte/Bruslés par fouldres", that is "The blood of the just shall be wanting in London/ Burnt by fire".[8]

Later, the Glorious Revolution of 1688, which brought William and Mary to the English throne, was also used to demonstrate the truth of astrological prediction. Such success is precisely what Bayle wished to denounce and to demystify. In his *Continuation* of 1705, Bayle attempts to show how the Catholic James II (from 1685-8) was manipulated by Protestant prophecies and influenced to leave his throne. Bayle's attention focused on a pamphlet titled *Mene Tekel ou jugement astrologique pour l'an MDCLXXXVIII dans lequel on montre par les principes de cette science la catastrophe prochaine du papisme en Angleterre, traduit de l'Anglais sur la copie de Londres*,[9] translated as *Mene Tekel: being an astrological judgment on the great and wonderful year 1688, deduced from the true principles of that art; shewing the approaching catastrophe of Popery in England*, work of J. Partridge, against the Roman Catholic J. Gadbury.

Bayle wrote to his Protestant friend, Basnage who was his new companion in the *Continuation,* "Vous êtes très assuré qu'il parut avant la fin de Décembre 1687 & cela vous persuade que la prédiction que l'on y trouve du déthronement de Jacques II Roy d'Angleterre n'a pas été faite après coup mais par une exacte connaissance des régles de l'astrologie" ("You can be insured that it was published before the end of December 1687 and it should convince you that the prediction of the dethronement of Jacques II had not been done after the event but through an exact knowledge of astrological rules").

In 1688 another text in French by the antipapist Partridge, in answer to Gadbury, was published in the same volume: "Courte réponse à un malicieux libelle appelé "Réplique écrite par John Gadbury, pour avancer le grand ouvrage".Trad de l'Anglais.[10] This is a translation of "A short answer to a malicious pamphlet, called a Reply, written by J. Gadbury [...] to help on the work".

The polemics between Gadbury and Partridge, belonging to opposite factions – Catholic and Protestant – seemed to Bayle to be the final confirmation that the astrologer is just a mercenary and that astrology has no proper message to convey. He writes: “Les pronostics des astrologues sont bien souvent inspirés par un esprit de faction”[11] (“astrologers' predictions are often inspired by a spirit of faction”).

The role of astrology and prophecy at a time of civil wars or of religious conflicts is of considerable concern, especially in the case of Nostradamus's prophecies.[12] Bayle says that Basnage, in his correspondence, mentions another booklet, *Lettre d'un Bourgeois de Londre [sic], Quacker de religion, à son colégue [sic] Mr. R.W., marchand à Rotterdam,*[13] where one could read “L'esprit lui a suggéré que dans le mois d'Octobre prochain [1688] il y aura dans ce Royaume un grand changement , que le mois suivant Guillaume d'Orange passera la Mer”[14] (“the spirit suggested to him that in next October, there will be in this kingdom a great change, that William of Orange will cross the sea”).

The name of the English Quaker William Penn (1640-1718), founder of Pennsylvania, also appears several times. It is likely, though, that such a text had no original English. We can find a similar example in 1665 with *Le Courrier de traverse ou le Tri-cométe observé à Oxfort en Angleterre, depuis le 22 Novembre iusqu'au 28 Janvier mil six cens soixante-cinq, traduit de l'Anglais de M. Vortfischer* [alias Nicolas Lasson].[15]

Bayle seems to react to astrology's success in prediction. Bayle was convinced that certain almanacs that he quoted had an influence upon the political situation in England and prepared the Revolution. It was already true, says Bayle, at the time of Cromwell: the predictive quality of almanacs was due to the relations of Cromwell with astrologers. As a matter of fact, in 1654/1655, Cromwell seems to have asked the French authorities to suppress a page of the *Fatum Universi,* published in Rennes, under the name of Petrus Allaeus, a latin treatise in *mundane* astrology, containing inappropriate developments upon England.[16]

Another argument in favor of astrology mentioned by Bayle (which shows that his work is not only interesting with regard to anti-astrological arguments), is the fact that astrology still had an impact in England. Bayle cites the *Astrometeorologia sana*[17] as an expression of astrology's lasting appeal. In part, its publication may have justified his own criticism: if there were no belief in astrology, what would be the use of his criticism of it?[18]

In the middle of the eighteenth century, English astrology, including the works of Goad and also Robert Boyle, was accessible in French mainly through the article “Influences”, in volume 8 of the *Grande Encyclopédie* by Diderot and d’Alembert (reprint) depending on the translation of Chambers’s *Cyclopaedia.*[19]

Comets, astrology and history

As a matter of fact, comets seem to represent both the strong and the weak points of astrology at the same time.[20]

1. Comets as the strong point.

a) Comets are an asset for astrology because they are a visible phenomenon, not reserved to the attention of specialists but apparent to the entire community.

b) Comets are also an asset because of the fact that they were not predictable, unlike planetary conjunctions or eclipses. By not being predictable, comets can indeed appear as a sign, a miracle of God. Indeed, the problem of comets is not an easy one, and Bayle will understand that through his bitter polemics with another French exiled Protestant, Pierre Jurieu to whom he will answer in particular through his 1694 *Additions aux Pensées diverses sur les Cométes ou Réponse à un libelle (*by Jurieu) *intitulé “Courte Revue des maximes de morale et des principes de religion de l’auteur des Pensées Diverses sur les Comètes*’, published in 1691, in a supplement to his *Pensées.* (*Reflections*). Bayle acknowledges the fact that comets appear to many people as a mark of Providence, a sort of spiritual astronomy of another sort than material and predictable astronomy. But comets do also appear in areas where people do not believe in God, says Bayle.

c) Comets are also an asset for astrology by being connected with clear interpretation and not with a more complex message. Indeed, the astrological “law” seems to be that a comet is an unfavorable sign. The significance of comets are more acceptable by astronomers than other astrological concepts, such as the zodiac signs, which were totally discredited at the end of the seventeenth century, mainly because of arguments based on the precession of equinoxes. The astrological discourse about comets is at least clearly formulated: comets are a recurrent phenomenon, supposed to always bring the same effects.

2. Comets as the weak point.

a) Comets become a weak point because their predictability was eventually established following the work of Edmund Halley and the "return" of "his" comet in the 1750s. Bayle, in his 1705 *Continuation,* alludes to this work, which would soon deprive comets of their apparently miraculous occurrence, which until now had forced the religious circles not to reject entirely their significance. "Si (Jean Calvin, Protestant author of a *Discours contre l'astrologie judiciaire,* 1549) avait su que les nouveaux astronomes nous ont appris qu'elles ne sont point formées d'exhalaisons de la terre & qu'apparemment elles ont une durée constante & peut-être aussi un cours régulier, il en eut nié entièrement les pronostic tout comme ceux des éclipses" *(Continuation,* 1705) ("If (Calvin) had known what the new astronomers have taught us since, that they are not made of the emanations of Earth and that apparently they have a constant duration and possibly a regular course, he would have entirely denied any prediction connected with comets, as he did for eclipses").

In fact by mentioning Calvin, Bayle betrays the fact that he is Protestant. Calvin was also referred to, although not directly named, by another seventeenth century French Protestant author, David Derodon, in his *Discours sur l'astrologie judiciaire.* (c.1660, Genéve).[21] According to such logic, the progress of astronomy is fatal for astrology and also causes religion to abandon astrology, which was thought to be using some divine miracle. There is here a certain irony: is it not a certain "superstitious" idea of religion, based on the temporary limits of science, which is under attack in the criticism of comets as unfavourable omens?

b) Comets are a weak point because they give a simplified idea of what astrology really is or at least wishes to appear to be. What weakens comets can also weaken the whole of astrology, which has included them in its corpus.

c) Comets are a weak point because it is rather an easy task to demonstrate that misfortunes are not especially related to comets. Actually, one could argue that comets appear at the same time as a theological or a scientific issue. Once comets become predictable, the theological argument ceases to work, and, moreover, if the correlation between comets and historical events is not explored and found to be related, it is astrology in general which is threatened. We shall insist on the attempts to prove that comets are not connected with misfortunes, especially in Bayle's works and on the real epistemological problem which lies behind such a debate.

Historical science has two problems, one connected with astrology, the other with politics. Such a debate underlines, in fact, certain weaknesses of history. If the level of historical analysis was higher, it can be argued that astrology would benefit and find more proper categories of classification. Therefore, to attack astrology implies simultaneously an attack against history and the way it apprehends events. On the other hand one could ask if history would have accumulated so many archives if not for the sake of astrological research. And, in fact, Bayle seems, in the first pages of his *Reflections,* to be sceptical about historians, whom he considers guilty of having encouraged and conveyed superstitions by being unable to distinguish between myth and reality, therefore transmitting unreliable information, including in the field of Chronology.

As a matter of fact, astrologers working on the effects of comets might be considered researchers of history, trying to discover certain historical laws.[22] The problem is also the proximity of history with politics. It was legitimate to try to understand the cause of revolutions and many books have been dedicated to the subject, such as the *Concordantia* of History and Astronomy by Cardinal Pierre d'Ailly (1414) or, in the late sixteenth century, the *Republique (*Book IV.II) by Jean Bodin. And in such works, astronomical configurations were also taken into account. When Charles I was executed in 1649, some astrologers like William Lilly thought that the reasons that explained the destiny of the English king could also work for the rest of Europe, especially in France with the disturbances of the 'Fronde' (1648-1653). One can imagine how such discourses could appear as dangerous for other monarchies.

The historical ambitions of astrology may also be connected with the chronological research of Isaac Newton,[23] who tried to base biblical chronology on certain celestial references. Astronomy, if not astrology, may appear as a threat to religious representations in the eighteenth and nineteenth centuries.

Comets versus judicial astrology

One has to distinguish between what Bayle says in 1681 and what he declares a quarter of a century later in his *III Reason, that Astrology which is the Foundation of particular Predictions from the Comets is most ridiculous.* In this work, Bayle develops a sophisticated argument:

> The whole detail of the Presages from Comets turning entirely upon the principles of astrology can't but be extremely ridiculous because these never was such a piece of Impertinence, never any thing so chimerical as astrology' etc [...]. The judgments founded upon Comets are to all intents null [...] Because they have no other foundation beside the principles of astrology.

Only the fact that a piece of knowledge is suspected of connection to astrology brings its discredit in Bayle's view. It seems, indeed, that Bayle accepts the attacks against astrology and does not endeavour to repeat them. Therefore, he says, "that the general Prejudice in behalf of astrology disparages the Authority founded upon great Numbers only".[24]

In the same way, Bayle, accepting the idea that astrology has no solid bases, quoting the *Logique of Port Royal,* concludes that if, however, astrologers get results, it cannot come from astrology. To Bayle, it is obvious that astrology is not a challenge: "If there be any author who has drawn his pen against astrology without striking it dead, he has undoubtedly perform'd a difficult exploit".

Chapter 43 is significantly called "Comment un horoscope se peut trouver véritable sans que les étoiles s'en mélent" ("Where it is explained how a horoscope can be found true, without the help of the stars"). And he makes a rule: "La prévision de l'avenir n'est pas plus facile à l'astrologue qui observe les prétendues régles de l'art qu'à celui qui ne les observe pas" ("Predicting future is not an easier thing to the astrologer who will respect the so called rules of his arts than to the man who does not care about them"). In other words, to Bayle, the work of the astrologer is one thing, the use of astrology is another. Bayle states that under the label "astrology" are hidden so many different factors. Certain writers on astrology use the success of the art of the astrologers to defend a certain vision of the world. "I'm sensible, he also writes, there's a vast number of fine Treatises upon the subject which detect the falseness and imposture of this wretched Art in the most convincing manner imaginable".[25]

Strangely enough, although Bayle connects comets with traditional astrology, his direct demonstrations against the comets do not refer to it but only to the simple question of the correlation of comets with calamities or evils. If comets are a part of astrology, why should he try to test their influence? In fact, Bayle knows very well that in a certain way, comets could, he fears, bring credit to the idea of a celestial influence as a separated body from astrology. So, in fact, Bayle tries to understand why some predictions from comets might appear as significant, that is with a certain appearance of truth: "Comparaison des années qui ont suivi les Cométes de l'an 1665 avec les années qui ont précédé la Cométe de l'an 1652".

Bayle considers the seven years following those comets. We are far from the idea that the effects should be immediate. This seems to us as an epistemological progress. The choice of seven years, however arbitrary, seems still rather pertinent because one can suppose that any cause needs a certain time to bring a complete process and a certain quantity of effects. For Bayle, it is necessary to accumulate data in order to check certain so-called laws so that astrology seems to be an incentive in favour of collecting informations and classifying them. Eventually, the real stake seems to be about the relationship between astronomy and history more than between astrology and politics. "Ne me dites point, je vous prie, que je n'ay pas pris un assez grand terme car il est du sens commun que si les Cométes présagent quelque chose, c'est pour les six ou sept premières années qui les suivent et c'est sur ce pied là que l'on prouve leur malignité par l'Histoire"("Do not argue that I took too large a period since it is common sense that if the comets announce anything, this will be for the six or seven following years and this is the way the demonstration about comets goes").

Bayle, in a manner of cross-examination, proposes to examine the period before instead of after the comet of 1652:

> Repassez un peu dans vôtre mémoire ce qui s'est fait dans l'Europe depuis l'an 1645 jusques à la Cométe qui parut sur la fin de l'an 1652 [...] Je trouve des maux epouvantables dans les années que j'ay choisies et paryticulièrement un esprit de sedition furieuse. J'y trouve le Roy d'Angleterre condamné à mort et décapité par ses propres sujets avec des circonstances horribles. [...] Je trouve la France déchirée d'une cruelle guerre civile [...] Il s'en faut de beaucoup que les sept années que j'ay prises à la suite de deux Cometes ne soient remplies d'autant d'événements facheux que les sept qui n'ont eté prises à la suite d'aucune Cométe mais au contraire au devant de celle de 1652.

Bayle ends: "Avouez donc, Mr, qu'il est des malheurs sans Cometes et des Cométes sans malheurs". In translation:

> Just remember all what happened in Europe since 1645 until the coming of the Comet, appeared at the end of 1652. [...] I find terrible harms for those years. I find the King of England condemned and executed by his own subjects [...] I find France divided by a cruel civil war [...] The seven years coming after the comets contain a lot less painful events [...] Let us admit that there are there are catastrophes without comets and comets without catastrophes.

But it is not enough that a correlation could work once, it has to be confirmed quantitatively every time that a same phenomenon appears – the same causes bringing roughly the same effects. The problem is that comets are far from being a convenient factor to check and Bayle considers all comets as one unique factor which has nothing to do with astrology, which considers the planets. Even an eclipse is a more clearly defined factor than a comet. The point is that astrologers themselves did not care which comet was concerned, which is a low level of astrology, a popular astrology more than a learned astrology: comets did not receive mythological names. And actually, the paradox was that, in the seventeenth century, rather confusing and unsophisticated representations of astrology, such as comets and the centuries of Nostradamus, were successful. Their success, hence, became suspect. If a knowledge which is irrational brings the same result as a sophisticated knowledge, is it not a proof that the whole field escapes to real science?

It remains that such a method of control seems valuable for testing whatever other celestial influences and their proposed correlations. Bayle seems to know only a few of the existing models that already in 1595, the French Claude Duret had reviewed critical in his *Discours de la Vérité des causes et effects des decadences, mutations, changements, conversions & ruines des Monarchies, Empires, Royaumes et Républiques*, Lyon B. Rigaud.[26] He does not care about the *Fatum Universi* system or about the type of research of Henry de Boulainviller. Bayle is using historical data to reject astrology but at the same time he opens the gate to the confirmation of other astro-historical models, past and future. In that sense, does not Bayle eventually belong to the reform movement of astrology – like Kepler, who also was critical, although quite interested by some comets of the beginning of the seventeenth century?

Bayle and the so-called decline of astrology

Comets were not the only topic treated by Bayle in his two volumes, it was an opportunity for him to attack traditional astrology also. In contradiction with the general representation of astrology in history, Bayle did not give at all the impression in 1705 that astrology was declining and he even tried to refute the argument that the survival of judicial astrology, in spite of so many attacks, was no proof of its intrinsic value. Bayle, in his *Continuation*, mentions the name of Eustache Lenoble, who in 1697 had published an important treatise on astrology, called the *Uranie ou Tableaux des Philosophes*. Thanks to Bayle, it was actually possible to discover Baron Lenoble who wrote on natal astrology and was forgotten by historians of French astrology. Another aristocratic supporter of astrology was Count Henry de Boulainvillers.. This French historian left a manuscript treatise on *mundane* astrology, *Histoire du mouvement de l'apogée du Soleil,*[27] while Lenoble remained in the field of individual charts. Actually, the astrological treatise of Lenoble was republished, after his death (1711) together with his other numerous works.[28] Lenoble was by no means alone in writing on astrology, and his *Tableaux des Philosophes* is an ambitious work including astrology on a much larger scale. Excerpts of his astrological work were given in Amsterdam as late as 1785 by Etteila, in his *Manière de se récréer avec le jeu de cartes nommées Tarots.*[29]

It is quite significant that in 1705 Bayle felt he had to reaffirm that he still sticks to his former position expressed twenty-five years earlier: "Si je persiste encore dans le mépris que j'ai témoigné pour l'astrologie". "Si c'est un préjugé favorable à l'astrologie de voir que les grandes lumières philosophiques du XVIIe siècle n'ont pu ruiner son credit". "Quoi qu'il en soit de toutes ces choses, je peux vous dire que depuis l'an 1681 que mon traité des cométes fut composé, je n'ai senti aucun changement dans mes opinions sur l'astrologie. J'ai déclaré en plusieurs endroits dans mon Dictionnaire combien j'étais convaincu de la vanité & du ridicule de cet art trompeur. Je vous déclare ici) l'heure qu'il est que je ne rabats rien etc". (If I still persist in the rejection I expressed in the past towards astrology". "If it is a favourable element on behalf of astrology to see that the great minds of the seventeenth century did not succeed in ruining its credit". "However, I can tell you that since 1681 when my treatise on comets was composed, I felt no change in my opinions *vis a vis* astrology. I have, in the mean time, declared in many places of my Dictionary how convinced I was of the vanity of this art etc.").

For Bayle, by attacking comets he attacked astrology. Bayle felt by no means that he was a witness of the decline of astrology at the beginning of the seventeenth century. In his dialogue of 1705, he agreed that the resistance of astrology could appear as a sign of its truth and he was forced to show that this apparent truth is mainly a delusion and its continuous credit the result of old habits, like in many other fields. As a matter of fact, it seems that Bayle gave the impression that astrology was in better shape in 1705 than it was twenty-five years earlier.

Bayle would probably not have initiated such a work if comets had not been credited with a certain success, in particular the coincidence of the 1618 comet and the beginning of the Thirty Years war. Bayle tried to explain that those who foresaw this war from its beginning could have done it just by knowledge of the political climate but the correlation remains significant even *a posteriori*. In fact, Bayle says that there is no need for any special predictive model in history, since events are predictable by mere observation. On the other hand, Bayle says that if there are general causes, the same type of events should occur everywhere in the world or at least in all places where a certain comet was visible and this he concludes, in his Abrégé, at the end of the *Reflections* of 1681, is false. "Si les cométes avaient la vertu de causer la peste et la famine [...] elles ravageraient toutes les parties de la terre sur lesquelles elles passent ou auxquelles elles se rendent visibles [...] Ce qui est faux" ("If comets had the faculty to cause pest and hunger [...] they would affect all parts of the Earth where they would be seen [...] which is wrong").

But Bayle did not try to prove that comets could not be the cause of a phenomenon other than calamities. He expresses a strong scepticism – things are not as they seem – which is by the way a conclusion of the Copernican revolution. Using a fake identity – and Bayle will do the same with the *Avis important aux Réfugiés sur leur prochain retour en France*,[30] after the revocation of the Edit de Nantes – is, as it were, a demonstration that one can believe things which do not exist. But the identity of Bayle was rather quickly discovered, although, Bayle insists, it was a matter of chance and the author of the text could well have remained unknown indefinitely. Truth, according to Bayle, is quite a relative and temporary statement as in the case of the nature of comets. But then one can wonder why Bayle is not also sceptical about proof against astrology.

The specific history of mundane astrology

We would like to underline the fact that for the historian of astrology, mundane astrology has to be treated quite differently from genethliacal/judicial astrology. But it is possible that the various experiments made by those who wanted to investigate the field of correlations between astronomical phenomena and historical events might have finally discredited traditional astrology, making astrology too vulnerable to a process of control while individual astrology remained much more difficult to falsify.

Bayle is a major element in the debate about the decline of astrology. In 1705, Bayle felt that astrology still had a certain impact but he did not expose the classical arguments against astrology, being content with just mentioning that successful attacks took place in the seventeenth century, like the one by Gassendi.

The historian of astrology is not bound to accept certain representations that astrological texts give of astrology. His duty is to explain certain processes and to make distinctions, which is not the case with astrologers and especially with anti-astrologers. The idea of just one astrology is indeed a mistake and does not help to approach the question efficiently. One would therefore suggest the use of the plural *astrologies*, or the necessity to specify which astrology it is referring to, even if the authors do not necessarily respect or are conscious of the essential differences. There is indeed a problem of terminology which has not yet been solved and which probably epistemologically handicaps the history of astrology: there is no sense in trying to approach astrology as a whole if it is not the case.

We think that mundane astrology, or as we call it "Astro-histoire",[31] has a different history from genethliacal astrology, even if the *Tetrabiblos* includes syncretically elements of various forms of astrology. While mundane astrology is mostly an applied astronomy, judicial astrology is based, for a significant part, on fake astronomy, starting with the correspondences between planets and signs of the zodiac, not to speak of other divisions as the decanates.

Mundane astrology itself, though, does not possess a coherent tradition and is not a single body of knowledge. Nevertheless, a common point between the various researches which took place in the sixteenth and seventeenth centuries is their astronomical orthodoxy, although sometimes using the data of the new astronomy. Judicial astrology, meanwhile, continues to rely on the old cosmology. However, the difficulties around the famous eclipse of 1654 were precisely due to the importance given to the Dragon's tail, which is not a concrete astronomical body. The conjunction of Saturn with the lunar node appeared to astronomers as a fantasy.

What Bayle said about comets though could apply to other astro-historical models and it is a fact that mundane astrology is more liable to be judged according to experience rather than plain judicial astrology since its concepts, both astronomical and historical, are easier to grasp and test. In that sense, nothing is more opposed to the comets than judicial astrology. Paradoxically, popular astrology – we do not speak here about the signs of the zodiac – is based on a sounder astronomical basis than learned astrology. Therefore, popular cometary astrology is easier to connect with both astronomy and history than judicial astrology.

Conclusion

Our conclusion is that astronomers and astrologers of that time might be considered as proper historians and should be included as such within a history of the historical discipline. In a way reactions in religious circles were an attack against historical and chronological research rather than a rejection of astrology itself. The failure of such experience became also, eventually, the failure of a real historical science.

Moreover, we think that the decline of astrology might be connected with the fact that events became more and more unpredictable, starting with the execution of the king of England. As long as society was predictable, astrologers could pretend to predict but when it became less and less so, astrology was discredited.

In the French commentary on Goad's *Astro Meteorologica Sana*,[32] it states:

> Si les astrologues se contentoient d'attribuer aux différentes situations des planetes, à leurs mouvements rétrogrades ou directs, le froid & le chaud, les pluyes & les tempêtes, ils pourroient mieux s'accorder avec les nouveaux Physiciens. Car ceux-ci se trouvent souvent si embarassez, quand il faut donner raison de leur diversité des mêmes raisons, je veux dire pourquoi un hiver & un été sont si différents d'un autre, qu'on leur ferait sans doute plaisir de leur montrer que les astres en sont la cause , selon leurs différentes combinaisons.[33]

Which can be translated as:

> If astrologers were just satisfied with dispatching cold and hot, rains and storms to the different situations of the planets, they would find some agreement with the new physicists, for they are often so embarrassed to explain some differences from one summer to another summer, etc., that they would probably be relieved to find the explanations of the stars and their combinations.

It is indeed rather obvious that a certain type of astrology tried to submit reasons or systematic explanations in fields where reasons were missing. One could wonder why non-astrologers did not try to study the influence of planets without referring to classical astrology instead of leaving such privilege to astrologers, but actually some astronomers were also concerned with explaining history through certain celestial parameters.

The case of Bodin is interesting, since in his *République*,[34] first published in 1575, he considers the relationship between history and astronomy. There was actually a chance for a certain type of astrology to find its way to recognition in a time when the empirical approach of history proved itself quite insufficient, *vis à vis* the unpredictable events such as the French wars of religion and the English civil war and the critical events for the monarchy in both countries. Hence Lilly's title: *Monarchy or no Monarchy*.

One can also wonder whether this statistical approach of astrological predictions proposed by Pierre Bayle, in 1681, has been followed by astrologers during the three next centuries. But it is a paradox that Bayle rejects the verdict of the majority to prove astrology and at the same time encourages statistical research which is based on quantities! As William Lilly thought, astrology has to be universal and an astronomical configuration cannot be limited to one country but has to bring effects in many countries at the same time. Thus Lilly announced, rather incautiously, that what happened in England with the (actually temporary) end of monarchy should also be noticeable in other countries, like France.[35] The problem was that the more astrology adopted a clear-cut methodology, the more it was exposed to criticism, and one can wonder whether this was one of the causes of its decline. As a matter of fact, the decline which is to be observed at the end of the seventeenth century is not concerned with individual or judicial astrology, which had already been discredited as a science but will continue under various forms, often mixed with geomancy, tarot and onomancy in the new century. Yet mundane astrology – of which comets are part – still nourished certain expectations, even among astronomers interested in history and by historians interested in astronomy.

On the other hand, the success of Nostradamus's *Centuries* as a substitute for mundane astrology should be noted. One should however mention the production, starting with the years 1740 of *Prophéties Perpétuelles* by T. J. Moult, unknown in England at the time,[36] in which a classification of years in groups of twenty-eight are proposed, which permits us to compare events occurring every twenty-eighth year.

Thus, as already stated, in a predictable world astrology was tolerated because it was not badly needed. But when the future of the world became more and more unpredictable, the burden fell upon astrology, which was not able to bring the expected solutions and demonstrate its legitimacy.

Endnotes

1. See P. Curry, *Prophecy and Power,* p.107.
2. *Miscellaneous Reflections occasion'd by the comet which appear'd in December 1680, chiefly tending to explore Popular Superstition, written to a Doctor of the Sorbon, Londres,* according to the title of the English translation which was published as late as 1708 and, regrettably without the aforementioned *Continuation* of 1705 (see commentary on the Avis au Lecteur de Bayle, in studies on P. Bayle *Pensées Diverses sur la Cométe*, Paris, 1994)
3. See our study "The revealing process of translation and criticism in the history of astrology", p. 211, *Recherches sur l'Histoire de l'Astrologie et du Tarot,* pp. 74-76, 120
4. Upon the reactions to Bayle's publications on Comets and especially Pierre Jurieu's, see, P. Rétat, Ed. Pensées Diverses sur la Cométe, Paris, 1994, pp. XXII-XXIII, using the work by A. Prat, Paris, 1911.
5. Paris, Louis Lucas, Etienne Ducastin et Veuve Prignard.
6. Brussels, Jean-Baptiste de Leeneer, Library of the Museum d'Histoire Naturelle, Paris (Chevreul collection), British Library 717 Q 10.
7. *Monarchy or no Monarchy in England*, London, H. Blunden, 1651, p. 37.
8. Translation and comment by Th.de Garencieres, *The true prophecies or Prognostications of Michael Nostradamus* etc, London, 1672, pages 82 and 380.
9. Bibliothèque Nationale de France, Nc 1419, British Library 1017 b 27.
10. British Library 1017 b 27 (1).
11. Chapter XLV.
12. See J. Halbronn," Les Prophéties et la Ligue" and "Pierre du Moulin et le théme du pape Antéchrist".
13. Bibliothèque Nationale de France, 4° Nc 1421.
14. P. 6.
15. Paris, J. Bouillerot.

16. See our study, "Astrologie et pouvoir", *Politica Hermetica,* 2003, "Yves de Paris, un capucin astrologue".
17. Published in London in 1690.
18. John Goad, Astro-Meteorologica sana, sive principia Physico-Mathematica, quibus mutationum aeris, aliorumque insigniorum natura effectuum ratio reddi possit, Londres, S. Tidmarsh, 1690 (cf P. Curry, Prophecy and Power, pp. 67-72 and .197) A first edition had been published in 1686.(British Library, 1480 d 15) This text was reviewed in Histoire des ouvrages des Savans, by H. Basnage de Beauval (to the questions of whom he answered in his Continuations) in December 1691, pp. 204-213 (reprint, Slatkine, 1969), and wasmentioned by Bayle in 1705 who learnt about it from that review.
19. See our study "Recherches sur l'Histoire de l'astrologie et du Tarot", in *Etteila, L'astrologie du Livre de Toth (1785),* Paris, Trédaniel, 1993 and for the influence of English astrology in France at a later period, *La vie astrologique il y a cent ans,* by P. Curry and N. Campion et J. Halbronn.
20. See our study: "Les variations d'impact des "cométes" en France. Etude bibliographique (fin Xve-fin XVIIIe siècles"), p. 60.
21. Copy at the Library of Rouen, France, and 1663 Deuxième édition veue, augmentée et corrigée, Genève J. A. et S. de Tournes, Bibliothèque Nationale de France, shelfmark, *R 33476.*
22. See our study on "Astrology & Revolutions in the seventeenth century", on website www.cura.free.fr
23. See our study "I. Newton et l'école précessionnelle française".
24. P. 45.
25. P. 27-33.
26. Cf our study: "Claude Duret et le Livre blanc de l'astro-histoire".
27. In 1711, published in 1947, Garges, Ed. Du Nouvel Humanisme.
28. *Les Oeuvres de Mr Le Noble,* vol. XVI & XVII, in 1718, in Rouen and Paris (Bibliothèque Nationale de France, microfilm M. 17370, 16 & 17) and 1726 (Bibliothèque Nationale de France, Paris, 8°Z 5591).
29. Vol. 4, pp. 152-164. See our study on Lenoble, *Recherches sur l'Histoire de l'astrologie et du Tarot,* with the reprint of the work of Etteilla, Paris, 1993, pp. 15-21.
30. See our *Texte Prophétique en France.*
31. See our study; "De l'astrologie à l'astro-histoire".
32. Rotterdam, 1691.
33. P. 209.
34. *Les six livres de la République*, Paris, Jacques Du Puys, in latin, in 1586 – *De Republica libri sex latine ab auctore reddita multa quam antea* locupletiores. Cum indice copiosissimo. Trad. du français, Lyon and Paris, J. Du Puys, BNF Fol *E 70 and in english, in 1606 – *The six books of a commonweale.* Translated out of French and Latine copies by R. Knolles, Londres, G. Bishop, the chapter II of Book IV is called: "S'il y a un moyen de scavoir les changemens et ruines

des républiques à l'advenir", that is " If there is a way to know about future changes and ruins of republics".

35. See Halbronn, "Astrologie et pouvoir".

36. See our study "Les Vaticinations perpétuelles: de l'agricole au politique (Thomas Moult)"; Cura.free.fr

Bibliography

Bayle, P., *Pensées diverses sur la comète,* Introduction P. Rétat, Paris, STFM, 1994.

Beaujot, J. P., Mortureux & M. Fr., "Genése et fonctionnement du discours: les 'Pensées Diverses sur la cométe de Bayle' et les 'Entretiens sur la pluralité des mondes' de Fontenelle", *Langue Française*, 15, September 1972, pp. 56-78.

Boulainvilliers, Henry (de), *Histoire du mouvement de l'apogée du Soleil* (1711), Garges, Ed. Du Nouvel Humanisme, 1947.

Carlson, W. R., "'Pensées' and 'Pensées diverses'. The art of persuasion in Pascal and Bayle", *French Forum*, 1979, pp. 137-146.

Curry, P., *Prophecy and Power: Astrology in Early Modern England,* London, Polity Press, 1989.

Curry, P., Campion, N., Halbronn, J., *La vie astrologique il y a cent ans*, d'Alan Leo à F. Ch. Barlet, Paris, Trédaniel, 1992.

Drévillon, H., *Lire et écrire l'avenir. L'astrologie dans la France du Grand Siècle (1610-1715),* Seyssel, Vallon, 1996.

Grenet, Micheline, *La passion des astres au XVIIe siècle. De l'astrologie à l'astronomie,* Paris, Hachette, 1994.

Guinard, P., "Eustache Lenoble (1643-1711): Un Bilan sur l'Astrologie à son déclin (avec des extraits de son *Uranie, ou les Tableaux des Philosophes*)", website: http://www.cura.free.fr

Halbronn, J., "Les historiens de l'astrologie en quête de modèles", website: http://www.cura.free.fr

Halbronn, J., "De l'astrologie à l'astro-histoire", website: http://www.cura.free.fr

Halbronn, J., "L'astrologie et les révolutions du milieu du XVIIe siècle", website: http://www.cura.free.fr

Halbronn, J., "Claude Duret et le "Livre Blanc" de l'astro-histoire, à la fin du Xve siècle", website: http://www.cura.free.fr (number 27).

Halbronn, J., "The revealing process of translation and criticism in the History of Astrology", *Astrology, Science and Society*, dir. P. Curry, Woodbridge, Boydell Press, 1987.

Halbronn, J., "Les historiens des sciences face à l'activité astrologique de Kepler", Congrès National des Sociétés Savantes, Bordeaux, 1979.

Halbronn, J., "Les variations d'impact des 'comètes' en France. Etude bibliographique 'fin Xve-fin XVIIIe siècles)", *La Comète de Halley et*

l'influence sociale et politique des astres, Actes du Colloque tenu à Bayeux, au Centre Guillaume Le Conquérant en Octobre 1986, Bayeux, 1991.
Halbronn, J., "Astrologie", website *Encyclopaedia Universalis* online
Halbronn, J., "L'empire déchu de l'astrologie au XVIIe siècle', "*Politica Hermetica,* 11, 1997.
Halbronn, J., *Le texte prophétique en France. Formation et fortune*, Villeneuve d'Ascq, Presses Universitaires du Septentrion, 2002.
Halbronn, J., "Astrologie et Histoire au XVIIe siècle", Colloque Astrologie et Pouvoir, in *Politica Hermetica,* 2003.
Halbronn, J., "Isaac Newton et l'école précessionnelle française", website: http://www.cura.free.fr
Halbronn, J., "Histoire des Religions et Phases astronomiques", website: http://www.cura.free.fr
Halbronn, J., "Misères de l'Histoire de l'Astrologie (Gaston Bachelard)", website: http://www.cura.free.fr
Halbronn, J., "Heurs et malheurs de l'astrologie mondiale française au XXe siècle" website: http://www.cura.free.fr
Halbronn, J., " Contribution de l'astrologie à la documentation de la science", *Encyclopaedia Hermetica,* website : http://www.ramkat.free.fr
Halbronn, J., " Pierre Gassendi et l'astrologie judiciaire. Approche bibliographique", in Pierre Gassendi (1592-1655), Actes du Colloque International, Digne, 18-21 mai 1992, *Annales de Haute Provence,* 323-324, 1993.
Halbronn, J., "Exégèse prophétique de la Révolution française", *Politica Hermetica,* 1994.
Halbronn, J., "Les variations d'impact des comètes en France. Etude bibliographique (fin Xve siècle- fin XVIIIe siècles)", Colloque *La Comète de Halley et l'influence sociale et politique des astres,* Bayeux, 1991.
Halbronn, J., "Comparaison du Tétrabible attribué à Ptolémée et de la *Mathesis* de Firmicus Maternus", *Homo Mathematicus, Actas del Congreso Internacional sobre Astrologos griegos y romanos*, Universidad de Malaga, 2002.
Halbronn, J., "Pierre du Moulin et le thème du Pape Antéchrist"; *Formes du millénarisme en Europe, à l'aube des temps modernes,* Actes du Colloque international de l'Association Renaissance, Humanisme, Réforme (Marseille, 10-12 Septembre 1998); dir. J. R. Fanlo & A. Tournon, Paris, H. Champion, 2001.
Halbronn, J., "Introduction bibliographique à l'Histoire de l'Astrologie Française", website: http://www.cura.free.fr
Halbronn, J., " Sur la véritable raison d'être des Dignités planétaires", website, *Encyclopaedia Hermetica,* website: http://www.ramkat.free.fr
Halbronn, J., "Yves de Paris, un capucin astrologue", website: http://www.cura.free.fr

Halbronn, J., "Les prophéties et la Ligue", *Prophètes et Prophéties au XVIe siècle*, Cahiers V-L. Saulnier, 15, Paris, Presses de l'Ecole Normale Supérieure, 1998.
Halbronn, J., "Pierre d'Ailly, des conjonctions planétaires à l'Antéchrist", Colloque Pierre d'Ailly, *Bulletin de la Société Historique de Compiégne*, 1993.
Halbronn, J., "Recherches sur l'histoire de l'astrologie et du tarot", in Etteilla, *L'astrologie du Livre de Toth (1788),* Paris, Trédaniel, 1993.
Halbronn, J., *Enquête sur Nostradamus,* Paris, Danicel, 2004.
Halbronn, J., "Nostradamus", *Dictionary of Western Gnosticism,* Leyde, Brill, 2004.
Halbronn, J., "Etudes autour des éditions ptolémaïques de Nicolas Bourdin (1640-1651)", in N. Bourdin, *Le Centilogue de Ptolomée*, Paris, Trédaniel, 1993.
Harran, Y. A., *Le lys et le globe, Messianisme dynastique et rêve impérial en France aux XVIe et XVIIe siècles,* Seyssel, Champ Vallon, 2000.
Labrousse, E., *L'entrée de Saturne au Lion. L'éclipse de Soleil du 12 Août 1654,* La Haye, M. Nijhoff, 1974.
Labrousse, E., "Quelques sources réformées des Pensées Diverses", *Notes sur Bayle,* Paris, Vrin, 1987.
Millet O., Intr. J. Calvin, *Advertissement contre l'astrologie judiciaire*, Genéve, Droz, 1985.
Moreau, P. F., "Les sept raisons des Pensées Diverses sur la Cométe", in *Pierre Bayle: la foi dans le doute,* dir. D. Abel et P. F. Moreau, Genéve, Labor et Fides, 1995.
Mori, Gianluca, *Introduzione a Bayle*, Ed. Laterza, 1996.
Mori, G., *Bayle, philosophe,* Paris, Champion, 1995.
Niderst, A., *Oeuves Diverses,* Paris, Ed..Sociales, 1971.
Pantin, I., "Rheticus et l'astrologie", Colloque Astrologie et Pouvoir, *Politica Hermetica,* 2003.
Simon, G., *Kepler, astrologue, astronome*, Paris, Gallimard, 1979.
Simon, Renée, Henri de Boulainviller, historien, politique, philosophe, astrologue (1658-1722).

Studying at the Sophia Centre, Bath Spa University College

The Sophia Centre

The Centre for the study of Cultural Astronomy and Astrology is an academic body within the School of Historical and Cultural Studies at Bath Spa University College. It is housed in a former eighteenth-century farm building known as The Sophia Centre. By studying at Bath Spa University College you will be working in a rapidly expanding institution close to one of England's most beautiful and historic cities.

Course information

The principal qualification offered at the Sophia Centre is the MA in Cultural Astronomy and Astrology. The MA is achieved in one year full-time or two-to-three years part-time.

Students may also obtain the awards of Postgraduate Diploma (PGDip) or Postgraduate Certificate (PGCert) by completing part of the course. Candidates who wish to attend individual modules only may apply as Associate Students.

Teaching is conducted in a seminar format and each module consists of ten three-hour seminars. The modules on offer include two which are compulsory (*Introduction to Cultural Astronomy and Astrology* and *Research Methods*) and four optional (*History of Astrology*, *Stellar Religions*, *Psychological Perspectives* and *Science and Scepticism*). Students may also take one of two modules offered by the Study of Religions department (*Sacred Geography* or *New Age*).

International Students

International students (non-EU residents) are required to study full-time. Students from the USA and Canada are eligible for federal loans and all students from outside the UK will receive help in finding accommodation. There are also a number of bursaries and scholarships available.

Entry requirements

The entry qualifications are normally a good BA degree and by interview. Mature students without a first degree may be considered on merit through the APEL programme and will be required to show that they are able to work at the appropriate level. Work experience and previous publications may be taken into account and applicants may be asked to write a 3,000-word academic paper.

Credit obtained at Bath Spa University College may be used towards qualifications at other universities, where appropriate. In certain cases credit from other universities may also count towards qualifications at Bath Spa, but such arrangements are discretionary and potential students should inquire in advance.

MPhil/PhD opportunities
The Centre also supervises research students who wish to study for the degrees of Master or Doctor of Philosophy (MPhil or PhD). The normal prerequisite is either a Master's degree (MA or MSc) or a good BA degree plus evidence of other work via publication. PhDs are obtained via supervised independent research, although students may be invited to attend MA seminars. PhD research takes either three years full-time or six years part-time.

Astrological research library
The Sophia Centre houses a library containing hundreds of major astrological publications, journals and newsletters from around the world which span over centuries. The library is currently in the process of being catalogued, and is available to students and by appointment to members of the public (reference only).

For further information, contact the Administrator:

The Sophia Centre
Bath Spa University College
Newton Park
Newton St. Loe
Bath BA2 9BN
United Kingdom
Tel: 00 44 (0)1225 876147
Fax: 00 44 (0)1225 876230
Email: sophia-centre@bathspa.ac.uk
or go online at www.bathspa.ac.uk/sophia/

The Centre for the Study of Cultural Astronomy and Astrology has been set up with funding from the Sophia Project (http://www.sophia-project.org.uk/).

Culture and Cosmos

www.cultureandcosmos.com

Culture and Cosmos is an independent peer-reviewed journal of the history of astrology and cultural astronomy, published in association with the Sophia Centre.

For details of subscriptions, back issues and contributors guidelines, please see www.cultureandcosmos.com,
e mail culture@caol.demon.co.uk
or contact

Dr Nicholas Campion,
the Editor,
Culture and Cosmos,
The Sophia Centre,
Bath Spa University College,
Newton Park,
Newton St.Loe,
Bath BA2 9BN,
England,
e mail n.campion@bathspa.ac.uk.